Yijiang Ding

Chinese Democracy
After Tiananmen

Columbia University Press • **New York**

Columbia University Press
Publishers Since 1893
New York

© 2001 UBC Press
All rights reserved
Paperback edition published 2002

Library of Congress Cataloging-in-Publication Data

Ding, Yijiang.
    Chinese democracy after Tiananmen / by Yijiang Ding.
        p. cm.
    Includes bibliographical references.
    ISBN 0–231–12565–8
    1. Democracy—China. 2. Social change—China. 3. China—Social
conditions. 4. China—Politics and government—1976– . I. Title.
    JQ1516 .D56 2002
    320.951–dc21

                                          2001037218

Printed in Canada on acid-free paper.

10 9 8 7 6 5 4 3 2 1

To Xiaomei, Han, and Shannon

Contents

Figures and Tables

Acknowledgments

I must first acknowledge the help of Dr. Ronald C. Keith, head of the Department of Political Science, University of Calgary. As my Ph.D. program supervisor, he offered me insights, comments, and suggestions in the course of writing and rewriting the earlier drafts of this book. He also provided me with important primary and secondary materials.

I also thank Dr. Mark O. Dickerson and Dr. Shadia B. Drury of the Department of Political Science, University of Calgary, Dr. Robert Ware of the Department of Philosophy, University of Calgary, and Dr. Victor C. Falkenheim of the Department of Political Science, University of Toronto, for their important suggestions and support. Two anonymous reviewers have made valuable comments on the manuscript, for which I am very grateful.

The project was assisted by a grant from the University of Calgary Research Grant Committee, which financed my trip to the East Asian Archive at the Hoover Institute, Stanford University, where I collected a large number of primary materials. During my stay at the Hoover Institute, I received great help from Julia Tung, chief librarian of the East Asian Archive, to whom I owe my thanks.

My editor, Emily Andrew of UBC Press, provided me with guidance and suggestions that contributed to the successful conversion of my Ph.D. dissertation into this book.

This book has been published with the help of a grant from the Humanities and Social Sciences Federation of Canada, using funds provided by the Social Sciences and Humanities Research Council of Canada. The Chiang Ching-kuo Foundation also generously provided funding.

Chapters 2 and 3 of this book developed from an article published in the *Journal of Contemporary China* 7, 18 (1998): 229-56. Chapter 4 is a much revised and updated version of an article published in *China Information* 12, 4 (1998): 44-67. I thank *China Information* and Taylor and Francis, publisher of the *Journal of Contemporary China*, for their permission to use these articles.

Chinese Democracy After Tiananmen

1
Introduction: Democracy in the Chinese Context

There has been much discussion by Western scholars of the issue of democracy in China from cultural, historical, ideological, and institutional perspectives. Focused sinological analysis of the Chinese concept of democracy has also been conducted by a few Western scholars. However, the emphasis of the Western scholarship has generally been placed on the cultural differences between China and the West, and on the particular cultural background and traditional values that have shaped the Chinese understanding of democracy and conditioned the unique Chinese approach to the issue. The dynamics of contemporary Chinese debates on democracy have not been given sufficiently comprehensive treatment. A somewhat static approach to the Chinese concept of democracy may also have distracted Western scholars from a thorough inquiry into the interrelationship between the concept of democracy and recent changes in social organization and political culture.

This book, on the other hand, attempts to describe and analyze a significant qualitative change in the intellectual conception of democracy in relation to the socioeconomic and cultural changes in contemporary China. While democracy is still very much a social as well as political construct, the concept now turns on a self-conscious dualism that distinguishes between state and society.

The traditional unity of state and society as foundation of the Leninist democracy has been challenged in both theory and practice by the reality of a multidimensional process of intellectual, socio-organizational, and cultural change. The concept of democracy now relates to the explicitly recognized contraction of the state and the expansion of autonomous social and economic life as indicated, for example, in the increasing reform focus on "small government and big society." The developing but unofficial theory of civil society is focusing attention on the organization of society into autonomous and horizontal social groupings. Actual organizational change has become manifest in the complex evolution of mass associations and the development of village self-government.

Intellectual understanding of democracy is vigorously exploring new dimensions of social and political pluralism. The idea of economic freedom characterizes individuals as players in the free market. The equality of different social interests is receiving attention in the formal differentiation of those interests that accompanies the processes of decentralization and marketization of the economy. Such differentiation meanwhile facilitates a focus on political pluralism. New theorizing on the dualism of state and society is contemporaneous with a new cognitive and cultural appreciation of people's independence from state authority.

The primary objective of this book is to analyze the change in the conceptualization of democracy as it relates to organization and political culture, to examine how the rethinking of democracy reflects the changing social and cultural reality, and to demonstrate that these different dimensions of change constitute a process of interrelated intellectual, social, and cultural development. The description and analysis, therefore, will cover these three apparently interconnected dimensions – the intellectual, the socio-organizational, and the cultural. The significant changes in these dimensions need to be further explored in order to establish meaningful connections among them.

Intellectual Background

The orthodox Chinese understanding of democracy follows an intellectual tradition that is entirely different from Western liberalism. It is very much confined to the ideological framework of Leninism, combined with elements of traditional culture. For a long time, this orthodox understanding of the meaning of democracy was shared by both the regime and mainstream Chinese intellectuals. Chinese scholars at the end of the disastrous Cultural Revolution remonstrated with the party leadership regarding their failure to exercise democracy on the party's own terms, rather than for holding a mistaken idea of democracy.[1] For this reason, the orthodox view can serve as the point of departure for the analysis of change, even though it is much less relevant today than it was before the 1980s.

To begin with, the orthodox Chinese concept of "the people" differs from the Western concept. While there is a general agreement that democracy literally means "rule by the people," that is also where the agreement ends between Leninism and liberalism. The liberal view of "the people" is all-inclusive, individualist, and plural, referring generally to all members of society and viewing society as an aggregation of individuals and a plurality of diversified social groups and interests. In the orthodox Chinese view, on the other hand, "the people" is both a social class concept and a collectivist or community-centred concept. Democracy is understood in two dialectical relations, expressed in two seemingly self-contradictory terms: democratic dictatorship and democratic centralism. Dictatorship and centralism are the two cornerstones of Leninist democracy.

Democratic dictatorship assumes a dichotomous view of society. "The people" refers to the ruling classes within society and is the opposite of the "enemy classes." Democracy and dictatorship are two sides of the same state system. Democracy is to be exercised among the people, while dictatorship is to be exercised over the enemies. In other words, "the people" is not all-inclusive; it denotes one part of society, and there is another part to which democracy does not apply. The "people's democratic dictatorship" is both the outcome and the continuation of the class struggle between the people and the enemy classes. Democracy and dictatorship are the two faces of the same proletarian state. For this reason, Chinese scholars used to identify "the democracy of the proletariat" with "the dictatorship of the proletariat" even when they tried to argue for a greater degree of democracy after the Cultural Revolution.[2] For a long time, dictatorship over the enemy classes was considered a primary function of the state.

Secondly, the orthodox idea of "the people" is a collective entity – a totality with fundamental and unified interests that transcend the interests of its individual members. These interests can only be represented in a highly centralized way by the vanguard party of the proletariat. Therefore democracy is considered to be dialectically related to centralism and is to be practised under the guidance of the centre, that is, the leadership of the party centre. This is termed "democracy guided by the centre." Democratic centralism, as Franz Schurmann pointed out, became the essence of the "practical ideology" of the Chinese Communists, in that it was embodied in the organizational structure of Chinese society.[3]

Schurmann also saw a difference between the Chinese and Soviet versions of democratic centralism. Unlike the Soviets, the Chinese appeared to regard democracy less as tied to centralism and more as an opposite tendency within a dialectical relationship. Democracy referred to "impulses coming from below," implying an upward transfer of authority and the release of "the spontaneity of the masses," in contrast to centralism, which implied "impulses coming from above." Schurmann found this to be one of the central contradictions that "marks the clash between the two great ideological currents" in Mao-era Chinese politics: revolutionary radicalism and bureaucratic conservatism. Mao Zedong, the supreme revolutionary leader, often sided with democracy, while Liu Shaoqi, former president of the state and a quintessential bureaucrat, tried to uphold centralism.[4]

Stuart R. Schram initially also noticed a difference between Mao's and Lenin's understandings of democratic centralism. Lenin appeared to be more in favour of centralized decision making by the party leadership and scorned the spontaneous tendency of the working masses toward economism. Mao, on the other hand, repeatedly praised "the spontaneity of the masses" and frequently resorted to mass mobilization to achieve revolutionary goals.[5] Later, however, Schram modified his opinion on Mao, and highlighted Mao's authoritarian aspect. He found that Mao's discussions of democracy and even his "mass line" had an "overriding emphasis on centralism." Mao's idea of democratic centralism, according to Schram in the 1980s, displayed "an obvious parallel ... with Lenin's thinking." While Mao oscillated between democracy and centralism, "he regarded centralized leadership as in the last analysis even more important than democracy."[6]

Observations made by Schurmann and Schram indicate that in pre-reform China, the leader created the official ideology on the basis of his own perception of society, social problems, and societal needs, and this ideology expressed itself in the political organization of society. The history of the Mao era has also shown that the kind of "great democracy" advocated by Mao Zedong in frequent mass revolutionary movements featured centrally directed mass mobilization instead of the kind of political participation practised in Western liberal democracies. Such mass mobilization always resulted in the strengthening of the absolute leadership of the party centre and the supreme leader.[7]

The orthodox democracy, therefore, is "the people" collectively pursuing their unified fundamental interests and exercising dictatorship over the enemy classes – a minority of people in certain socioeconomic and political categories. Based on the principles of dictatorship and centralism, the orthodox democracy effectively emphasizes the unity of interests both among the people and between the people and the Communist Party leadership. In essence, democracy means rule by the party centre in the interest of the people. Theoretically, the party has no special interest of its own and acts solely on behalf of the most fundamental, unified, and long-term interests of the people.

Mao Zedong himself expounded on the structure of interests in socialist society as unity among three different kinds of interests – those of the state, the collective, and the individual – reflecting the ownership system prior to the contemporary economic reform. In Mao's analysis, state ownership was the advanced form of public ownership, collective ownership was a step toward state ownership, and private ownership was no more than a tolerated remnant of old society. "Contradictions among the people" were acknowledged, but assumed a secondary position, and were considered "questions involving the distinction between right and wrong among the people," originating in economic, cultural, or ideological underdevelopment. Such contradictions basically indicated negative aspects of life, whose positive aspects were related to unity. The way to handle such contradictions was Mao's well-known formula: "unity – criticism – unity," which meant "to start off with a desire for unity and resolve contradictions through criticism or struggle so as to achieve a new unity on a new basis."[8]

While Deng Xiaoping rejected Mao's revolutionary radicalism, he clearly shared Mao's emphasis on the fundamental unity of interests in a socialist society ruled by the Communist party-state. In a 1979 speech on the importance of the "four cardinal principles," he said: "Under the socialist system, individual interests are subordinate to collective interests, the interests of the parts are subordinate to the interest of the whole ... This is because, in the final analysis, the interests of the individual and of the collective are in unity with each other under the socialist system, so are the interests of the parts and of the whole."[9] Such emphasis on the unity of interests has obscured the conceptual distinction between the state and society and justified the Communist Party's unchallengeable control of political power.

A number of Western scholars have noticed the importance of the unity of interests to the Chinese understanding of democracy, and related it to the traditional cultural focus on social harmony. For example, Andrew Nathan's discussion of Chinese democracy traced its root to a culturally conditioned misunderstanding of the Western concept. In his opinion, the Chinese traditionally emphasized the "fundamental harmony of interests" between the ruler and the ruled, and popular support for a powerful government, rather than individual rights, diverse social interests, and limited government. Consequently, the Chinese understanding of democracy was essentially substantive rather than procedural in nature. It was defined by how the interests of the people were served, not by a competitive leadership selection procedure that established a formal contract to rule for a fixed period. It was clear, as Nathan suggested, that the Communist regime's concept of democracy was fundamentally similar to the pre-Communist understanding of democracy.[10]

Brantly Womack pointed out that democracy was accepted as a meaningful Chinese ideal in spite of the fact that it was alien to the Chinese cultural and political tradition. Its acceptance was, however, "clearly related to common assumptions that were already present in the Chinese political culture," just like the Chinese acceptance of communism as a radical Western ideology. Therefore, democracy in China had to be understood in its own terms and in relation to its own cultural heritage, instead of being judged by Western standards. He suggested that there was a "depth of continuity" in Chinese thinking, and outlined some important assumptions underlying the Chinese approach to the issue of democracy. The most important of these was "the concept of order and ethical behaviour" based on "community rationality, rather than the abstract rational individual." This in turn led to assumptions about the regime's moral responsibility, unity and centralization, the "governing mission" of the intellectual elite, and moral education rather than institutional means to control government behaviour. Democracy came to mean "care for the people" as a moral obligation of the ruler toward the ruled, rather than institutionalized control of political authority by the people themselves. The mass line – the party's "quasi-democratic system" – was no more than a moral pressure on the regime to serve the interests of the masses.[11]

Robert X. Ware outlined some of the major differences between the Chinese and Western concepts of democracy. In his opinion, "democracy with Chinese characteristics" differed from the Western concept in five important ways. It emphasized goods instead of rights, the collective instead of the individual, practice instead of procedure, objective interests instead of subjective interests, and social mobilization instead of voluntary participation. Unlike Nathan, who appeared to view the Chinese concept as a misconception, Ware allowed for far more cultural variation in the concept of democracy.[12] In spite of their disagreement on the validity of the Chinese concept, these authors all explored one very important dimension of democracy in China: cultural continuity.

Beginning in the early 1980s, however, the importance of both dictatorship and centralism gradually eroded in scholarly debates on democracy. The idea of dictatorship had previously been marred by its implication in the "gang of four" theory of "all-round dictatorship" during the Cultural Revolution. It suffered a further blow when in 1979 the regime leadership found it politically necessary to declare that, though some individual enemies of the revolution remained, their numbers were too small to constitute enemy classes. Therefore, enemy classes no longer existed in China, and class struggle was no longer the main contradiction of Chinese society.

Without enemy classes, "the people" ceased to be a social class concept and became more or less all-inclusive, and dictatorship lost its main target and rationale. The regime leadership continued to insist on dictatorship as a principle of socialism, on the grounds of the existence of individual political enemies – "counterrevolutionaries" – within and "international hostile forces" outside China. Many in the intellectual circles, however, came to see dictatorship as unnecessary or even harmful.[13] This contributed to a virtual disconnection of democracy and dictatorship, and the discussion of democracy in its own right, without the baggage of dictatorship.

Few people could criticize the principle of dictatorship without any modifications, since dictatorship has always been upheld by the regime as one of its "four cardinal principles." Excessive dictatorship was criticized, while dictatorship itself was generally assumed to be a legitimate function of the state that though once important was now outdated or limited to certain areas, such as criminal justice. This assumption can be observed in two theoretical developments directly connected to the downgrading of dictatorship. First, the function of the socialist state was redefined in scholarly discussions. The emphasis shifted from the dictatorship to "the management of public affairs" or "social management" *(shehui guanli).* Dictatorship was no longer regarded as a primary function of the state. The state in the post-class-struggle era, it was argued, should concern itself mainly with the management of society, rather than dictatorship over class enemies.[14] Second, since class struggle was no longer important, the main internal dynamics of and motivation for social change were now found to be "the contradictions among the people." This type of social contradiction required social management and reconciliation instead of dictatorship.[15]

Like dictatorship, the principle of centralism also came under attack in the early 1980s. The main reason was that the highly centralized monopoly of power by the Communist Party was now viewed as a major obstacle to economic and political reform. The reformist regime led by Deng Xiaoping, Hu Yaobang, and Zhao Ziyang recognized the need for a limited degree of decentralization and division of power. It advocated functional separation between the party and government bureaucracies, as well as between government and enterprises. Nevertheless, the regime never abandoned the idea of "unity between centralism and democracy." Many people in the intellectual circles, on the other hand, came to view centralism as the harmful antithesis of democracy and discredited it in the scholarly debates on political reforms.[16] This was a significant intellectual development because not only was the theoretical connection between centralism and democracy questioned and rejected, but the very idea of unity – a key value in the orthodox democracy that rationalized centralism – was challenged. This paved the way for a growing emphasis on pluralism rather than unity, corresponding to the shift of focus from class struggle to "contradictions among the people."

To sum up, in the early 1980s, the nature of the socialist society and the basic functions of the socialist state began to be raised as issues in the scholarly discussions. The disappearance of the enemy classes triggered a series of theoretical developments. "The people" changed from a social class to a nearly all-inclusive group, which was identical to "society." Class struggle was replaced by "contradictions among the people" as the main dynamic for social change. The primary function of the state consequently changed from dictatorship over the enemies to managing public affairs for the whole society. Though these scholarly discussions were still largely confined to the orthodox ideological framework, the significant theoretical development within that framework paved the way for radical conceptual breakthroughs in the late 1980s.

Social Background

China's pre-reform economic and social organization corresponded at least in form to the orthodox ideological concept of democracy, which justified domination of society by a highly centralized state power. Economically, all industrial and agricultural production was conducted on the basis of public ownership and regulated through central planning. Socially, nearly the entire population was organized by the state into various kinds of "work units" *(danwei)* such as industrial and commercial enterprises, rural "production brigades," academic and educational institutions, and government offices.[17]

This social organization characterized the integration of society into the state system and had two basic features. First, its structure was vertical and hierarchical, like a huge pyramid made up of a number of vertical control systems. Every individual belonged to a work unit, which was assigned a bureaucratic rank within a vertical system. Horizontal, cross-system social interaction and mobility were highly restricted. This kind of economic and social cellularization and encapsulation enabled the state to penetrate deeply into the life of individuals and to exercise effective control of society.[18]

Second, decision-making power was highly centralized, with rather limited grassroots flexibility and discretion. The vertical systems helped the state assume broad economic and political control. The range of lower-level decision making was largely limited to the realm of central policy implementation. For example, peasants in pre-reform China had to grow the kinds of crops designated by the central authority, in spite of unfavourable local conditions and often at huge economic losses. Factories were not able to buy badly needed materials and equipment from nearby enterprises if the latter belonged to a different bureaucratic system.[19]

Grassroots participation in the political process was also severely restricted. Articulation of individual and group interests was constrained by the organizational structure and took distorted forms – often realized through personal connections, focused on limited flexibility in policy implementation, and restricted to state-designated channels. A study of political participation in pre-reform China conducted by Tianjian Shi has indicated that the lack of grassroots participation in the political process created an "institutional setting" for an abnormal form of interest articulation. Individuals had to exploit the restricted flexibility in policy implementation available to the grassroots work units in order to pursue their private interests, and typically tried to lobby grassroots cadres through personal connections. In the absence of effective checks, cadres in grassroots work units took advantage of the situation and turned their power into a source of income.[20]

Corresponding to economic statism and social regimentation was a culture of collectivism that denied individuality and creativity, and a culture of dependence that assumed that the state should be fully responsible for the livelihood of all individuals. Every adult in the pre-reform era was assigned a position in a work unit within a vertical system, and was likely to stay within it for the rest of his or her life. Whether one liked it or not, one could not choose, change, or even quit a work unit of one's own free will. A person in pre-reform Chinese society was therefore often described as "a tiny screw in the giant machine of revolution," or "a drop of water in the great ocean." These images were frequently evoked in the "Learn from Lei Feng" movement, which was a central piece of official propaganda during the 1960s and 1970s, aimed at fostering loyalty to the party-state by promoting the collectivist culture. These images of the individual reflected the reality of social encapsulation.

Reciprocally, the state provided crucial goods and services, including housing, health care, child care, education, and a pension. In urban areas, many basic necessities, such as rice, flour, pork, beef, eggs, cooking oil, sugar, salt, matches, clothing, coal, and certain vegetables, could be purchased only with state-issued coupons or "purchase cards." Most of these goods and services were allocated to the individuals through their work units. This kind of relationship between the individual and the work unit made people reliant on the highly paternalistic state both economically and psychologically, and contributed to a culture of dependence. Virtually every adult individual belonged to a work unit. An inquiry into a person's identity and social status generally began with the question, "Which work unit do you belong to?" The state – through the work unit – was not only the only source of a livelihood, but also the primary object of psychological identification: the individual belonged to the state.

This situation began to change when the economic reform started in 1979. The main measures of the reform were various forms of economic decentralization – first in agriculture and then in urban economy – and the gradual opening of China to foreign investors. The changes in Chinese society in the early 1980s prompted some Western scholars to look for new models to analyze organizational as well as ideological change in China. Lowell Dittmer, for example, suggested that the post-Cultural-Revolution "ideological deradicalization" reversed the relationship between ideology and organization. Schurmann's model, in which society was restructured in accordance with the official ideology, was no longer applicable. The political system was now reconceived to respond to the new political reality, which was the end of radicalism. The official ideology was therefore "redefined to be an expression of the institutional interests," and the main function of organization changed from maintaining ideological conformity to practical management of economic affairs.[21]

Peter R. Moody Jr. pointed out that the political changes in the late 1970s and early 1980s started a process of depoliticization and deradicalization.

The rise of pragmatism was indicated by economic liberalization, and accompanied by a "limited expansion of formal democracy" in the rather circumscribed reform of the people's congress system, which strengthened the role of the National People's Congress and allowed direct elections of local-level people's representatives. These changes, according to Moody, indicated the decline of ideology and the transformation of the Chinese regime from totalitarian to authoritarian. In this process, the party came to consider itself "less a revolutionary vanguard and more the representative of all the people." The Leninist notion of popular sovereignty remained, but the Maoist idea of radical revolutionary dictatorship was discarded.[22]

Since the early 1980s, wave after wave of economic decentralization has resulted in the continuous shrinking of the role of central economic planning and the fast growth of the non-state sectors. At present, state-owned enterprises account for only about one-third of China's industrial production. This situation has meant growing economic freedom for society, and the increasing dependence of the state on the non-state sectors for its revenue. A State Taxation Administration report revealed that tax revenue from China's private enterprises reached 44.1 billion yuan (US$5.3 billion) in the first nine months of 1997, an increase of 23 percent over the same period in 1996. Meanwhile, tax revenue from foreign investment soared by 32 percent to 77.8 billion yuan (US$9.4 billion). At the end of 1997, China had about 28.8 million private businesses, which employed about 61 million people.[23]

As the economy is being more and more liberalized, it becomes harder for the state to maintain direct control over the masses. The primary social effect of the economic reform has been the dramatic growth of individual economic freedom and independence. The reform has removed large sections of the population from the state sector into the non-state sector, thus liberating them from direct organizational control by the state. State control over those remaining in the state sector has also been significantly weakened as a result of various decentralization measures. Medicare reform and the recent housing reform, for example, have progressively reduced the state's leverage over the lives of individuals. While state control over social and economic resources is weakening, the amount of such resources controlled by individuals is increasing.[24] These socioeconomic changes have gravely undermined the organizational structure based on work units as a means of control over individuals. A realm of social and economic life that is not directly controlled by the state has developed, which in turn has created conditions for the development of autonomous grassroots communities and horizontal social groupings.

The outline above serves as a background for the following chapters, which further explore the context of the conceptual evolution of democracy in social and cultural development in contemporary China. Chapters 2 and 3 focus on the intellectual circles' rethinking of democracy before and after the 1989 Tiananmen incident, and offer a detailed analysis and documentation of the development of ideas occurring in the scholarly debates. Chapters 4 and 5 describe and analyze two areas of organizational change that form an important part of the emerging social reality to which the intellectual rethinking of the state-society relationship is responding. Chapter 4 discusses the emergence of large numbers of associations, a phenomenon that has caught the attention of both Chinese and Western scholars. It attempts to construct a picture of associational activities through a review of available evidence, and to explore the roles of China's associations in the changing state-society relationship. Chapter 5 discusses village self-government as a facet of the reorganization of rural society. It analyzes the factors that contributed to the emergence of village self-government, the nature of the self-governing organizations, their internal and external functions and relationships, the distinction between democracy and self-government, and the political significance of village self-government in the changing state-society relationship. Chapter 6 explores the political culture dimension of the change in the state-society relationship and begins to place the changes discussed in Chapters 2 through 5 into a larger sociocultural context. It attempts to demonstrate that the evolution of contemporary China's state-society relationship is manifested not only by intellectual and organizational changes, but also by an increasingly pronounced cultural distinction between society and the state, as indicated by ordinary people's alienation from orthodox values and beliefs, and by the rise of individualism and materialism.

In 1989, some believed that China's political reform process had been violently short-circuited. Indeed, the regime downplayed political (as distinct from economic) reform, but few would dispute that China is now in the midst of a very important transition, which has been described in qualified terms as "soft" authoritarianism or "authoritarian pluralism."[25] At its root, however, has been an extraordinary change in the intellectual conception of democracy. While there has been a growing interest among Western scholars and Chinese intellectuals in the development of civil society in China, the development of ideas has not yet been fully described and analyzed in the related sinological literature. Increasingly, democracy is understood as the control of a limited state by an independent society and the accommodation and coordination of diverse social interests through a political process predicated on the dualism of state and society. This evolving pluralism constitutes a significant departure from both traditional political culture and the Leninist concept of democracy.

Objectively, the intellectual development has taken place in the context of social and cultural changes. Subjectively, the scholarly discussions have self-consciously responded to the changing reality by attempting both to provide its theoretical justification and to prescribe its "right" course of development. The purpose of this book is to describe and analyze these specific developments in the Chinese cultural context and the apparent connections among the intellectual, social, and cultural dimensions of change. I hope that this analysis will contribute to the scholarship on the subject of Third World democratization and socio-cultural transformation.

2
Pre-Tiananmen Intellectual Rethinking of State and Society

In the late 1980s, the intellectual circles in China were engaged in intense debates concerning the political reform. New ideas were proposed, indicating important rethinking of democracy in terms of the changing state-society relationship. Increasing emphasis was placed on societal autonomy and plurality of social interests. Correspondingly, the meaning of democracy also changed from the party-state's monopolistic representation of unfied social interests to political participation by an autonomous and pluralistic society. The brief period of post-Tiananmen political backlash failed to inhibit further development and widening acceptance of the new ideas on the state-society relationship and the meaning of democracy among a new generation of Chinese intellectuals in the 1990s.

Western discussions of the state-society relationship in China have mostly focused on social and economic change instead of the formal intellectual change. Nevertheless, a number of scholars in the West have explored the Chinese rethinking of issues relating to democracy and the state-society relationship. The scale of this reconception, however, necessitates a more comprehensive and focused analysis than has thus far been offered. In his analysis of the 1986 debate on the political reform, Benedict Stavis revealed that disagreements between intellectuals and the regime on the issue of democracy were already quite obvious at that time.[1] In the late 1980s, the intellectual circle's discussion of democracy redefined the concept of society and its relationship with the state.

The growing importance given to society was directly connected with the intellectual developments discussed in Chapter 1, including the shift of focus from the now non-existent class struggle to the "contradictions among the people," the change of "the people" from a social class to a largely all-inclusive concept almost identical to society as a whole, and the change of the state's functional focus from dictatorship to managing public affairs.[2] These earlier developments provided the foundation for the emergence of new ideas about the state and society that explicitly or implicitly challenged orthodox Leninist notions of democracy.

The regime leadership has consistently held the orthodox view that democracy is based on the unity of interests both among the people and between the people and the Communist Party, and that the party rules on behalf of the unified interest of the people. The stress on the unity of interests is incompatible with a conceptual distinction of society from the state, and justifies the party's monopoly of political power. The idea of democracy based on the unity of interests, however, was rejected by many scholars in the late 1980s. Available evidence indicates that it was challenged in three ways. First, the validity of the idea of unity as the foundation of democracy was directly questioned. Second, society was increasingly viewed as a separate entity from the state. Third, society itself came to be regarded as a plurality of equally legitimate social interests.

Criticism of Unity

The issue of unity was raised in early 1986 at a conference on political reform organized by *Zhongguo Shehui Kexue* (Chinese social sciences), an influential journal published by the Chinese Academy of Social Sciences (CASS), the top social science institution in China and a leading think tank for the regime. The participants at this conference maintained that one major mistake made by Stalin was his conclusion that after the elimination of enemy classes, a socialist state would be highly unified and devoid of conflicts of social interests. They suggested that "the issue of 'interest pluralism' *(liyi duoyuan zhuyi)* is worthy of our study and investigation."[3] After the conference, a large number of articles appeared in official newspapers and academic journals, attacking the orthodox idea of the unity of interests. Several related arguments were presented in these articles.

First, the orthodox idea of unity was criticized for ignoring an important social reality, which was the obvious existence of different interests in society.[4] Second, arguments were made against "imposing unity" upon people with different interests – a common practice in line with the Leninist orthodoxy. Instead, the principle of minority rights should be upheld and included in the idea of democracy, assuming that different interests in society were equally legitimate and deserved equal protection.[5] Third, "overemphasis on the unity of interests" vindicated highly centralized decision making and consequently contributed to the supremacy of the state over society. Such emphasis obstructed social and economic development, inasmuch as the latter was predicated on the modern market economy, which required the recognition of diverse interests and individual rights and freedoms.[6] Because it justified centralized decision making by a powerful state, the emphasis on the unity of interests was blamed for the lack of democracy in China. The last point deserves special attention since it directly relates to the new meaning of democracy that was emerging from the scholarly discussion.

Several authors tried to establish a negative correlation between unity and democracy, in two interrelated but different approaches to the issue of democracy. One argument focused on the state-society relationship and suggested that the difference of interests between the state and society provided a basic motivation for democracy, which was to provide a mechanism for society to protect itself against arbitrary rule by the state. In other words, democracy was the institutional guarantee that the rule of the state served the interests of society, rather than the state itself. The rationale for democracy, therefore, derived from the recognition of the difference of interests between the state and society. Emphasis on the unity of interests between the state and society, on the other hand, implied that the people's interests would be completely embodied by the state, thus making it unnecessary for people to exercise their democratic rights.[7]

The other argument focused on the diversity within society itself. Recognition of pluralism in social interests was a precondition for democratic politics, because the purpose of democracy was to allow articulation of various interests by people of different social groups. In other words, democracy was a decision-making process that was open to the participation of multiple groups. The motivation for democratic participation lay in the difference of interests among social groups and the need to voice these differences in order to pursue group interests. The past emphasis on the unity of interests, on the other hand, created "a false sense of social unity," which removed the need for democratic participation.[8]

During this period, emphasis on the difference rather than the unity of interests as the foundation of democracy became a well-established opinion among scholars and gained some official acceptance, as evidenced by scholarly discussions on the state and society. Even *Hongqi* (Red flag), a conservative journal run by the Communist Party's Central Committee, published an article that somewhat reluctantly acknowledged "a certain lack of complete unity of interests in the relationship between different regions, ethnic groups, social groups, and even between the state, groups, and the individual." Interestingly, the author replaced "the collective" *(jiti)*, a standard orthodox term, with the more trendy term "groups" *(qunti)* in the orthodox formula of interests. While the collective transcends the individual, a group merely connotes a simple aggregation of individuals.[9]

Differentiation of Society from the State

The conceptual differentiation of society from the state appeared to be an extension of the earlier arguments for decentralization and division of power within the state system. Theoretically, when decentralization exceeds the boundary of the state system, power is transferred from the state to society. In the late 1980s, more and more people began to argue that truly effective decentralization would have to involve transferring some power to an increasingly autonomous society. This new intellectual position was noted by Merle Goldman and X.L. Ding. Both authors touched upon the important issue of state-society differentiation and social pluralism in their analyses of the activities of a small group of leading intellectuals who formed an informal network and undertook the Promethean mission of disseminating the ideal of democracy in China. These "critical intellectuals" to some extent still held to the traditional, elitist idea of their role in the political system, believing that it was their moral duty to remonstrate with the regime leadership. Nevertheless, their attitude toward the regime and their understanding of democracy and the state-society relationship changed significantly during the 1980s: from emphasizing moral persuasion and trying to humanize Marxism, to advocating individual rights and freedoms, societal autonomy, political and legal checks on power, and institutionalized democratic procedures.[10]

In early 1986, an article in *Zhengzhixue Yanjiu* (Political science research), a journal published by the Institute of Political Science in the CASS, expressed the view that the past measures of decentralization were ineffective chiefly because they "focused only on the allocation of power among different levels of government," while the problem of excessive centralization could be solved only by "giving power back to society" *(huan quan yu shehui)*. The word "back" indicated the liberal as well as Marxist idea that the power of the state originated in society: to transfer power to society was to return it to its source. Such a transfer of power was deemed necessary because the state had become too powerful. The author made a strong argument for the necessity of distinguishing between government and non-government affairs and establishing legally defined boundaries of government power, so as to limit the government and provide legal protection for the autonomy of social and economic life.[11]

This new position on the state-society relationship was supported by several leading scholars of the time. For example, Yan Jiaqi, then head of the Institute of Political Science in the CASS and a top advisor to Premier Zhao Ziyang, suggested that different levels of government should have legally defined powers and that the state should give up its total control of society, allowing individuals and mass associations autonomy from the state. He proposed a "four-direction division of power": (1) horizontally, between legislative, executive, and judicial, and between the party and the government; (2) vertically, between different levels of government; (3) between government institutions and mass associations in society; and (4) between government and the public, in the form of popular participation. This pro-posal included not only the division and decentralization of power in the traditional sense but also devolving some power to non-governmental organizations. In his proposal, Yan was clearly considering the political implication of the large numbers of associations that were emerging in China at that time.[12] Su Shaozhi, another leading scholar and head of the Institute of Marxism-Leninism in the CASS, pointed out that, contrary to what Marx had assumed, the existing system in China really amounted to "state socialism," under which the party "developed into an omnipotent structure in charge of everything." Consequently, social and political life became "a unified domain," and this system "suffocated democracy and freedom." In his opinion, freedom and democracy required the separation of social and political life, and a decrease of the power held by the party and the state.[13]

During this period, the most systematic theory for the separation of the state and society was proposed by Rong Jian, a prominent young scholar from Renda (the People's University), who later became a main participant in the debate on neo-authoritarianism. Rong published several articles in 1987 and 1988, in which he reinterpreted Marx's position on the relation-ship between civil society and the political state and proposed a theory of "state-society dualism" *(eryuanhua)*. This quasi-Marxist position justified the ongoing economic reform by suggesting that social and economic free-dom was a necessary stage of political development in Marxian social evo-lution. Rong's idea of dualism also provided a rationale for giving power back to society, as advocated by many scholars.

Rong explained that, according to Marx, the state originated in society and came to control society when society lost its self-control in its internal conflicts. Once society regained its "self-consciousness," a two-step historical process would begin, during which "society will take back the power of the state." First, society would "regain the power of economic self-determination from the state." This would result in state-society dualism, with the state dominating political life while society enjoyed economic freedom. Second, society would regain political power and come to control the state through democratization. This would result in the "withering away of the state." In this way, the state-society relationship would undergo three evolution-ary stages in a Hegelian negation of the negation: (1) the unity of the two through state domination; (2) dualism, or separation of the two; and (3) final unity through the "withering away of the state."[14]

Pre-capitalist society featured a high degree of integration of society into the state system. "A great achievement of capitalism," in the opinion of Marx as interpreted by Rong Jian, "was to have completed the process of the separation of civil society from the political life of the state."[15] Civil society here was understood as a separate sphere of social and economic freedom. The key to the development of civil society, therefore, was to separate social and economic life from the political life of the state. Rong believed that China was now entering into the second stage of the state-society relationship, in which it faced the task of achieving dualism. Since China had never been through capitalism, the separation of the state and society would have to be achieved through the economic and political reforms. Rong emphasized: "The purpose of the reform is to complete the dualism."[16] In other words, reform should aim at creating a separate sphere of social and economic freedom – a civil society in China.

Some scholars outside mainland China noticed this Chinese discourse on civil society. For example, Shu-Yun Ma discussed how "civil society" as a historical Marxian term was interpreted by some Chinese scholars in the late 1980s, and reviewed subsequent discussions of civil society by exiled Chinese scholars.[17] He Baogang, on the other hand, emphasized the contemporary political implications of mainland discussions of civil society through a comparison with similar discussions in Taiwan. Both authors indicated the development of a new understanding of the state-society relationship among some Chinese scholars.[18]

Rong Jian's theory of state-society dualism as a reform Marxist justification for the separation of the state and society and for economic freedom enjoyed much support among Chinese scholars and provided a theoretical foundation for a general consensus on the development of the state-society relationship in China. Two central issues emerged in the discussions on the state-society relationship, representing two interrelated perspectives. The society perspective emphasized the need for economic freedom. The state perspective focused on the need to change the role of the state. Both could be derived from the theory of dualism.

Economic Freedom

The issue of economic freedom was raised by many authors in the late 1980s. Its chief political justification lay in being a precondition for political freedom and democracy. For example, an article in *Gongren Ribao* (Worker's daily), a newspaper run by the official trade union, argued, "if the economy is controlled by a centralized power and without freedom, political freedom is merely empty talk."[19] A *Zhongguo Shehui Kexue* (Chinese social sciences) article also suggested that the growth of democracy depended on the development of a free market.[20] Sometimes, the presence or absence of economic freedom was made a criterion for the distinction between autocratic and democratic politics. The former was "the politicization of social and economic powers," while the latter was "the separation of social and economic powers from the political power."[21]

Several authors attempted to establish a "natural" connection between free market economy and political democracy, in order to argue that the former would pave the way for the latter. The market economy was said to "naturally favour equality ... in economic relations" and require economic players to be independent, free, and equal. This in turn would foster demands for political freedom and democracy, since democracy as a kind of political relationship reflected the economic relationships of the free market.[22] It was therefore suggested that any kind of democracy – whether socialist or capitalist – would require a highly developed market economy as its precondition and its foundation.[23]

Some cited Marx's idea of communism as "communities of free people" as evidence that the kind of socialism envisioned by Marx was built on the basis of free, contractual relationships, whereas in China, socialism was "grafted" onto a "society of ascribed status" *(shenfen shehui)*. Reform, in this sense, would replace social relationships based on ascribed status with free contractual relationships.[24] Liao Xun, a well-known economist from the CASS, held that economic organizations in socialist society should also be "communities of free people," since societal autonomy was what socialism really meant.[25] Without exploring the meaning of "freedom," these authors identified the freedom of individuals in a market economy with Marx's "communities of free people" and, in a dramatic twist of logic, turned Marx's idea of communism into a justification of a market economy based on freedom of contract. This reflected a tendency among some Chinese scholars to use Marx to justify totally non-Marxist claims in order to stay politically correct.

Ironically, the argument for economic freedom as a condition for democracy often seemed to assume that the current priority was economic freedom and development rather than political democratization. Indeed, this underlying assumption was implicit in Rong Jian's theory of dualism, and became explicit in the 1988-89 debate on neo-authoritarianism. In the opinion of Barry Sautman, this debate well illustrated the significant change in the conceptual framework within which the Chinese discussion of democracy was conducted. One international event during the debate was a cross-Pacific video conference held by the cultural section of the American Embassy in Beijing in late 1988. Scores of Chinese scholars attended and several American scholars were invited to participate via satellite. The participants in the debate made their arguments for or against democratization in terms and concepts that were familiar to Western political scientists, rather than loading their arguments with Leninist jargon. Both sides tried to theorize and justify their positions from a non-Marxist perspective. They both assumed what the regime always tried to deny, namely, its authoritarian nature. This discussion demonstrated how far removed the Chinese intellectuals were from the orthodox ideology.[26]

During the debate on neo-authoritarianism, its proponents and the proponents of democratization disagreed on the current priority of and the timing for democratization, but not on the meaning of democracy. They all agreed that democracy should be the political expression of individual freedom and equality, and that economic freedom was a necessary foundation for democracy. Prominent advocates of neo-authoritarianism, including Wu Jiaxiang, a member of the central government's Policy Research Office, clearly shared Rong Jian's view on the three evolutionary stages of the state-society relationship. Their "neo-authoritarianism" was essentially the same as his "state-society dualism." The distinction they made between traditional authoritarianism and neo-authoritarianism, which corresponded to Rong's first and second stages, highlighted their emphasis on the need for economic freedom. Neo-authoritarianism was an authoritarian regime that was determined to promote economic modernization through the development of a free market economy. In their view, economic freedom fostered by an authoritarian state, the so-called East Asian model, was the only way for China to develop the social, economic, and cultural preconditions for its eventual democratization. Their argument against immediate democratization was based on the perceived lack of such necessary preconditions in contemporary China, and the fear that, in their absence, democratization would bring political disruptions that would derail economic development.[27]

The Role of the State
The issue of the role of the state was first raised in the early 1980s. Discussions at that time focused on changing the function of the state from dictatorship to the management of society, so as to catch up with the reality that enemy classes had ceased to exist and that "contradictions among the people" had replaced class struggle as the primary motivation for social change. In the late 1980s, however, emphasis gradually shifted to "giving power back to society." The main argument now was that the role of the state should be weakened, limited, and "societalized" *(shehuihua)*, meaning that the social management function of the state should be partially replaced by self-management of societal players through "giving power back to society." Many scholars proposed that power should be transferred from government to non-government organizations – a reference to the emergence of a large number of mass associations.[28]

For example, an article in *Tianjin Shehui Kexue* (Social sciences in Tianjin) defined "societalization of government functions" as "the transfer of many affairs formerly controlled by the government to localities, enterprises, social organizations, and mass associations." This, according to the author, was a "general trend in the transformation of the state" in both socialist and capitalist countries," alluding to reforms in Eastern Europe and the rise of neoliberalism in Anglo-American democracies, where the ruling parties pushed for government downsizing, privatization, and market deregulation. In socialist countries, the author suggested, this tendency resulted more from the self-conscious efforts of the state to withdraw from social and economic life, because "the basic task of the socialist state is to self-consciously create material and spiritual conditions for its own withering away," and "the societalization of government functions is the only way" to that end.[29]

One might argue that using mass associations as a means of social control was part of the traditional "mass-line" approach to the relationship between government and the masses, which was a kind of state corporatism that underlined the fundamental unity between the state and society and reserved decision-making power for the state. However, the rationale behind the societalization of government functions differed fundamentally from the mass-line tradition in emphasizing the separation between the state and society and the need for societal autonomy. The mass-line approach aimed at strengthening the power of the state, while societalization attempted to weaken it.[30]

During this period, a well-publicized formulation for changing government functions was "small government and big society" *(xiao zhengfu, da shehui)*, which was said to be first proposed by Liao Xun.[31] Liao cited both Marxism and Western liberalism to justify his proposal. The liberal principles of personal freedom and limited government assigned a very circumscribed role to government in an autonomous society. Marx, on the other hand, accepted utopian socialist ideas of small government and societal autonomy, and believed that communism as "communities of free people" could be fully realized only after the "withering away of the state." In Liao's opinion, the Soviet model of socialism was in fact a model of statism, which was in direct opposition to the Marxist view of socialism because it was a model of complete state domination over society.[32]

A much discussed example of "small government and big society" was the "Hainan model," the Chinese government's experiment of making Hainan Island – now Hainan Province – a Special Economic Zone. While there is evidence that a liberal perspective existed among some scholars, who viewed Hainan as an experiment in limited government and legally protected individual rights and freedoms,[33] the Marxist theory of the state-society relationship as expounded by Rong Jian appeared to be a more widely accepted rationale for "small government and big society." For example, an article in *Shehui Kexue* (Social sciences) suggested that "small government and big society," as a necessary stage in "giving power back to society," would be both an inevitable outcome of the "dualist differentiation of society from the state" and in complete agreement with the Marxist idea of the "withering away of the state."[34]

To sum up, in the late 1980s, the idea of an autonomous society free from state control was proposed by many scholars in China. A Marxist theory of civil society and its relationship with the political state was developed to justify a degree of separation of society from the state. This theory – termed "state-society dualism" – suggested that the state should abandon part of its power over society in order to allow members of society to enjoy a degree of freedom in social and economic life.

Civil society in China was hotly debated among Western scholars after the Tiananmen incident in 1989. In his analysis of the Chinese discourse on civil society in the late 1980s, Shu-Yun Ma suggested that Western scholars generally believed that the Chinese intellectuals at that time were almost totally unaware of this issue. However, the available evidence not only supports Ma's claim that the Chinese discussion on civil society appeared as early as 1986, well before the date "most Western scholars may have assumed," but also indicates that these discussions went well beyond the questions of how the term had been used by Marx, how it should be translated into Chinese, and what its implicit meanings were.[35]

In the late 1980s, some Chinese scholars were already using the Marxist concept of civil society to argue for the development of an autonomous sphere of social and economic life in China. However, the meaning of "civil society" as defined by Chinese scholars during this period was rather weak and passive. Instead of a well-organized political society confronting the state, as some Western scholars often used the term to describe the situation in Eastern Europe, civil society was no more than a depoliticized sphere of social and economic life, while the state was given the power to dominate the political life of society. The focus then was not on the right of society to participate in the political process, but on limiting state power to the political sphere: separation rather than participation. In this sense, the societal autonomy being proposed was still quite limited, reflecting the political reality in China in the 1980s, when society was gaining more and more economic freedom, but the state retained tight control of the political sphere.

The relationship between such a civil society and political democracy was ambiguous at best. Indeed, this concept of civil society was employed to justify neo-authoritarianism. Nevertheless, the definition of democracy based on societal autonomy differed fundamentally from the orthodox idea of democracy based on the unity of interests between the state and society, in that state control of society was now rejected as autocratic politics, and societal autonomy itself was regarded as democracy at its early stage of development. The contemporary economic and political reforms were subsequently viewed in essence as efforts to create an autonomous society and pave the way for the advanced stage of democracy: political freedom and mass participation.

Pluralism and the Differentiation of Social Interests

While the conceptual differentiation of society from the state challenged the unity of interests between the party and the people, the concepts of interest differentiation *(liyi fenhua)* and social pluralism *(shehui duoyuan-hua)* broke away from the idea of fundamental unity among the people. This break was theoretically related to the earlier shift of emphasis away from class struggle. The discussions on the "contradictions among the people" in the early 1980s already tended to exceed the orthodox meaning of the term in that the negative connotation attached to such contradictions was replaced by an implicit recognition of the legitimacy of different social interests. In the late 1980s, this implicit recognition developed into a general acceptance of interest differentiation and social pluralism.

The issue of interest pluralism *(liyi duoyuan zhuyi)* was raised during the conference on political reform organized by *Zhongguo Shehui Kexue* (Chinese social sciences) in early 1986.[36] This conference marked the beginning of the series of attacks on the orthodox idea of unity discussed earlier in this chapter. Initially, proponents of social pluralism generally tried to establish as fact that every society was made up of different interest groups, since individual members of society inevitably formed social groups in accordance with their shared interests.[37]

A few people expressed the view that different interests had always existed in socialist society, and simply came into the open and multiplied as a result of the economic reform.[38] What appeared to be the mainstream opinion soon began to assume that interest differentiation and pluralism were the inevitable outcome of the economic reform and the process of modernization, an idea that was clearly borrowed from the modernization paradigm proposed by Western sociologists such as Talcott Parsons. Economic reform directly resulted in economic pluralism, which in turn contributed to the emergence of social groups with distinctly different interests. This position was held by many scholars, including Wang Huning of Fudan University, Zheng Yongnian of Beijing University, and Min Qi, a political scientist who coordinated the first national survey of political culture in China in 1987.[39]

Unlike the arguments for the separation of the state and society, which were primarily based on the Marxist theory of the state-society relationship, the idea of pluralism appeared to be more influenced by the Western theory of modernization and political development. This assumed a causal relationship between economic development, differentiation of social structures and interests, increased demand for participation, and the development of a rational and efficient political system through structural-functional differentiation and democratization.

Assuming interest differentiation and pluralism as faits accomplis resulting from the economic development since the beginning of the reform, some Chinese scholars proposed that the essence of the economic reform was to "reorganize," "readjust," and "coordinate" the relationships among different social interests, so as to "create equal opportunity," "mobilize productive initiatives," and resolve conflicts of interest.[40] Their discussions seemed to acknowledge the uneven impact of the economic reform, the acute feeling among many people that the reform benefited others far more than themselves, and the fear that the conflicts of interest between social groups might escalate into social crises. For example, Min Qi warned that interest differentiation and social pluralism would lead to increasing demands for political participation, which, in the absence of established channels for interest articulation, would result in a "participation crisis," a term borrowed from American comparative politics literature describing the lack of institutional resources to handle fast-increasing demand for participation in developing countries.[41]

The solution to the potential crises was said to be "political modernization" – a process of political and institutional development concurrent with economic, social, and cultural development, leading to the establishment of a "rationalized political authority" *(lixinghua de zhengzhi quanwei)*, in order to keep pace with social and economic modernization.[42] It was suggested that this rationalization of political authority had two different, and sometimes conflicting, dimensions: efficiency and democracy. Efficiency required structural differentiation and functional specialization as well as system integration and institutionalization, again expressions borrowed from American comparative politics literature describing the modernization of political systems and the consolidation of modern political institutions. Democracy required the opening of the political system to mass participation, making it responsive to societal demands. Although there was general agreement on the meaning of political modernization, there was clear disagreement on the priority given to these two dimensions.[43]

Those who held that the current priority should be efficiency rather than democracy believed that democracy required certain social, economic, and cultural conditions that were underdeveloped in China. In this circumstance, pushing for democratization would intensify rather than alleviate existing social conflicts and jeopardize economic development.[44] Those who preferred democratization, on the other hand, believed that the only way to avoid social crises was to allow mass participation and develop "political pluralism" *(zhengzhi duoyuanhua)* to permit different social groups to press for their demands within the political system. It is obvious that the efficiency versus democracy debate shared the general theme of the neo-authoritarianism debate; indeed, the idea of efficiency was used to justify neo-authoritarianism. With a degree of approval from the Zhao Ziyang regime (1987-9), the notion of "social consultation and dialogue" *(shehui xieshang duihua)* was proposed as a limited opening of the political system. Social consultation and dialogue was explained as a system of interest articulation by different social groups, recognizing the diversity of interests in society.[45] Some of its proponents held that its purpose was to facilitate "input" and "output" between the political system and the social environment, using Western systems analysis jargon.[46]

In addition to social consultation and dialogue, political pluralism – a much more radical idea – was proposed by some scholars. Min Qi, for example, believed that it was necessary to modify the current one-party system in order to allow the new social forces to participate in the political process and to head off a participation crisis.[47] An article in *Tansuo: Zhesheban* (Exploration: Philosophy and social science edition) also argued that pluralism of social interests required differentiation of political institutions and the separation of powers, a process that was "usually accompanied by the emergence of multipartyism."[48] An article in *Shulin* (Books) went so far as to praise the "bourgeois democratic system" as the "best achievement of political civilization that has been made by mankind so far," and to suggest that China's political reform should aim at the establishment of a "pluralist democratic political system with social interest groups as its main participants and checks and balances as its core content."[49]

The idea of political pluralism as an integral part of democracy corresponding to economic and social pluralism indicated another important change in the Chinese understanding. Democracy came to mean a process of accommodation, coordination, and compromise of interests, in contrast to the politics of class struggle, which suppressed the expression of different interests.[50] In the same way, democratization came to be understood as "a process of admitting different interests into the political process." A balance of different interests was preferred over domination by one interest because the former would create favourable conditions for democratization.[51] In line with this understanding of democracy were the proposals that various mass associations should become autonomous representatives of different societal interests, and that the people's congress system should be modelled after Western parliaments and act as "coordinators of social interests."[52] Some of these discussions were reviewed by Kevin J. O'Brien in his analysis of the Chinese debate on the possible role of the National People's Congress in a Chinese system of democracy and on the change to its structures necessary to make it an effective legislative body.[53]

This understanding of democracy also implied that democracy was the politics of peace and stability, in contrast to class struggle, which was the politics of violence and instability. "Political coordination" *(zhengzhi xietiao)* was explained as a system of "consultation and compromise" based on the principles of "peace and moderation" and of "seeking common ground while maintaining differences" *(qiutong cunyi)* – a traditional mass-line formulation that was now employed to emphasize political tolerance as an element of democracy. Democracy was said to be able to ensure political stability because it "was capable of comprehensive coordination of the various interests and demands of the modern society."[54]

There was clear agreement that democracy was in essence a process of peaceful accommodation, coordination, and compromise of diversified social interests. This understanding is similar to the meaning of democracy as explained by a number of contemporary Western political scientists.[55] The influence of Western political science theories was indicated by the terminology, vocabulary, and the overall rationale of these Chinese scholars.

To sum up, the acceptance of the plurality of social interests, together with the conceptual differentiation of society from the state, profoundly influenced the Chinese intellectual circles' understanding of the meaning of the economic reform and political democracy in the late 1980s. The economic reform came to be understood both as the gradual separation of society from the state and as the readjustment of relationships among different social interests. These can be viewed as two dimensions of the same reform process, in which large sections of society are being freed from direct state control, new social interests have emerged, and they are adapting themselves to one another and to the state.

In the same way that the economic reform was understood as the readjustment of economic and social relationships, the political reform was viewed as the readjustment of political relationships. Those who focused on the state-society relationship viewed democracy as societal freedom from the state at its early stage, and societal control of the state in its advanced form. Those who emphasized pluralism and the differentiation of social interests viewed democracy as a process of accommodation, coordination, and compromise of interests. These were two related changes from the orthodox Leninist democracy.

This new understanding of democracy was well illustrated by "the first nationwide conference on the building of democratic politics" held in Changsha in 1988. The participants expressed the view that democracy was "in essence society's control of the state," and that democratization was required by the development of social pluralism. Since "each group has its own interest and has the right to press for its interest" in the political system, it was necessary to seek common ground among the majority through negotiations and democratic procedures. This was said to be "the negation of the political system in which a power standing above society exercises unified control of all aspects of social life."[56] To a large extent, the changing intellectual climate of the late 1980s evidenced by these scholarly debates contributed to the 1989 pro-democracy movement in China.

3
Post-Tiananmen Discussions

The 1989 Tiananmen incident was a crucial test of the vitality of the new ideas about the state and society developed in the late 1980s. Immediately after 4 June, almost all of these ideas were attacked in both the official media and academic journals. People who had advocated them were completely silenced. Many of those who had pioneered them belonged to either what Goldman termed the "democratic elite" – Hu Yaobang's intellectual network and their associates – or Zhao Ziyang's "think tanks." Both groups were purged after the incident. Their members were jailed, fled overseas, or simply ceased publication in academic journals. In her book, Goldman described the fates of some of these scholars, which partially explained why most of these people became silent.[1]

However, the new ideas about the state and society not only reappeared soon after they were criticized, but gained greater acceptance among the intellectuals. Even the most sensitive issue, political pluralism, was raised again. The revival of these ideas also coincided with the appearance of a large number of new names in Chinese academic journals, indicating the emergence of a new, post-Tiananmen generation of Chinese scholars. The following is a list of authors cited in this chapter, most of whom appeared in Chinese journals after the Tiananmen incident. Their affiliations were not always available, as Chinese journals do not always provide this information. Quite a few of the scholars were domestically trained PhDs and in their thirties:

Bao Xinjian, Shangdong Provincial Social Science Association
Cai Tuo
Chen Binhui, Xiamen University
Chen Shi
Chen Zhen, Shandong University Law Faculty
Cui Peiting, professor, CPC Central Party School

Deng Zhenglai, chief editor, *Zhongguo Shehui Kexue Jikan* (Chinese social science quarterly)

Fan Yongfu

Gan Yang

Gong Zhihui, Nanjing Institute of Politics

Gu Benhua

Guo Daohui, chief editor, *Zhongguo Faxue* (Chinese legal science)

Guo Dingping, professor of political science, Fudan University

He Zengke, PhD in political science, associate researcher, Institute of Modernity, the CPC Central Bureau of Compilation and Translation

Jia Dongqiao, Department of Political Science, Northwestern Normal University

Jing Yuejing, associate professor of political science, People's University

Li Jing, CPC Sichuan Provincial Party School

Li Jingpeng, professor of political science, Beijing University

Li Shenzhi, former vice-president of the CASS and former head of the Institute of American Studies

Liu Wujun, Department of Law, Beijing University

Liu Zuoxiang, associate professor, Northwestern Institute of Politics and Law

Lu Pinyue, professor, Southeastern University

Lu Xueyi, researcher and director, Institute of Sociology, CASS

Ma Changshan, Heilongjiang Provincial Bureau of Civil Affairs

Shi Xianmin, PhD in sociology awarded by Beijing University, Shenzhen Institute of Administration

Shi Xuehua, PhD in political science awarded by Fudan University, associate professor, Hangzhou University

Sun Guohua, professor of law, the People's University

Sun Li

Sun Liping, professor of sociology, Beijing University

Sun Xiaoxia, Department of Law, Hangzhou University

Wang Huning, professor of political science, Fudan University

Wang Jiangang, the China Youth Institute of Politics

Wang Jianqin, assistant professor, Central Cadre Institute of Politics, Law, and Management

Wang Puli

Wang Song, professor, East China Normal University

Xie Hui

Xie Pengcheng, Graduate School of the CASS

Xie Qingkui, professor, Beijing University

Xu Guodong, professor, Central South Institute of Politics and Law

Yan Qin

Yin Guanghua, General Office of the Central Commission for the Size of the State Institutions

Yu Keping, PhD in political science awarded by Beijing University, associate researcher, Institute of Modernity, the CPC Central Bureau of Compilation and Translation

Zhang Chengfu

Zhang Hailing

Zhang Jingli

Zhou Duo, former chief of the Office of General Planning of the Stone Group Corporation

Zhou Yezhong, PhD in law, professor, Law School, Wuhan University

Zhu Changping

Zhu Xueqin

From Hibernation to Revival

The Tiananmen crackdown was followed by a criticism campaign, which targeted key concepts such as state-society dualism, marketization, giving power back to society, economic freedom, individual freedom, social pluralism, political pluralism, and checks and balances. In the second half of 1989 and throughout 1990, the criticism campaign more or less dominated the official and academic publications. However, a year after the Tiananmen incident, dissenting voices began to reappear in academic journals. For example, in mid-1990, *Zhongguo Faxue* (Chinese legal science) carried several articles discussing democracy and the rule of law. One author claimed that during the "preliminary stage of socialism" – a term coined by the regime to justify a private sector economy in China – it was still necessary to fight for freedom, democracy, and civil rights, ostensibly for their realization in the higher stage of socialism.[2] Another author emphasized the similarities between "socialist democracy" and "bourgeois democracy" and declared that "democracy is a spiritual wealth that belongs to the whole of mankind," which therefore should not be monopolized by capitalist countries.[3] An article in *Ningxia Shehui Kexue* (Social sciences in Ningxia) suggested that the lack of institutionalized participation was responsible for the 1989 social unrest. The author cited Samuel P. Huntington's theory of the relationship between institutionalization and participation to justify the necessity of establishing democratic procedures so as to avoid "participation crisis" and political alienation caused by "participation failure." Such use of Western political science terminology recalled the pre-Tiananmen debate on political modernization.[4]

In 1991, the criticism campaign clearly began to flag. Unorthodox ideas reappeared in terms that were more or less acceptable to the regime leadership. More and more articles appeared in academic journals and leading newspapers to challenge the orthodox views expressed during the criticism campaign. For example, in clear reply to the revival of "proletarian dictatorship" amid the "anti-bourgeois liberalization" campaign, an article in *Fujian Xuekan* (Fujian journal of learning) repeated the old argument that the function of the state was not merely "class suppression," but primarily the management of public affairs for the whole society.[5] Taking advantage of the regime's increased tolerance of academic discussions on the issue of human rights, an article in *Shehui Kexue* (Social sciences) pointed out that democracy meant the recognition of individual rights: there was no sovereignty of the people to speak of if people did not enjoy their human rights.[6] A *Guangming Ribao* (Guangming daily) article expressed the view that democracy was a process of articulation, exchange, and coordination of social interests, and that the so-called people's fundamental interest was simply the "optimal point of combination" of different social interests.[7] An article in *Zhengzhi yu Falu* (Politics and law) carefully distinguished between the "restriction of power" and "checks and balances" in order to justify the former.[8] Liberal-minded scholars who had lain low for almost two years were again feeling out the boundaries of the regime's tolerance.

While 1991 saw cautious testing of the political waters, 1992 saw dramatic change in the political climate, caused primarily by Deng Xiaoping's *Nanxun* (southern tour) speeches. Deng probably intended no more than to revive the sluggish economy and to gain back some ground that had been lost to the more conservative elders. Nevertheless, his speeches triggered a wave of articles in the official media throughout China criticizing the "left," meaning orthodox Leninism, and demanding the "liberation of the mind," a watchword for the liberals since the beginning of the reform. In June, the official party newspaper *Renmin Ribao* (People's daily) carried an article by Rong Yiren, who was then president of the All-China Federation of Industry and Commerce and later became vice-president of the PRC. Rong reasserted the famous Dengist slogan that "practice" was "the sole criterion of truth," implying that the conservative backlash had failed to address the country's economic problems.[9] In July, the "anti-left" and "liberation of the mind" themes were further played up in a *Renmin Ribao* editorial.[10] One immediate effect of this sudden and surprising change of climate was the revival of all the key ideas about the state and society that had developed in the intellectual circles in the 1980s – their hibernation ended quite abruptly.

Most discussions of the state-society relationship in the 1990s focused on a few familiar topics, namely, the role of the government, societal freedom and independence, social pluralism, and political pluralism. However, the issue of civil society now attracted much greater attention than before and some new ideas were proposed, apparently stimulated by the Western interest in civil society in China in the early 1990s.

Changing the Role of Government

Changing the role of the government was by now an old and safe topic: it had received the regime's approval and did not suffer from criticism in 1989-90. The regime's focus was on downsizing government institutions to make them more efficient, and to allow a degree of deregulation of market activities. Many intellectuals, however, used this topic to break the post-Tiananmen silence on the state-society relationship and to revive those ideas criticized in 1989-90. Their chief interest was in limiting government power and giving society more freedom and independence. Articles on this topic had appeared in newspapers and journals since the late 1980s, i.e., pre-Tiananmen, written by both scholars and officials, including top regime leaders such as Premier Li Peng. However, a careful reading of these articles reveals the difference between the regime leadership and the scholars.

In May 1992, Chen Shi, who had defended economic freedom in 1986, suggested, again in *Gongren Ribao* (Worker's daily), that direct government intervention in the economy contributed to the problem of "big government, small society." Government, he proposed, should be the servant rather than the leader of the reform. Management of society ought to be its sole function and most of its direct economic functions should be eliminated. Its role in the economy should change from that of a player to that of an impartial rule-maker and referee. *Gongren Ribao* is a newspaper controlled by the All-China Federation of Trade Unions and is known for frequently taking liberal, unorthodox positions. For example, when Wang Ruoshui, a former chief editor of *Renmin Ribao* (People's daily), was criticized for his support of humanist Marxism and barred from publishing in *Renmin Ribao*, he began publishing in *Gongren Ribao*.[11]

In July, *Renmin Ribao* published an article by Premier Li Peng on the reform of county-level government institutions. Li proposed the formulation "small bureaucracies providing big service" *(xiao jiguan, da fuwu)*. He was concerned with cutting the size rather than the power of government, and showed no interest in transferring power to non-governmental actors. Nevertheless, he agreed that the government should reduce its direct intervention in the economy, so as to allow "a greater proportion of adjustment by market." In Chinese political vocabulary, "adjustment by market" *(shichang tiaoji)* differs greatly from "market economy" *(shichang jingji),* and means using the market as a complementary measure in a planned economy. Li's position therefore signalled only a reluctant and limited acceptance of the market. In a recent article, Lu Xueyi, a researcher and director of the Institute of Sociology of the CASS, recalled that "small bureaucracies providing big service" had been a failed attempt made by "some people" – Li Peng's name was of course not mentioned – to sabotage "small government and big society." Lu revealed that the problem with that formulation was found to be its focus on government instead of society, placing the former above the latter. He pointed out that the policy was impracticable because if government continued to function in a "big" way, it was impossible to make bureaucracies "small."[12]

A month after Premier Li Peng's article, a *Renmin Ribao* editorial went far beyond his proposal to suggest that there should be a clearly defined boundary limiting the power of the government in social and economic affairs.[13] A signed article in *Renmin Ribao* went even further than the editorial and demanded "giving the power back to enterprises and to the market" *(huanquan qiye, huanquan shichang)*.[14] By this time, the conservative premier, ostensibly suffering a serious illness, had been relieved by acting premier Zhu Rongji. The widespread rumour was that he was politically sidelined. Urged by Deng Xiaoping, the regime leadership led by Jiang Zemin abandoned the conservative economic policies of 1989-91 and adopted the "socialist market economy."

This change of policy orientation was greeted by a large number of articles discussing the proper role of government in a socialist market economy. The authors included both scholars and government officials. In these articles, "changing the role of the government" was discussed in relation to the broad topic of the state-society relationship. It was equated with the idea of "small government and big society," and was explained as a movement from political "monism" *(yiyuan)*, meaning the centralized domination of economy and society by the state, to the "dualism of politics and economy, the state and society, and the government and citizenry." The term "monism" had been used in a positive sense by the late party chairman Mao Zedong during the Cultural Revolution. Mao referred to the highly centralized leadership of the Communist Party as "the monist leadership" *(yiyuanhua lingdao)*. Chinese scholars in the 1990s regarded the change from monism to dualism as part of the process of political modernization as well as the transition of society from tradition to modernity.[15]

It was suggested that a legally defined boundary of state power was necessary in order to turn an "unlimited government" into a "limited government."[16] Some warned that "the cycle of decentralization and recentralization of power purely between government institutions" must not be repeated.[17] Not only the size of the government but also its role had to be reduced to the point that the government would "only be concerned with what has to be done by the government."[18] It was also suggested that changing the role of the government would promote the development of civil society by contributing to the separation of the state and society, while civil society in turn would create a "social momentum" for the change.[19]

Yin Guanghua, a member of the Central Commission for the Size of the State Institutions, acknowledged that though there would still be many difficulties in actually changing the role of the government, "on the issue of [the need for] the government to give power back" to societal players, "a general consensus has been reached throughout society."[20] This "general consensus" was indicated by the vocabulary of the officials participating in the discussions. They generally used the term "giving power back" *(huan-quan)* to refer to the transfer of power to non-governmental organizations, as if they were aware that power originated in society, not the state.

Developing Civil Society

Unlike "small government and big society," the concept of civil society never received official recognition. Nevertheless, the term appeared in scholarly discussions in the 1980s and became a hot issue in the early 1990s, with many scholars offering their opinions on it. This growing interest in civil society was clearly influenced by the Western interest in the subject. Chinese scholars participating in the discussions often cited Western authors and summarized Western views on civil society. For example, an article in *Zhongguo Shehui Kexue* (Chinese social sciences) discussed the historical evolution of the concept of civil society and reviewed a large number of ancient, modern, and contemporary Western authors, including Aristotle, Cicero, Aquinas, Locke, Rousseau, Kant, Montesquieu, Paine, Hegel, Marx, Talcott Parsons, Antonio Gramsci, Jean Cohen, Andrew Arato, Jonathan Turner, and Jürgen Habermas.[21]

In the discussions, the reform Marxist theory of state-society dualism proposed by Rong Jian in 1987 was clearly revived, though Rong's name was never mentioned, perhaps to avoid possible political controversy; Rong, as an active participant in the pre-Tiananmen debate on neo-authoritarianism, appeared to have lost favour with the regime. (Rong subsequently put his dualism theory into practice by becoming a successful businessman and a millionaire.) The issue of changing the role of the government was also connected to the need to develop civil society in China.

In November 1992, Deng Zhenglai, known as one of the authors of a popular book series published in the mid-1980s titled *Zouxiang Weilai* (Toward the future), started the journal *Zhongguo Shehui Kexue Jikan* (Chinese social science quarterly), with himself as chief editor. Though the journal was printed in Hong Kong, most of its contributors were scholars in mainland China. In the opening issue, Deng Zhenglai and Jing Yuejing, a professor of political science from Renda (the People's University) in Beijing, published an article on civil society, which they defined as "a private sphere of autonomous economic and social activities based on the principle of voluntary contract, and a public sphere of unofficial participation in politics."[22] The inclusion of "a public sphere of unofficial participation" marked their departure from Rong Jian's idea of civil society, which was economically free but politically passive. Based on this more active definition, they proposed a relationship of "positive interaction" *(liangxin hudong)* between the state and society. In this relationship, civil society would play an active role in protecting societal freedom, opposing state domination, developing social pluralism, and promoting democracy.[23]

In their opinion, the previous focus on the transformation from one type of political authority to another *(quanwei zhuanxing)* – highlighted by the pre-Tiananmen debate on democratization versus neo-authoritarianism – failed to recognize the fact that the main difficulty with China's political modernization was the lack of "dualist structure" in the state-society relationship. In other words, achieving state-society dualism was a prerequisite for democratization. Therefore it was necessary to shift attention from transforming the nature of the authority to the development of societal autonomy and civil society.[24]

They envisaged a two-step development of civil society. The first step aimed at setting up a dualist structure in the state-society relationship and developing civil society in the private sphere. The second step was characterized by the "expansion of civil society from the private sphere to the public sphere," the development of "positive interactions" between the state and society, and, consequently, democratic politics.[25] This seemed to resemble Rong Jian's two-step historical process of "giving power back to society," and indeed, they incorporated some of Rong's step-two targets into their own second step. However, Deng and Jing's step two was similar in essence to Rong's step one, since it was part of the development of civil society based on state-society dualism, rather than state-society reintegration through democratization and the "withering away of the state" (Table 3.1).

Deng and Jing's article marked the opening of heated discussions on civil society and the state-society relationship. In August 1993, more than forty scholars attended a conference on civil society in Shanghai titled "The Symposium on Civil Society and China's Modernization." The participants in the conference exchanged their understandings of Western theories of civil society as expounded by such classic theorists as Hegel and Marx, as well as by more contemporary authors such as Antonio Gramsci, Jürgen Habermas, Jean Cohen, and Andrew Arato.[26] The proposed shift of focus from the transformation of the nature of the authority to the development of civil society, and the idea of positive interaction between the state and civil society, appeared to receive wide support.

For example, Guo Dingping, a political scientist from Fudan University in Shanghai, agreed that the development of civil society had to precede the transformation of the nature of the authority – a code for democratization – since the latter had certain economic, social, and cultural preconditions that could only be created through the development of civil society.[27] Lu Pinyue, a professor at Southeastern University, held that "if society itself does not have a system of self-management," efforts to transform the political system would only result in a vicious circle in which "decentralization

Table 3.1

Two-step process: Deng Zhenglai and Jing Yuejing compared with Rong Jian

	Step one	Step two
Rong Jian	• Transfer of economic power to society • State-society dualism • Civil society based on economic freedom	• Transfer of political power to society • Reintegration of state and society through democratization • The "withering away" of the state
Deng Zhenglai and Jing Yuejing	Similar to Rong's step one: • State-society dualism • Civil society within the private sphere	• Continuation of state-society dualism • Civil society's expansion into the public sphere • Positive interaction between state and society • Democratization

leads to anarchy; recentralization leads to stagnation" (*yi fang jiu luan, yi tong jiu si*).[28] In other words, transformation from authoritarianism to democracy depends on the ability of society both to impose order on itself through self-management, and to maintain a positive balance of power with the state. Such abilities could only be attained through the development of civil society.

Meanwhile, there was some disagreement on the meaning of "positive interaction": did it signify a cooperative or a competitive relationship with the state? Deng and Jing proposed a combination of civil society's "positive ability to participate" and its "negative ability to check and balance."[29] Others, however, tended to prefer one to the other. For example, some scholars contended that positive interaction meant constructive engagement, not antagonism; dualism required a contractual relationship based on mutual respect. Cooperation and mutual complementarity, rather than "the people versus the government," was the appropriate model for civil society in China.[30] These arguments generally emphasized the common interests between the state and society. On the other hand, some scholars held that the essence of positive interaction lay in checks and balances between the rights of the people in society and the power of the state, and that the basic structure of modern society was a division of power and checks and balances between the state and society.[31] This disagreement somewhat resembles the difference between two Western models of China's state-society relationship: civil society and corporatism. The former emphasizes societal independence and confrontation with the state; the latter depicts a relationship of dependence and cooperation between the state and society.

Rong Jian's influential theory of dualism remained the basis of broad agreement on the meaning of civil society and the evolution of the state-society relationship. Civil society was generally viewed as a sphere of social and economic life separated from the political life of the state. Within this dualist structure, civil society was seen as a dynamic process of development instead of a static model. It was believed that different elements of civil society could be achieved in stages. For example, Lu Pinyue suggested that the economic, social, and political elements of civil society could be attained in three stages.[32] Meanwhile, a few scholars proposed more stringent criteria for civil society, and emphasized property rights, a contract system, and a relatively high degree of social organization as crucial elements of civil society. The more rigid definition led to the conclusion that civil society was yet to be developed in China.[33]

In spite of these differences, everyone seemed to agree that China needed a civil society; the term itself came to symbolize a combination of economic, social, cultural, and political elements that were considered preconditions for democratization. These elements included economic freedom; autonomous social organizations; a political culture that valued individual rights and freedoms, equality, and independence; and the ability of society to manage its own affairs and to participate in the political process. In short, the development of civil society came to mean the establishment of the foundation for democracy.[34]

Legal scholars joined political scientists and sociologists in these discussions and became influential. Their theoretical justification for the rule of law was anchored in the "social origin of law." This theory of the relationship between law, society, and the state was pioneered in China by Guo Daohui, a prominent legal scholar and chief editor of *Zhongguo Faxue* (Chinese legal science), in a series of articles published between 1993 and 1995. Guo suggested that legal rights originated in "spontaneous social rights," which were transformed into legal rights through the law-making function of the state.[35] Therefore, "law" *(fa)* differed from "laws" *(falu)* in that law was the common will of society, while the state-made laws were in essence the expression of law.[36] He made two parallel distinctions: one between "rule of law" and "rule by law," and the other between "socialism" and "statism." Rule of law was found in socialism, which placed both society and law above the state. Rule by law and statism, on the other hand, signified the state domination of society. He concluded that socialism demanded "giving power back to society" and state-society dualism, supporting Rong Jian's theory.[37]

A similar idea was expressed by Ma Changshan, a legal scholar affiliated with the Heilongjiang Provincial Bureau of Civil Affairs, who distinguished the "form of law" from the "essence of law." The former reflected the will of the state, but was determined by the latter, which embodied the demands of civil society. The orthodox notion of law as originating in the "will of the ruling class" was incorrect because it mistook the form of law for its essence and justified the state domination of society. The development of civil society presupposed the liberation of society from state domination.[38] The same idea was proposed in an award-winning article in *Faxue Yanjiu* (Studies in law), which expressed the view that "civil law" was the law of civil society, based on property rights and a contract system. Both of these, according to the author, were abridged and abrogated by public ownership and economic planning, which were the means of the state domination. The author held that true "small government and big society" meant the replacement of state domination with the separation of the state and society, the implementation of a market economy, and the development of civil society in China.[39]

The rule of law was discussed in terms of the state-society relationship by a number of other legal scholars, who generally supported Guo Daohui's idea of law as originating from society instead of the state and his distinction between statism and socialism. Some expressed the opinion that, instead of embodying the will of one social class, law actually resulted from coordination, compromise, and common understanding among different social interests. The development of dualism and the emergence of civil society in China would be a process of establishing the rule of law in China, since law expressed the interests of civil society. Democratization would replace "the supremacy of the state" with "the supremacy of law."[40] These discussions provided a legal science perspective on the issue of the state-society relationship and democracy in China.

Social Pluralism and Political Pluralism

The idea of social pluralism received some official approval at the party's thirteenth congress in 1987, came under attack in the 1989-90 criticism campaign, and reemerged in 1992. Subsequently, social pluralism again received widespread attention. Many people, such as Deng Zhenglai, Jing Yuejing, Guo Daohui, and Ma Changshan, mentioned it in discussions of related issues, and other scholars focused on it. People generally agreed that a market economy inevitably led to social pluralism. It was suggested that, in a pluralist society, the common interests of society resulted from compromise between particular interests, and that democracy as the political expression of such common interests could only grow out of the free and equal articulation of interests by different social groups.[41]

The possibility of a participation crisis was again raised. The need for proper institutionalized channels of interest articulation to meet societal demands was suggested, indicating the persistent influence of Western modernization theory.[42] It was argued that the emergence of social pluralism demanded "political integration," and that a pluralist society needed to develop "common understanding" on basic political values and procedures.[43] These arguments appeared to emphasize the integrative function of the political system in avoiding the possible social disintegration that could be caused by a participation crisis.

A few people discussed the recent social structural changes in China. They believed that the social differentiation occurring in China was not merely functional, but amounted to a "reconstruction of society." It was a complete departure from a society of ascribed status dominated by the state. The emergence of group interests based on the "individualization of social interests," it was argued, promoted the "consciousness of group interests," which in turn would foster democratization.[44]

A new "structure of interests" consisting of individual, group, and social interests was proposed, explicitly challenging Mao's orthodox structure of interests, which was made up of the interests of the state, the collective, and the individual. The new structure gave individual interests primary importance. Group interests were regarded as aggregations of individual interests, and both were deemed particular interests. Social interests, on the other hand, were the general interests of society that stemmed from various particular interests and were shared by most individuals and groups. The proponents of the new structure held that the problem with the orthodox structure of interests was that it replaced social interests with the interests of the state, which were in themselves a kind of particular interest that might or might not be transformed into the general interests of society. Indeed, they might even be contrary to the general interests of society. The state could legitimately intervene in social affairs only in the name of social interests, not for the interests of the state themselves.[45]

It is clear that "group interests" in the proposed new structure, shared by groups of individuals, were quite different from "collective interests" in the orthodox structure, which are unified interests of a collective entity that transcended those of its individual members. The former term conveyed liberal individualist values and a pluralistic view of society, whereas the latter conveyed collectivist values and a monolithic view of society. In his analysis of the Chinese debate on the rule of law and human rights in relation to the changing structure of interests, Ronald C. Keith also noticed the increasing reform focus on the "rights and interests" of different social groups at the expense of the traditional emphasis on the "rights and obligations," a change with profound implications for the development of China's legal system. The ascendance of rights and interests and the gradual separation of rights from obligations were also clear indications of the steady advance of liberal individualism and the continuous decline of traditional collectivist values in contemporary China.[46]

Unlike social pluralism, political pluralism was one of the most sensitive issues in China's political discourse and had been the target of the most vicious attacks in the 1989-90 criticism campaign. However, the issue was raised again in many subsequent discussions on democracy. For example, the criticism of political monism by some scholars contained an implicit argument for political pluralism, since monism *(yiyuan)* is the opposite of pluralism *(duoyuan)*. There was also discussion of the emergence of increasingly independent social groups that demanded participation in the political process; entrepreneurs and intellectuals received special attention. Some scholars suggested that economic and social pluralism would eventually lead to pluralism in the structure of political power. Some proposed that China should adopt Western-style competitive campaigning in political elections, and even an American-style balance of power and checks and balances among the three branches of government: the National People's Congress, the State Council, and the Supreme Court.[47]

Specific suggestions also included the introduction of "the mechanism of free competition" into politics, and the subsequent transformation of the current party system into a "one-party-dominant system," similar to the party system in Japan before the 1990s, which would allow smaller parties to act as political oppositions so as to create a "stabilizing mechanism" for a pluralist society.[48] Many agreed that pluralism was inherent in the meaning of democracy, understood as a process of coordination, concession, and compromise among different social interest groups, and proposed the concept of "socialist political pluralism" – an attempt to legitimize "political pluralism" by prefixing it with "socialist."[49] Even Wang Huning, a professor of political science at Fudan University who now serves as a senior policy advisor to the current regime leadership, agreed that political pluralism was a necessary principle of modern democracy.[50] We can see that political pluralism was generally accepted as an inevitable outcome of social pluralism and a necessary ingredient of democracy. The thrust of these discussions indicates an agreement with Brantly Womack's theoretical speculation on a "party-state democracy" with distinctly Chinese institutional features.[51]

The broad trend in China's intellectual development in the past two decades has been a growing acceptance of liberal individualist values and beliefs in the analysis and evaluation of Chinese society and its relationship with the Chinese state. This can be seen in a series of debates on issues related to political development in China. The acceptance of Western liberalism by mainstream intellectual circles was most clearly demonstrated in the recent debate on the value of individual freedom and human dignity in China's economic modernization. This debate started in November 1997, when a long article commemorating the death of Isaiah Berlin, a well-known British liberal thinker, appeared in *Nanfang Zhoumo* (Southern weekend), a Guangzhou newspaper. A few months later, in the foreword to an edited volume, Li Shenzhi, a leading scholar, former vice-president of the CASS and former head of its Institute of American Studies, claimed that the experiences of over two hundred years of socioeconomic development in the West as well as China's experiences in the past hundred years had provided sufficient proof that liberal values and beliefs were the best and the most universally applicable.[52]

The subsequent debate between the "liberals" and the "new leftists" illustrated a return to a previous theme: what should be the current priority for China – individual freedom and economic modernization, or social justice and political democratization? Some people fear that the emergence of a new left among Chinese intellectuals in recent years may represent a conservative backlash against the economic reform or the reincarnation of the orthodox Leninists – the old left – among the younger generation of Chinese intellectuals. However, many new leftists are Western educated, and there are indications that most of them are strongly influenced by such Western ideologies as neo-Marxism and democratic socialism, which are sharply critical of orthodox Leninism and the Soviet model of socialism. Ideologically, the new leftists are very much the descendants of the humanist Marxists who were ruthlessly attacked by orthodox Leninists during the 1983-84 debate on humanism and alienation. Their call for "social justice" should not be interpreted simply as a backlash against economic reform. It is a negative response to the polarization of Chinese society during the past two decades of rapid industrialization, and a call for more equal distribution of wealth on behalf of those social groups that have benefited little from China's fast economic development. While the liberals demand greater economic freedom for individuals, the new leftists feel that this would contribute to greater polarization of Chinese society. As one prominent new leftist put it, the issue is not whether to have reform, but how reform should be carried out.[53]

Politically, new leftists are just as critical of the authoritarian regime as the liberals are. Both groups deem lack of democracy a major source of political corruption. Some new leftists have accused the liberals of trying to justify the possession of huge amounts of wealth by a few people, and accuse the current regime of representing only the interests of the rich. Liberals, on the other hand, believe that the problem is not too much economic freedom, but too much political interference and political corruption – the abuse of power by officials. In a recent article, Zhou Duo, a prominent political activist who was imprisoned after the Tiananmen incident, suggested that the two groups represent the "central left" and the "central right" that are taking shape in China's political spectrum.[54] Their debate shows that contemporary Chinese scholars are thoroughly familiar with various Western schools of thought, a result of the continuous introduction of Western ideas into China in the past two decades.

Conclusion

In the late 1980s, many Chinese intellectuals rejected orthodox Leninist democracy, which was based on a monolithic view of "the people" and justified centralized control by the party-state. Two key concepts were developed: state-society dualism and social pluralism. Society was conceptually differentiated from the state and came to be understood as comprised by a plurality of legitimate social interests. The role of the state was to be limited to the realm of political life and to the provision of necessary services to society. This new understanding of the state and society contributed to the conception of democracy as the control of the state by an autonomous society and decision making conducted by different social groups through peaceful coordination and compromise. However, the notion of civil society developed in this period was passive: a depoliticized sphere of social and economic life that was not dominated by the state, while the state controlled the political process. Often, this notion demanded only economic freedom under an authoritarian state. Economic freedom, viewed as a condition for economic development, was given priority over political freedom, while democracy remained an ideal for the future.

The progressive development of these new ideas was only briefly interrupted by the political backlash of 1989-90. Beginning in 1991, these ideas not only were revived but continued to develop among Chinese intellectuals – now largely a new generation of scholars. Stimulated by Western debates, civil society became the subject of heated discussions and replaced transformation of the nature of the authority as the perceived key to China's political modernization. A more active role was proposed for civil society and gained wide intellectual acceptance; it now included both a private sphere of economic freedom, as previously suggested, and an "unofficial public sphere" of political participation. This resulted in a closer connection between civil society and democracy. "Civil society" came to mean a combination of economic, social, cultural, and political preconditions for democracy that were to be obtained in a dynamic process of development.

In view of the political reality in China, it is quite understandable that the focus of scholarly attention turned in the 1990s from transformation of authority to the development of civil society. Many now believe that the latter is the key to political modernization. Apart from recognizing the political reality, the scholarly focus on civil society also undoubtedly reflects the changes in socioeconomic reality, such as the rapid development of the private sector economy, associational activities, and grassroots self-government, which have begun to draw attention from the outside world only in recent years.

What is puzzling is that, while the regime appears to be highly repressive toward political dissidents, the reemergence and development of the ideas discussed in Chapters 2 and 3 seem to indicate a greater tolerance toward the academic community. This raises questions concerning both the authors cited in this chapter and the overall relationship between the intellectuals and the regime.

Of the scholars listed at the beginning of this chapter whose institutional affiliations are known, some two-thirds are from institutions of higher education, including universities, various institutes of politics, and the graduate school of the CASS. However, we cannot say that other groups are less important. For example, the chief editors of *Zhongguo Faxue* and *Zhongguo Shehui Kexue Jikan* clearly played crucial roles in the development of cutting-edge ideas. Of those whose personal information is not available, five published in newspapers, which seldom provide such information. However, the ability to publish in nationwide newspapers such as *Guangming Ribao, Renmin Ribao, Jingji Ribao,* and *Gongren Ribao* usually indicates a degree of prestige. Most of the others published in university or provincial social science journals, indicating possible affiliations with the respective universities or provincial social science academies.

Taken as a whole, these authors and their ideas are quite influential in this important theoretical area. Individually, their influence is demonstrated by their ability to publish in prestigious journals and newspapers, and to introduce new ideas that incited responses from others, as demonstrated by Rong Jian, Deng Zhenglai, Jing Yuejing, and Guo Daohui. Collectively, their influence can be seen in the intellectual focus of attention created by their discussions. In China, the intellectual locus may sometimes directly affect the political atmosphere, as demonstrated in the months prior to the 1989 Tiananmen incident. Their influence is also evidenced by their long-term intellectual impact. For example, the pre-Tiananmen discussions on the state-society relationship clearly affected the post-Tiananmen discussions.

There is strong evidence that the Chinese scholars participating in these debates are highly aware of one another, as shown by frequent discussions among them on specific ideas. A welcome new tendency now is that authors pay more attention to crediting the ideas they have cited. This is reflected in the increased number of notes in their articles, which document both interactions among Chinese scholars and the existence of Western influence. Academic conferences have also played a role in building connections among scholars. Jing Yuejing's report on the first nationwide conference on civil society offered a vivid description of this type of interaction among Chinese scholars.[55] On the whole, the active interactions among the intellectuals make them more influential as a group.

If the intellectuals involved in this discussion are influential, and their ideas are clearly unorthodox, then the question is: why does the regime tolerate them? In my opinion, the answer lies in the nature of the present regime and its relationship with the intellectuals.

As a result of the decline of the Communist ideology and the weakening of the party-state, the present regime has lost much of its radicalism and become selectively repressive. Instead of indiscriminate persecution of certain social categories, as was the case until the end of the 1970s, the regime now targets only those who have directly challenged its rule, while leaving alone those who do not constitute an immediate threat. To use Merle Goldman's words, the current regime "has neither the will nor the capacity" to exercise comprehensive control over the intellectuals.[56] Meanwhile, the post-Tiananmen political alienation, combined with unprecedented opportunities in the market economy, has increased the independence of the intellectuals and their distance from the regime. Consequently Chinese intellectuals today are "changing from their traditionally dependent and close relationship with government to one of increasing autonomy." They now seek to use their "independent channels to influence society directly rather than indirectly through political patrons."[57]

Seemingly paradoxically, while the intellectuals appear to have become more alienated from the regime, there is also evidence of a closer partnership between them, in that the regime actively seeks their advice in such consequential areas as human rights and legal system reform. In recent years, virtually all the important issues concerning the politics and economics of the reform have been subject to heated intellectual debates, which undoubtedly influenced the policy-making process. In fact, the partnership between the intellectuals and the regime does not necessarily negate the increasing independence of the intellectuals. An interesting illustration of this paradoxical relationship is that between Professor Wang Huning and President Jiang Zemin. Wang is said to have twice rejected Jiang's invitation to Beijing to serve as his policy advisor, before finally accepting it. This may indicate Wang's reluctance to get too close to the regime leadership even though his advice has been actively sought by the latter.

It is of course necessary to be aware that the Chinese scholars reviewed in the above chapters belong to the relatively liberal part of the intellectual community. The relatively conservative part of that community is represented by journals such as *Zhenli de Zhuiqiu* (The pursuit of truth). On the whole, however, the conservative journals appear to be less influential among the younger generation of intellectuals than the large number of journals published by academic institutions, which are considered to be more "academic" – meaning less orthodox.[58]

Given this changing relationship between the regime and the intellectuals, it will be interesting to observe how the current leadership responds to the further development of the new political ideas that have already fundamentally challenged the Leninist orthodoxy.

4
Emerging Civil Society: Associations

The Chinese scholars debating the state-society relationship in the 1980s and '90s were not talking about hypothetical situations in abstract terms. They were, instead, fully aware of the social context of their discussions, and frequently referred to social and economic changes. The significant withdrawal of the state from society and the gradual emergence of a realm of social and economic activities that was not directly dominated by the state has changed the organization of society, especially in areas related to market economic activities. These societal changes illustrate the altered state-society relationship while having provided the social context for the conceptual evolution of that relationship. Such proposed ideas as state-society dualism, societal autonomy, economic freedom, and social pluralism were not merely constructs employed for the sake of developing new theories. Rather, they described and rationalized the emerging new social reality. All the key elements in the new intellectual understanding of democracy have both responded to and justified the new social reality in contemporary China.

The Chinese regime has also recognized the new social reality to an extent in its own Marxist terms. A theory of "the preliminary stage of socialism" was proposed in the late 1980s to acknowledge a mixed economy containing a fast-growing private sector. In the early 1990s, the regime proposed the further idea of a "socialist market economy" to justify replacing central planning with the market as the main mechanism regulating economic activities. The regime has also recognized the significant changes in the organization of society that have accompanied the retreat of the state as the development of "grassroots democracy" *(jiceng minzhu)*. Both "autonomous" associations of the masses and "villagers' committees" *(cunmin weiyuanhui)* in rural areas are often officially referred to as evidence of grassroots democracy in contemporary China.

The "reorganization of society" discussed here and in the next chapter refers to the erosion of the work unit system as a form of social organization within the state's vertical control structure, and the development of new structures and organizational forms to partially replace it. The signs of this development are found mainly in two areas: (1) the emergence of horizontal groupings in associational activities, and (2) the development of autonomous quasi-government organizations – village self-government – in rural areas.

Though there are obvious differences between these two types of organization, to the extent that they are both part of the transformation of the old organizational structure and of the movement toward greater societal autonomy, the current discussion will treat them as different manifestations of organizational change on the same conceptual level. Chinese scholars have regarded both as constituting parts of the "big society" corresponding to the "small government."[1] Some Western scholars have also noticed the similar roles played by associations and village self-government institutions in contemporary China's political development. B. Michael Frolic, for example, suggested that the rise of associations and the development of village self-government were both manifestations of "state-led civil society" in China.[2]

The emergence of a large number of associations *(shehui tuanti* or *shetuan)* has caught the attention of both Chinese and Western scholars. A number of studies have been made, and there has been disagreement on the appropriate model for the analysis of organizational change in contemporary China. The following discussion focuses on the social reality that underlies the different models, and attempts to construct a relatively complete picture through a comprehensive review of existing evidence, including several previous studies. I argue that not just one model, but a selective application and combination of several, is required to represent the complicated social reality in contemporary China, namely the reorganization of Chinese society, the emergence of horizontal social groupings, and the development of a realm of organized social life that is increasingly autonomous and pluralized. Such an emerging reality is reflected in the scholarly discussions of "societal autonomy" and "social pluralism."

The Emergence of Associations

There has been a dramatic increase in the number of associations since the early 1980s, though there is some discrepancy in the reported numbers. A 1990 *Beijing Ribao* (Beijing daily) article reported that there were 1,800 nationwide associations and 100,000 local associations. An article in *Qiushi* (Seeking truth) also confirmed that the total number of associations in China exceeded 100,000 in 1991.[3] According to Guo Dingping, a professor of political science at Fudan University, as of 1992, there were

1,400 nationwide associations, 19,600 provincial-level associations, 160,000 county-level associations, and "countless associations below the county level or within large work units."[4]

A case study conducted in Xiaoshan County, Zhejiang Province, in 1991-92 by Gordon White, Jude Howell, and a group of Chinese scholars from the CASS, found that before 1979 there were only four associations in this county. All of them were official "mass organizations," which were part of the pre-reform organizational structure of the state. The 1980s witnessed a fast increase in the number of associations, and in 1990, the total number of county-level associations reached ninety-nine.[5] A 1993 study conducted by some CASS scholars in Nanhai County, Guangdong Province, showed that the quick growth of county-level associations was sometimes accompanied by the emergence of an even larger number of associations below the county level. The Nanhai study showed that there were almost 200 associations in Nanhai County in 1988, nearly three-quarters of which were below the county level.[6] Given the fast pace of growth and the large number of sociogeographic units below the county level, it is likely that the total number of associations in China could well be in the hundreds of thousands.

This phenomenon raises a number of questions. What has given rise to it? What is the nature of these associations? What kind of relationship do they have with the state? What roles do they play in the social and political life of ordinary citizens? In what way have they altered the organizational structure of the Chinese society? What is the appropriate state-society model to explain them?

A generally held opinion is that the emergence of such large numbers of associations is directly related to the development of a market economy in the course of economic reform. The reform has resulted in the shrinking of the state and the weakening of the old organizational structure through which the state traditionally exercised control over the population. In general, the social and economic resources controlled by the state have been diminishing, while those controlled by individuals have greatly increased.[7] Large numbers of people have left the state sector for the non-state sector, and have consequently removed themselves from the direct control of the state through the old organizational structures. For those remaining in the state sector, state control is also weakened as a result of various measures of decentralization and economic reform.[8]

For example, the development of a market economy has significantly weakened the function of the work unit as the provider of basic necessities and social programs. For a large number of people, the work unit has simply ceased to be the main source of income. The reform of the labour system and the development of a labour market have made it much easier for individuals to find jobs outside their work units, even if they do not choose to abandon the work unit altogether. Indeed, one of the goals of the current reform of state-owned enterprises is to relieve them of their social welfare functions so as to make them more competitive in the market. As a result, even individuals who remain in the state sector depend much less on their work units than ordinary people did in the pre-reform era. The organizational structure based on work units as a means of control over individuals is therefore greatly weakened.[9]

These changes, on the one hand, have made it increasingly difficult for the state to use the old "direct command" mechanism and organizational structure to control and regulate the social and economic activities of individual citizens. It now needs to create a new mechanism of indirect control. On the other hand, individual members of society now identify themselves less and less with their work unit. Those who have gained a degree of economic independence now feel the need to develop new group identities so as to associate themselves with others and to articulate and seek satisfaction of their particular interests.[10] In other words, the development of associational activities stems from both the breaking down of the old organizational structure and the differentiation of interests – the development of social pluralism – that is taking place in Chinese society.

Several studies have shown that the emergence of these associations has been the result of both official promotions from above and individual initiatives from below, though the two sides obviously hold different expectations for the roles of various associations. The situation that gives rise to an association varies from case to case and consequently they are organized in different ways. Some associations are initiated by groups of private individuals to pursue certain common interests. Others are organized by the government, for the purpose of social management and economic development.

Typically, cultural and intellectual associations tend to be self-initiated. This is reflected in the case studies of both Xiaoshan and Nanhai. Such associational activities are largely apolitical and therefore free from government interference.[11] X.L. Ding's discussion of the institutional basis of the "counterelite" provides us with examples of the different types of intellectual group that developed as early as the mid-1980s. Such groups include "cliquish" *(tongren)* journals, writer groups for book series, semi-autonomous professional associations, and even private research institutes founded by groups of intellectuals for the purpose of expressing their ideas.[12] More recently, self-initiated associational activities also include unofficial religious and semi-religious groups, and even political groups. These will be discussed below under "Elements of Civil Society."

Other associations result from official initiatives. The Xiaoshan case

indicates that the local government, instructed by higher-level state organizations, has taken an active role in organizing associations in areas
directly related to market economic activities. Such associations aim at the
regulation of social and economic activities by the state. One example is
the Xiaoshan County Cement Manufacturers' Association *(Shuini xiehui).*
The county has sixteen cement manufacturers located in different townships, under different levels of leadership, and in different forms of ownership. In 1986, the county government set up the Cement Manufacturers'
Association in order to implement unified regulation of this industry by
the county government.[13] Another example is the county Consumers'
Association *(Xiaofeizhe xiehui),* which was organized by the county government's Industrial and Commercial Management Bureau (ICMB) to supervise the market activities of business enterprises.[14]

A less obvious example is the self-employed labourers' associations *(Geti
laodongzhe xiehui).* In 1982, the central government instructed local governments to organize such associations.[15] The Xiaoshan County association,
however, was allegedly organized by the self-employed labourers themselves in 1983, in response to the call from the central government. The leadership of the association was initially made up entirely of self-employed
labourers. Because it lacked official status, the association experienced
great difficulty dealing with government institutions and enterprises on
behalf of its members. In 1986, the association was said to have asked the
county government to turn it into a "semi-official" association, thus placing itself under the leadership of the county ICMB.[16] In this way, the central government intention was fulfilled apparently through local societal
initiatives.

These examples demonstrate that an association may be completely self-
initiated or set up by an agency of the state. Different associations in China
may also have various relationships with the state.

Evidence of Corporatism
In China, evidence of corporatism is found chiefly in the fact that the state
has deliberately set up a system of control of associational activities
through the network of state institutions, and allows only one association
for each sector or area of social life. The state's intent to control is quite
obvious in the Chinese law concerning the organization and the operation
of associations. The State Regulation for Registration and Management of
Associations stipulates that every association must register with the government and must have a state organizational unit as its "supervisory organization" *(zhuguan bumen)* in order to be legally registered,[17] and that the
supervisory organization is responsible for the daily management of the
association under its supervision.[18] These legal stipulations set up formal
corporatist relations between the state institutions and associations and

provide a legal basis for state control through supervisory organizations. One might say that from a strictly legal perspective, all Chinese associations are supposed to be "official."

However, the actual control of an association by its supervisory organization varies. A two-variable approach has been adopted by a number of scholars to define the relationship between an association and its supervisory organization: the degree of personnel overlap between the two and the source of funding for the association. They conclude that China's associations fall into three different types: some are "official," some are unofficial or "popular," and most are "semi-official."[19] The leaders of an official association are all appointed by the supervisory organization and are cadres on the state payroll – usually leading cadres of the supervisory organization. The association's funding also depends entirely on the supervisory organization. An unofficial association has no personnel overlap with its supervisory organization and depends completely on its own funding. A semi-official association may receive part of its funding from the supervisory organization, but the key members of its leadership are appointed by the supervisory organization.[20]

It appears that the distinction between official and semi-official associations may not be very meaningful, since in both types, the supervisory organization has the power to appoint leading personnel of the association and to control its activities. For example, sixty-nine of the ninety-nine

Table 4.1

County-level associations in Xiaoshan: Degree of officialness by area of activity

	Official	Semi-official	Popular	Total
Political	6	2		8
Economic		20		20
Science and technology		42		42
Culture and education			9	9
Sports			9	9
Health			2	2
Social welfare		1		1
Religious			2	2
Social		1	2	3
Public affairs		3		3
Total	6	69	24	99

Source: Wang Ying, "Zhongguo de shehui zhongjianceng: shetuan fazhan yu zuzhi tixi conggou" (The intermediary level of Chinese society: Development of associations and the rebuilding of the organizational system), *Zhongguo Shehui Kexue Jikan* (Chinese social science quarterly) no. 6 (February 1994): 25.

county-level associations in Xiaoshan were considered semi-official by the two-variable measurement (see Table 4.1). Yet 736 of the leaders of these associations – the vast majority of the leadership – were appointed by their supervisory organizations.[21]

Table 4.1 also indicates that official and semi-official associations seem to be concentrated in the realms directly related to politics and economics. This will be analyzed later. The categorization of associations by their functional purposes was made by Gordon White, who defined a political association as one that "primarily functions as an instrument of political-administrative regulation, mobilization, communication and control." Examples include the Trade Union, the Communist Youth League, the Women's Association, the Self-employed Labourers' Association, and the Private Entrepreneurs' Association. Similarly, a consumers' association is economic, a poets' association is cultural, and an association of certain scientists is an intellectual association.[22]

A closer look would reveal the official nature of some semi-official associations. For example, in the Xiaoshan County study, all industry associations, such as the Cement Manufacturers' Association, are categorized as semi-official. These associations, however, are organized by the government and function as official organizations. Economic reform has resulted in the development of large numbers of enterprises that are under different government organizations and different ownership systems. Industry associations have been set up by the government for the purpose of effective management of each industry. The membership of these associations is usually all-inclusive. Their main function is to facilitate government coordination of enterprises in different industries.[23]

A similar case is Xiaoshan County's Self-employed Labourers' Association, which is also termed semi-official. However, Chinese scholars participating in the study revealed that it functioned as a work unit or supervisory organization for all self-employed households. Membership is legally compulsory: every self-employed labourer with a government-granted business license must belong to this association. Case studies in Beijing and Tianjin confirm the official nature of such associations in big cities.[24] They serve as *the* official organization for certain types of people: the only one that the state allows, and membership is required. In other words, it is an organization of state control over a particular section of the population that, because of the economic reform, has moved out of the traditional work unit system.

It is clear that a more accurate measurement of the degree of officialness of an association should include not only its source of funding and the way its leadership is selected, but also factors such as whether it is the only association officially designated for certain types of people, whether membership is voluntary or compulsory, and whether its chief function is to facilitate state control over society. This more comprehensive assessment would likely place many of the semi-official associations into the category of official associations, especially those involved in political and economic activities.

The state assignment of representational monopoly is an important feature of corporatism, as evidenced by the efforts of the state to control the number of associations. The State Regulation for Registration and Management of Associations stipulates that a new association that is the same as or similar to an existing association is not allowed to set up within the same administrative district.[25] Strict enforcement of this regulation would create an ideal multilevel corporatist system, in which only one official association would target each social category within each sociogeographic unit. As we have seen, for example, in 1988, there were close to 200 associations in Nanhai. The county government's Civil Affairs Department decided that there were too many and ordered 102 associations, mostly below the county level, to disband or merge with others. This was said to be for the improvement of organizational quality. It also effectively eliminated duplications: in one township alone, fifteen cultural and sports associations were ordered merged into two.[26]

Efforts to reduce the number of associations were also observed at higher levels, in the name of eliminating duplications. For example, when a private entrepreneurs' association was set up in the city of Xiamen that competed with the Self-employed Labourers' Association under the city ICMB, the city government appealed to the central government, which ruled that this kind of duplication was not allowed and ordered the new association to stop operation. This government effort, in the words of Unger and Chan, was "in true corporatist fashion."[27]

Politically, many of China's associations have been deliberately used by the state to create a new organizational structure and system of control, which can supplement or partially replace the old direct control system and organizational structure. For example, industry associations as a new means of industrial management were proposed by a top regime economist and actively promoted by the government, in a deliberate effort to adapt the Japanese experience. The declared purpose of such associations was to assist the state to exercise "indirect leadership ... over various kinds of enterprises."[28] At higher levels of government, where the bureaucracy is large and the division of labour between offices is specific, government industrial offices have been directly transformed into such associations. For example, the city of Shanghai turned fourteen government industrial bureaus into industry associations in 1992.[29]

It is clear that associations of this type constitute a new form of organization set up by the state for the purpose of social management. They target social categories of economic actors – various kinds of enterprises and entrepreneurs. Though the associations are given a limited degree of freedom, corresponding to the change from direct command economy to socialist market economy, the state must be able to exercise control over their organization and activities. Therefore, these associations must be official. On the other hand, employing associations to exercise indirect control of society and economy represents a retreat of the state from its former position of direct command. Ronald C. Keith, for example, noticed that the development of corporatism was part of the state effort to accommodate societal interests and to manage society more effectively "in a time of regime decline."[30]

Several scholars have noted the intended dual function of China's associations: to serve both as tools of the state to control various social groups and as a means of interest representation for their members. However, there is disagreement over whether these functions coexist in harmony or conflict. Chinese scholars mostly emphasize the harmony of the two functions, while Western scholars appear to focus more on the conflicts between them.

A number of Chinese scholars have expressed the opinion that the two functions are well combined in China's associations. Sun Bingyao, a scholar from the CASS who participated in several case studies on grassroots associations, held that in China, associations "do not represent certain independent social groups to confront the government." In his opinion, associations in China indicate a combination of "state-guided corporatism from above" *(guojia zhudao de zishangerxia de jituanzhuyi)* and "corporatism from below based on unofficial relationships" *(minjian guanxi de zixiaershang de jituanzhuyi),* and consequently demonstrate characteristics of both.[31] Guo Dingping suggested that the harmony of the two functions was determined by the fundamental unity of interests between the state and society, evoking the old Leninist idea, and that China's political system would not allow the existence of Western-style pressure groups. He proposed an "Asian corporatism model" *(Yazhou xiezuozhuyi mushi)* for China's associations – a model supposedly adopted by other East Asian countries as well.[32]

Many Chinese associations clearly state in their constitutions that they aim at helping the government to manage society. For example, a self-employed labourers' association must "assist the government Taxation Bureau and the Industrial and Commercial Management Bureau by urging its members to pay taxes according to law." Private entrepreneurs' associations must "assist relevant government offices to supervise private enterprises." From industry associations to scientific and academic associations, all pledge to do a good job fulfilling those responsibilities authorized by the government. Such stated objectives apparently support the argument for the harmony of functions.[33]

However, conflicts of interest are evident in spite of the emphasis on harmony and cooperation. Associations in China are often caught between the government and their own membership: to fulfil their duty to the former often means sacrificing the interests of the latter. Ma Changshan, a legal scholar affiliated with the Heilongjiang Provincial Bureau of Civil Affairs, noted that the current Chinese law on associations enhanced the tendency of government offices to make associations into extensions of the government administrative system. He argued that the primary function of associations should be to serve as "representatives and champions of social group interests." For this reason, "they should have independence," but the tendency to make them administrative entities "has weakened their independence." He suggested that the law should be amended to allow them greater freedom.[34]

A typical example of the conflict of functions is found in the role played by the labour union. It has always been an official association controlled and funded by the government. However, the economic reform has resulted in a differentiation of interests between enterprise management and employees. Tension between the two has increased. Widespread labour unrest has been frequently reported, especially in recent years, when state-owned enterprises began to lay off millions of their employees. According the media reports, more than 10,000 incidents of labour unrest occurred in 1994. In the first half of 1995, nearly 13,000 labour disputes were referred to arbitration committees set up by the government – a 66 percent increase from the same period in 1994. The Asian financial crisis further worsened the labour situation, and large-scale labour protests have now become rather regular in China.[35] This has put the official labour union in a difficult position. To continue functioning as a means of state control would completely discredit it among its members, but to try to protect the interests of its own members would frequently put it in confrontation with the state. Surveys conducted by Chinese scholars and by the All-China Federation of Trade Unions (ACFTU) itself revealed that most members had a low regard for the official union, because union branches were controlled by the party leadership of enterprises and were ineffective in protecting the interests of employees. The surveyors concluded that emphasis on "unity of interests" and concentration of power in the party leadership had contributed to the union's decline.[36]

In this circumstance, labour unions at different levels have felt pressure to serve the interests of their members. In 1994 it was reported that 200,000 workers at state enterprises in the northeast went on strike as a result of government efforts to lay off employees and the failure of some enterprises to pay wages. In the city of Fushun, some local union branches "broke loose from the central control and led the strikes."[37] At the national level, this situation was illustrated during the drafting of the Labour Law, when the ACFTU "fought an uphill battle to secure legal protection for workers' rights and benefits," in opposition to powerful state bureaucracies such as the Economic Planning Commission and the Trade Commission, which were in charge of economic development.[38] After the adoption of the law, Xue Zhaojun, the ACFTU's vice-president, declared at an NPC Standing Committee meeting that the trade union had shifted its emphasis to protecting workers' interests and gaining trust among the workers. She reportedly urged that the union branches "be turned into 'homes of workers' instead of departments of the government."[39]

A similar shift of emphasis was also observed in the behaviour of the Federation of Industry and Commerce (FIC) *(Gongshangye lianhehui)* and the entrepreneurs' associations within the FIC system. The FIC is the national association officially designated by the state to serve as a bridge between the state and the private business owners. The FIC is supposed to play two roles, namely, to help the government exercise indirect control over the private sector economy and private entrepreneurs, and to articulate the interests of large private entrepreneurs. However, in recent years, the FIC has displayed a tendency to focus on its interest-serving function at the expense of its control function.[40]

In big cities such as Beijing and Tianjin, the FIC branches reportedly are actively engaged in the advocacy of membership interests: "The [FIC] seems to carry out its advocacy function almost too well and its control function far less so. District [FIC] chapters are so zealous in pursuing their members' interests that they actually undermine city-level authority."[41] In Nanhai County, the Private Entrepreneurs' Civic Association *(Minjian qiyejia gonghui)* has become a champion for owners of private enterprises. It has mediated between its members and their employees during labour disputes and promoted the political status of private enterprise owners, helping three of them get elected to the county People's Congress, and six of them to the county's People's Political Consultative Conference.[42]

According to a case study conducted in Hainan Province by a group of scholars from the CASS, both the government-sponsored Hainan General Chamber of Commerce *(Hainan Zong Shanghui)*, which was the successor to the provincial FIC, and the privately sponsored Hainan Entrepreneurs' Association *(Hainan sheng qiyejia xiehui)* pledged to protect the "legitimate rights and interests" of their memberships through participation in the provincial policy-making process on behalf of memberships. Their activities include organizing regular meetings between their members and government officials, conducting research, filing reports, and making policy recommendations to the provincial government on issues concerning the interests of their members.[43]

Instances of this nature lend plausibility to the idea of a transition toward "societal corporatism" proposed by several Western scholars.[44] Some

Chinese scholars have also noticed a transition from "state-guided corporatism from above" toward "corporatism from below based on unofficial relationships." It is obvious that the emergence and increasing awareness of social group interests, and the resulting tension between an association's control and service functions, are responsible for the transition. In other words, interest differentiation has increased the pressure for greater autonomy in associational activities. The scholarly discussions of social pluralism and societal autonomy have clearly reflected this development. Having dual functions is not a stable condition: in the dynamics of state versus societal corporatism, one function tends to predominate. Meanwhile, a transition toward societal corporatism does not necessarily mean a less-official status for an association. What is necessary is a change of its functional focus.

A conflict of functions has also been observed in the self-employed labourers' associations in big cities, but with a different outcome. In this case, the control function has been emphasized at the expense of the interest-serving function. In large cities like Beijing and Tianjin, such associations serve mainly as a means of government control over self-employed individuals. Consequently, members of such associations regard them as police – "more dangerous than helpful." These associations were often in striking contrast with the FICs in the same cities, which were able to actively promote their memberships' interests and consequently gained popularity among their members.[45]

This contrast between the self-employed labourers' associations and the FICs, in the opinion of Nevitt, indicated the interests of government officials at lower levels. The district-level government within big cities viewed private enterprises as an important local economic resource base for itself and therefore strongly backed the local FIC's effort to protect the interests of private business owners. The large number of self-employed labourers, on the other hand, were viewed with suspicion and regarded as a potential source of trouble. The selective support of local associations, Nevitt observed, was evidence of local state power. Unger and Chan also noticed that the demonstration of independence and pursuit of membership interests by business associations in some smaller cities or counties were backed up by local government, which was engaged in empire-building against the higher levels of government. In other words, an alliance emerged of the local state and local society "against the encroachment of the central state: an alliance of interests on behalf of local protectionism."[46]

One question raised by the idea of an alliance of local interests against the higher levels of government is that of the roles played by the local state and local society in this type of alliance. Nevitt appears to suggest that the local state has been dominant, manipulating local associations for its own purposes. The membership interests of the local associations are promoted by the local state only when they coincide with its own interests, as in the case of self-employed labourers in Tianjin. This explanation supports the idea of local state corporatism. Unger and Chan, on the other hand, noted that local private business owners "have their own reasons" to support the local state against higher levels of government, and that pressure from memberships was a factor in explaining the behaviour of local associations. In his study, Unger examined the different degrees of autonomy displayed by different associations, and concluded that not only the interests of the local state, but such factors as the association's geographic and administrative location, its degree of financial independence, the social status of its constituency, whether its membership was voluntary or compulsory, and whether its supervisory organization was an administrative agency or a non-administrative organization, all contributed to different degrees of autonomy.[47]

The problem with the theory of local state corporatism is that it cannot explain the tendency of some local union branches and entrepreneurs' associations to demonstrate independence not only of the central state, but of the local state as well. Pressure from the membership rather than manipulation by the local government appears to better explain the behaviour of these associations in playing an active role in promoting and protecting membership interests. Local associations may not be altogether passive in the so-called alliance of local interests. They may be active players, pressuring the local government into confrontation with the higher levels of the state in some cases and rebelling against local officials in others, as demonstrated by some recent incidents of labour unrest. In other words, grassroots pressure may be as responsible as local state interests for the tension between different levels of government and the fragmentation of the overall corporatist system.

The demonstration of independence by local associations renders the idea of local state corporatism questionable. A combination of localism and the tendency toward societal corporatism – "local societal corporatism" – is probably a better model for the behaviour of some local associations. Societal corporatism is understood here as the autonomy from the state gained by associations within the corporatist system, in contrast to state corporatism, in which the state retains tight control over associational activities. Local societal corporatism is indicated by the fact that the state control of associational activities tends to be progressively weaker as we move from higher to lower levels, and from the centre to the provinces. For example, the provincial-level FICs in big cities such as Beijing and Tianjin are controlled and funded by the Communist Party's United Front Department. The associations within the FIC system at lower levels tend to be more self-funded and under less government control.[48]

In Xiaoshan, the Private Entrepreneurs' Association *(Siying qiyejia xiehui)* is partially funded by its own members.[49] In Nanhai, the Private Entrepreneurs' Civic Association *(Minjian qiyejia gonghui)* is said to be "completely separated from the government," not even supervised by the county ICMB. The Nanhai situation may also reflect the influence of Hong Kong in Guangdong Province; there are more private enterprises in Guangdong and the local government there adopts a more laissez-faire attitude toward them.[50] The same is true of the Private Enterprise Civic Association *(Minban gonghui)* in Wenzhou, a well-known entrepreneurial centre. It is established and operated by a group of successful private business owners and only nominally linked to the FIC.[51] Whereas in big cities such as Beijing and Tianjin, the associations of self-employed labourers are mainly a means of government control, in some smaller cities and in counties, they begin to voice the interests of their members.[52]

The Nanhai case study indicated that associations at the township level are generally more independent than those at the county level, for several reasons. The size of the township government is relatively small, which has limited its ability to supervise associational activities on a regular basis. Also, many of the township- or village-level associations are cultural, an area where the government may find it unnecessary to intervene. As a result, even those township associations that are categorized as semi-official are largely unofficial in nature: their leadership is made up largely of individuals without official status, they are mostly self-funded, and their chief function is to meet the needs of their members.[53]

To sum up, there is evidence of various types of corporatism in contemporary China. State corporatism, local corporatism, and a tendency toward societal corporatism coexist within China's transitional society. There is an indication that the state is deliberately setting up a system of indirect control through various associations. The associations within the corporatist structure have, however, shown a tendency toward greater independence and a greater focus on serving membership interests. The subtypes of corporatism help describe the overall corporatist structure: the idea of local corporatism introduces a useful explanatory variable, the tension between different levels of government, and the transition toward societal corporatism helps explain a dynamic process of change within the corporatist structure.

On the whole, the various models of corporatism all emphasize harmony, cooperation, and problem solving within the existing corporatist structure, but are inadequate for other dynamic aspects of associational activities. They may not account for the rapid proliferation of unofficial and voluntary associations in spite of the controlling effort of the state, nor for the increasingly confrontational approach taken by some local groups, reflecting the growing social tension created in the course of the economic reform. These phenomena are clear indications of an emerging civil society in China.

Elements of Civil Society

Civil society has been a key concept in the scholarly discussions on the contemporary state-society relationship, and one of the agreements reached in them is on the need to develop civil society in China. The scholarly discussions, in fact, have served to theorize a new social reality, which is the emergence of civil society in contemporary China. Elements of an emerging civil society can be found both inside and outside the existing corporatist structure. Civil society as a realm of autonomous social organizational activities obviously can overlap with the concept of societal corporatism, since corporatism as an institutional arrangement connecting the state and society does not exclude the possibility of societal autonomy within the corporatist structure. Furthermore, the emergence of localism in China has fragmented the corporatist structure, which, combined with the tendency toward societal corporatism, is likely to produce elements of civil society with pluralist inclinations.

Figure 4.1 illustrates the extreme complexity of this fragmented system. If thousands of associations within this system shifted from being instruments of state control to independently articulating group interests, would it be a development of corporatism or pluralism? It would be hard to tell. The difference between a fragmented and localized societal corporatism and a civil society with pluralist inclinations becomes terminological. A transition to one is a transition to the other.

Figure 4.1

Relationships within a fragmented corporatist system

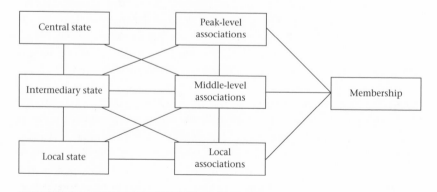

Note: Lines indicate interconnections and interactions.

In addition to the transition toward societal corporatism, indications of an emerging civil society are also found outside the corporatist structure, in the form of legally registered but completely unofficial associations, associations that are not legally registered or "illegally registered," independent intellectual networks, unregistered labour organizations – core groups in many wildcat strikes – religious and semi-religious groups, and even independent political groups.

The fact that the government at different levels sometimes finds it necessary to cut the number of associations indicates that the "ideal" number necessary for a corporatist system is often exceeded. However, the state has apparently been unsuccessful in controlling the number of associations. For example, during the "anti-spiritual pollution" campaign, the central government "ordered a nationwide check on professional associations," but once the campaign ended, such associations again mushroomed.[54] What was even more unacceptable to the regime was that some associations were organized by private individuals without permission from the government. An article in the official party journal *Qiushi* (Seeking truth) angrily referred to this "problem" with associations as evidence of "bourgeois liberalization."[55]

The Ministry of Civil Affairs also complained that many associations had been established without being properly registered, and lamented the lack of effective measures for implementing the law on associations. One problem was that many "purely private associations" *(chun minjian shetuan)* did not have clear professional characteristics, and consequently did not know which government agencies should be their supervisory organizations. Another problem was that the organizers of some associations managed to secure support from certain senior officials through personal connections and started publicizing their associations in the media without even bothering to register. In other cases, the organizers used illegal means to get registered. For example, the Chinese Peasant Literature Society *(Zhongguo nongmin wenxue she)* registered with a forged government document and published as many as fourteen issues of *Nongmin Wenxue Bao* (Peasant literature news) before the forgery was found out. In Shaanxi, the provincial "artists' association" *(meishujia xiehui)* was "split" into eighteen provincial associations of essentially the same nature, a clear violation of the legal restriction against duplications.[56]

A *Beijing Ribao* (Beijing daily) article reported that there were too many associations nationwide and that too often, several similar associations were found in the same area of social activities. The article noted that this was especially true of associations engaged in cultural and intellectual activities.[57] Table 4.1 illustrates that at the county level, unofficial associations are concentrated in the areas of cultural life, whereas most official and semi-official associations are directly related to politics and the economy. The state control of associational activities appears looser in non-political and non-economic areas. This may indicate that the state is either less interested in or less capable of controlling associational activities in areas outside politics and the economy. There is a clear tendency for society to create more and more associations, and the government may find it difficult to put a stop to this growth. For example, after being drastically reduced to around 100 in 1988, the number of associations in Nanhai County reached 129 in 1993. In Hainan Province, the number of associations at and above the county level more than doubled between 1992 and 1996 from 414 to 872.[58]

Legally, even a purely self-organized and self-funded association must place itself under a supervisory organization. However, it appears that this requirement can be easily circumvented, at least in some cases. X.L. Ding remarked that the relationship of an association with its supervisory organization was often set up through personal connections solely for registration purposes.[59] Moreover, because the supervisory organization has no clearly defined roles or obligations, it may be strongly interventionist or almost completely laissez-faire in dealing with the association under its supervision.[60] The supervisory organization can be merely a "state work unit to hang on to" *(guakao danwei)* in order to guarantee the legitimacy of an association.

Unofficial associations can start as a small group of friends with common interests in certain cultural or intellectual activities. In order to register with the government and become lawful, members of the group explore various personal connections so as to find a government organization willing to serve as the supervisory organization. A typical example in the late 1980s was the Beijing Institute for Research on Social and Scientific-Technological Development, headed by Chen Ziming and Wang Juntao, who displayed acrobatic skills in their efforts to find an official sponsor for their organization and for the publication of their journal.[61]

More recent examples of such unofficial groups include the China Social and Economic Investigation Centre founded in Beijing by a PhD student from Beijing University. The Centre operated for a few years and became famous for supplying *Beijing Qingnian Bao* (Beijing youth news) with its survey reports on hot social issues, until the government banned the Centre in 1994 for conducting a controversial survey on Deng Xiaoping.[62] There are also networks of intellectuals around privately sponsored academic journals such as *Zhongguo Shehui Kexue Jikan* (Chinese social science quarterly), *Xiandai yu Chuantong* (Modernity and tradition), and *Dongfang* (Orient), or informally organized "readers' clubs." Members of these unofficial networks shared a common interest in promoting social change. Some regularly held conferences in major Chinese cities, and readers' clubs often meet regularly at bookstores. One such club is the Sanwei Readers'

Club, which holds regular meetings of over a hundred people, mostly professors, students, officials, and journalists, every Saturday afternoon at the Sanwei Bookstore in downtown Beijing. During such meetings, the participants engage in heated discussions on issues concerning China's economic and political reforms, including human rights and democracy.[63] Existence of such groups indicates that it is not too difficult to set up an unofficial association and to find a supervisory organization. An association of this nature is usually quite independent: its relationship with the supervisory organization is largely nominal.

The Chinese law is flexible about what kind of "state unit" *(guojia danwei)* can serve as a supervisory organization, and allows nationwide official associations, such as the ACFTU, the Women's Association, and the Federation of Industry and Commerce, to supervise other associations.[64] Generally, when an association is founded by another association, it is one step further removed from direct government control, as in the case with many chambers of commerce *(shanghui)* set up by local FIC branches. This appears to have become a strategy for some official associations to achieve a degree of independence from the state, and this practice is likely to contribute to the proliferation of associations.[65]

Legal ambiguity sometimes causes confusion in the relationship between the supervisory organization and the association under it. For example, when the Chinese Women Entrepreneurs' Association *(Zhongguo nü qiyejia xiehui)* reelected its leadership in October 1988, its supervisory organization – the Chinese Enterprise Management Association *(Zhongguo qiye guanli xiehui)* – declared the election result null and void. This led to a dispute over their relationship, in which the former declared that it was not under the "administrative leadership" of the latter.[66] A more recent case involved a lawsuit brought by the China Confucius Foundation against the Chinese Ministry of Culture, for the Ministry's alleged "illegal" interference in the activities of the Foundation and violation of its property rights.[67]

Apart from associations that are unofficial in nature but legally registered, there is also evidence of various "illegal" or semi-underground associations. For example, wildcat labour associations mushroomed throughout China and were responsible for hundreds of strikes. These labour organizations usually call themselves "workers' employment agencies" or "workers' mutual help associations" to avoid suspicion. The authorities were said to have "refrained from taking action ... for fear of provoking a labour crisis."[68] Recent evidence has indicated that similar associations also exist among peasants in many rural areas. The past few years have witnessed frequent large-scale peasant protests against heavy tax burdens, often with thousands of participants. An investigative report internally published by the State Council's Rural Research Centre revealed that many of these protests were organized by secret peasant associations, which frequently called themselves "burden-relieving groups" *(jian fu zu)*. The activists in these groups, some of whom become popular leaders among peasants, are called "burden-relieving representatives" *(jian fu daibiao)*. Some large-scale protests have been triggered when local government officials attempted to detain popular peasant leaders. In one incident, protestors held several local law enforcement officers hostage until the release of their leader, who was charged with "organizing mass tax revolts" *(ju zhong kang shui)*. It was reported that the central leadership ordered local government officials to refrain from using force to crack down on the peasants, for fear of escalating violence.[69]

It has also been reported that large numbers of underground publications exist, and that when the regime finds a book politically unacceptable, it has great difficulty detecting where the book was printed. A CPC and State Council circular on the "cultural market" issued in December 1994 demanded that "the sources of the publications must be checked and their distribution channels cleared." A *Renmin Ribao* (People's daily) commentator noticed that some illegal publishers and booksellers formed syndicates and networks and had "complicated political backgrounds," adding that the task of eliminating them would "remain arduous for a long time."[70]

A 1997 *China News Digest* interview of Tong Yi, veteran dissident Wei Jingsheng's secretary and interpreter between September 1993 and February 1994 when Wei was temporarily released from prison, revealed that there were networks of intellectuals within the private sector. These networks were capable of setting up private research institutions, commissioning translations and possible underground publication of politically sensitive books by Western political scientists (such as *China's Crisis* by Andrew Nathan), and connecting the young college graduate with Wei Jingsheng right after Wei's release from prison. It is not clear how extensive such networks are and how they interact with, and influence, the intellectual community as a whole.[71]

In addition to cultural and intellectual groups, religious and quasi-religious groups have also caught the attention of both the regime and the Western media. Though the Chinese government officially denies the existence of semi-underground "house churches," it is generally believed that members of such religious groups outnumber the membership of the officially sanctioned Christian churches. In recent years, nationwide networks have developed that provide systematic training for pastors of house churches. Millions of Chinese have joined these Christian groups in spite of discouragement and sometimes harassment by local officials.[72]

The recent crackdown on Falun (Wheel of Law or Dharma Wheel) Gong and a number of smaller cults has highlighted the widespread existence of semi-cultural, semi-religious organizations. In city parks throughout China, it is quite common to see groups of people practising various kinds of breathing exercises *(qigong)*. Millions of people, including many high-ranking party, government, and military officials, participate in such group activities, and there are now hundreds of *qigong*-related semi-spiritual groups in China. All claim to promote public health through *qigong* exercises. Almost all of them, including Falun Gong, have been legally registered, but conduct their activities with almost complete independence from their supervisory organizations. Most such groups are small and localized, but a few have grown into large nationwide organizations with millions of members, like Falun Gong.

The regime is apparently considering banning another such nationwide organization: Zhonghua Yangshen Yizhi (China Health and Wisdom Promotion) Gong, or Zhong Gong. This organization is in many ways very similar to Falun Gong. Its spiritual guru is a *qigong* master called Zhang Hongbao who founded it in 1988. Zhang claims to have supernatural healing power, just like Li Hongzhi, the spiritual leader of Falun Gong. Li was said to have prevented the earth from exploding, at the request of President Jiang Zemin, but Zhang's claim is much more modest: he cured President Jiang's arthritis. Under Zhang's guruship, Zhong Gong has developed into a large organization with a hundred branches throughout China that claims twenty million members. The organization runs a conglomerate, the Tianjin-based Unicorn Group Inc., which makes health food products and employs 400,000 people nationwide.[73]

While the state has cracked down on those that are perceived as a political threat or as engaged in illegal activities, most such organizations remain untouched. Even the much publicized suppression of Falun Gong has been passively resisted by much of the population, revealing the inability or unwillingness of many grassroots state organizations to mete out harsh punishment to people participating in such groups.[74]

The most dramatic example of an unofficial group engaged in political activities has been the China Democracy Party (CDP). The CDP seized the opportunity of President Clinton's visit to China in June 1998 to announce its establishment and applied to the Zhejiang provincial government for registration as a lawful organization. The application was turned down. A few members of the CDP were detained a week following Clinton's departure, but interestingly, most of them were released after two days. Those who remained in police custody were let go at the end of August amid domestic protests and international pressure. This relatively benign outcome appears to have encouraged the dissident organization to further press its demand.

In mid-September – less than a month before the planned signature of the International Covenant on Civil and Political Rights (ICCPR) by China

(China had declared its intention to sign in March), the CDP launched a nationwide effort to register itself simultaneously in nine provinces. In late October, after China signed the ICCPR, two other provinces received the CDP's application, bringing the total to twelve. The Chinese government appeared to be caught by surprise. Most provinces rejected the application and detained the applicants. Some, however, initially accepted the application and told the applicants to await further study *(yanjiu)* of their applications. In December, the central government signalled a crackdown to the provinces, and a few leading CDP members were arrested and sentenced to long prison terms. In spite of this setback, the CDP continued its activities. In February 1999, it declared the founding of four more provincial branches, claiming to be a national organization with sixteen provincial branches and hundreds of active members.[75]

In fact, the CDP is not the only independent political group that has appeared in the past few years. For example, an organization of intellectuals in Beijing called Alliance for China's Development *(Zhongguo Fazhan Lianhehui)* claimed to have 4,000 members and held weekly meetings to discuss sensitive political issues. In October 1998, the Beijing municipal government ordered it to dissolve, but the organizers of the group reportedly refused to accept the order. There are also a few groups actively involved in grassroots social unrest. For example, an organization called the Society for Reducing Taxes and Saving the Nation was said to be responsible for large-scale peasant unrest in Hunan Province in January 1999. The Association to Protect the Rights and Interests of Laid-off Workers has been active in labour unrest.[76]

To sum up, signs of civil society are found both inside and outside the existing corporatist structure. Within that structure, civil society coincides with the transition toward societal corporatism and is enhanced by the emergence of localism. Outside that structure, it is indicated by the existence of unofficial associations, independent intellectual networks, various kinds of "illegal" associations, and religious and semi-religious groups, as well as a few political and dissident groups.

Theoretical Considerations
The 1989 pro-democracy movement evoked various responses from Western scholars and raised the issue of change in China's social organization, especially the possible emergence of civil society. Much of the Western scholarship on the contemporary state-society relationship in China employs one of two seemingly opposite concepts: civil society and corporatism. Inspired by the pro-democracy movement, some Western scholars proposed applying the concept of civil society to China. Others, however, rejected the idea of an emerging civil society and suggested a more corporatist development.

For example, Martin Whyte held that a civil society was already "emerging and consolidating" in China, as evidenced by the development of "a bewildering variety" of autonomous associations, which, he believed, were at least partially responsible for a series of confrontations with the state during the 1980s.[77] Similarly, Gordon White observed that mass associations were no longer merely "bridges" between the state and society but were gaining autonomy in the representation of societal interests. The political dilemma of the economic reform, in his opinion, was that the socioeconomic foundation of the current regime was undermined by rapid social differentiation, demonstrated by the "flowering of associational life."[78] Others, such as Barrett L. McCormick, Su Shaozhi, and Xiao Xiaoming, accepted the idea of an emerging civil society while pointing out that its growth was rather weak and its future prospects were uncertain.[79]

However, the definition of civil society itself has been a source of contention and confusion. "Civil society" is sometimes used in a strong European liberal sense to mean an independent political society voicing its demands in a public sphere, and sometimes used in a minimal Hegelian/Marxian sense to mean a modern bourgeois society, a private sphere of autonomous social and economic activities separated from the political life of the state.[80] Gordon White suggested that the minimal definition of civil society appears to be more applicable than the strong one in China, where civil society is directly related to the development of the market and the process of economic modernization. The common ground between the two meanings of civil society should, however, be recognized; individual rights and freedoms are basic to both. While the view of civil society as a political society in the public sphere focuses on political rights and freedoms, civil society as an autonomous bourgeois society in the private sphere stresses economic rights and freedoms, the structural foundation for the former.[81]

In addition to this disagreement, there is also no consensus on the relationship between an emerging civil society and the state. For example, Heath Chamberlain suggested that civil society differs from society in that it emphasizes the common good rather than parochial interests, and therefore it cannot be defined solely in terms of its independence of, and opposition to, the state. Historically, civil society is "as much a creature of the state as it is of society."[82] In the same spirit, Tony Saich cautioned against overemphasizing the democratic implications of an emerging civil society, which, without the "civilizing" effect of a morally acceptable state, might restore the "state of nature" instead of leading to a democratic order.[83]

In general, civil society is defined in terms of confrontation or at least separation between the state and organized social activities. The concept of civil society, therefore, crucially includes the development of autonomous or semi-autonomous organizations in society. For this reason, those who saw more harmony, cooperation, and dependence in the contemporary Chinese state-society relationship than competition, antagonism, and independence tended to embrace the concept of corporatism instead. They pointed out that the term "civil society" implies too much independence from and confrontation with the state, whereas in China the relationship between the state and the new economic players as well as the large number of associations is marked by harmony and dependence. Therefore, they found corporatism a better analytical model.

For example, Dorothy J. Solinger expressed the opinion that the economic reform resulted not in a separation of the state and society, but in a growing mutual dependence between the new economic actors and the bureaucratic state, and their subsequent merger.[84] The same opinion was also expressed by Jean Oi, who observed that political power and economic operations were often combined at the local level, where government organizations acted like quasi-corporate entities.[85] A number of studies of associational activities have also emphasized the corporatist nature of the relationship between the state and associations. Jonathan Unger and Anita Chan, for example, suggested that the rapid development of associational activities in China could be explained as the emergence of a state corporatist structure and the gradual transformation of that structure from state to societal corporatism, a process of development similar to that in other East Asian countries. The concept of societal corporatism had originally been proposed by Philippe C. Schmitter as a post-liberal phenomenon, in contrast to the pre-liberal state corporatism. Unger and Chan pointed out that the East Asian experience indicated that societal corporatism could be the result of a transformation from state corporatism.[86] In their case studies of the associations of private entrepreneurs, Christopher Earle Nevitt and Kristen Parris also focused on the corporatist nature of such associations.[87]

However, the apparent opposition between civil society and corporatism can be misleading: civil society refers to a realm of organized social activities outside the state, which imply a certain kind of state-society relationship, while corporatism refers directly to a particular connection between the state and society. The conceptual distinction between civil society and corporatism therefore needs to be clarified.

People who have applied the concept of corporatism have mostly used Schmitter's definition.[88] It should be noted that Schmitter viewed corporatism not as the opposite of civil society, but as an "institutional arrangement for linking the associationally organized interests of civil society with the decisional structures of the state." His notion of societal corporatism suggested the possible coexistence of corporatism and independent social organizations – components of civil society. He made two primary distinctions that are useful in clarifying the relationship between civil society and corporatism: between corporatism and pluralism, and between state corporatism and societal corporatism.[89] Civil society as autonomous social organizational activities is logically opposed to state corporatism only. It is in opposition to corporatism of both types only when it implies a pluralist relationship with the state.

The distinction between corporatism and pluralism includes the following key elements: (1) whether the number of associations is limited or unspecified; (2) whether one association is designated by the state and has a representational monopoly within a social category, or many associations compete for articulation and representation; (3) whether they are hierarchically ordered; (4) whether their membership is compulsory or voluntary; and (5) whether the state exercises a degree of influence over their leadership selection. What is noticeable is that the autonomy of associations does not rule out corporatism, because societal corporatism allows it. Logically, cooperation does not exclude independence. The distinction between state and societal corporatism is whether the corporatism is a system of state domination or is arrived at through societal competition and pressure. For example, the state-designated representational monopoly can result from the power of the state to appoint an association as the only official one. Alternatively, the state may simply recognize the monopoly status of a powerful association. Similarly, the state's influence over an association's leadership selection can result from either the state's imposition or "a reciprocal consensus on procedure." On the other hand, state subsidies are usually a sign of dependence.[90]

Another variation of corporatism is local corporatism, which has been found useful in the discussion of China, where the tension between different levels of government supposedly has caused fragmentation of the structure. Kenneth Lieberthal, for example, suggested that the weakening of the central authority in the post-Mao era resulted in a "general fragmentation of authority in the system."[91] A localized corporatist system requires one association for each social category within each geographical unit and at each level of government, as described by Jonathan Unger and Anita Chan: "Each successively lower layer of regional government in China – the province, city, county, township and village – increasingly comprises a small empire which holds levers of control over the organizations and activities within its own borders."[92] Given the size of the Chinese state, this fragmented corporatist system, if fully developed, could contain millions of component units. Such a large number, plus the fragmentation of hierarchical ordering, implies the possible growth of pluralism within the system.

To sum up, the models basically centre on two concepts, civil society and corporatism, each of which contains subtypes and variations. Civil society may be European liberal or Hegelian/Marxian, and may imply a societal corporatist or a pluralist relationship with the state. Corporatism may be state or societal and has a variation in the form of local corporatism. Civil society and corporatism are not necessarily opposite concepts and are not mutually exclusive. On the contrary, societal corporatism constitutes a conceptual overlap between them, as illustrated by Figure 4.2. In spite of their apparent disagreement as to its nature, the proponents of civil society and corporatism both indicated a degree of change in the relationship between the state and society and in the way society is organized. As B. Michael Frolic pointed out, such a change could be characterized as "state-led civil society," which, as an "Asian type of political development," was a form of corporatism. Jonathan Unger also noticed the conceptual overlap between societal corporatism and civil society when he discussed the role of chambers of commerce in China.[93] The emerging social reality underlying the scholarly debate is the breakdown of the pre-reform-era direct control structure and its replacement by a new mechanism of indirect control, in the case of state corporatism, or by a growing degree of independence of the new societal players, in the case of "emerging civil society" or "transition toward societal corporatism."

In my opinion, no one of these models can provide a sufficiently comprehensive account of the complex reality and dynamic nature of associational activities in contemporary China. What appears to be the case is the coexistence of opposite tendencies. While the state is actively promoting state corporatism as a new mechanism of control to partially replace the direct command system, some of the newly emerging societal forces have already shown a tendency to free themselves from this state control. Sometimes the effort to become autonomous can enjoy limited success, given the state's deliberate withdrawal from certain areas of social life, the complexity of the state system itself, and the constant tension between different institutions and between different levels of government. These substantially weaken the state's control and leave the door open for certain societal

Figure 4.2

Corporatism and civil society: Subtypes and variations

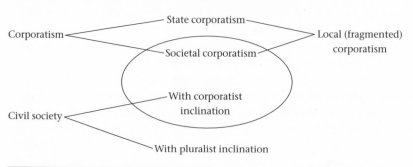

Note: The circle indicates a conceptual overlap.

forces to organize themselves without much state interference. Such a complicated social reality requires a selective combination and application of several of the models discussed above.

Conclusion

During the past twenty years of the economic reform, an important aspect of the restructuring of the Chinese society has been the emergence of large numbers of associations, which are playing an increasingly important role in the state-society relationship. Different analytical models have been proposed to describe the relationship between associations and the state at various levels, and between associations and their own members. The concept of corporatism emphasizes harmony and cooperation between the state and society, with a limited number of official associations functioning both as the means of state control over different social categories and as official representatives of different societal interests. The concept of civil society, on the other hand, focuses on the autonomy of associations as the means of articulating social interests independent of or in confrontation with the state.

The concept of corporatism probably offers a better general description of associational activities in the areas of political and economic life, where associations are limited in number, usually enjoy official status, and form nationwide hierarchical systems. Their memberships are either compulsory or highly inclusive within their respective social categories, and their leadership selection is largely controlled by the supervisory state organizations. In short, they fulfil all the major criteria for associations within a corporatist system. The fact that the Chinese state at different levels has been promoting a system of state corporatism can be observed both in the legal stipulations regulating and limiting associational activities and in the way the state has acted toward associations, including its efforts to set up official associations, to control associational activities for its own purposes, and to reduce the numbers and duplications of associations.

Meanwhile, several tendencies provide evidence of tension and dynamic change within this corporatist system, to the effect that the overall corporatist structure is being fragmented by localism and the transition toward societal corporatism. First of all, among some major national associations, a shift of functional focus has occurred. They are becoming increasingly independent agents acting on behalf of their memberships rather than being used as a means of state control. This transition has been fuelled by the emergence and increasing awareness of social group interests, and the consequent tension between an association's control and service functions. In this circumstance, one function tends to prevail over the other, leading to the dynamics of state versus societal corporatism.

Second, state control is often weaker at lower levels of government administration. Grassroots branches of some national associations tend to have greater independence. While local state organizations may find it beneficial to support the pursuit of group interests by some associations within their localities, pressure from the membership rather than manipulation by the local government better explains why local associations actively protect and promote membership interests. Grassroots pressure may be as responsible as local state interests for the tension between different levels of government and the fragmentation of the overall corporatist system.

The model of societal corporatism creates a conceptual overlap between corporatism and civil society, since corporatism as a particular way of connecting the state and society does not necessarily exclude the possibility of societal autonomy. This overlap becomes especially obvious when the transition toward societal corporatism coincides with the emergence of localism, creating the phenomenon of "local societal corporatism." Societal autonomy is further enhanced by localism.

Finally, the state appears to be less capable of controlling associational activities in areas outside politics and the economy. Its corporatist effort is more successful in political and economic areas than in cultural, intellectual, and spiritual areas, where unofficial and voluntary associations have thrived, creating a largely autonomous realm of organized social activities. The concept of corporatism, therefore, can be better applied to the former areas, while the concept of civil society is probably applicable to the latter, insofar as associational activities are concerned. It is clear that the search for elements of civil society should not be limited to the official or semi-official associations in political and economic areas or to the existing corporatist structure. Even in the realm of politics, independent group activities appear to be on the rise, stimulated by the growing social tension that accompanied economic development and the recent economic downturn, and by increasing influence and pressure from Western countries.

Hence, no single-model approach can adequately explain associational activities in China. The size of the Chinese state, the complexity of the relationships involved, and the wide variety of phenomena that have been observed clearly require a combined approach, employing different concepts and models, to the analysis of this aspect of change in social organization.

The complex reality of associational activities generally points to some broad trends of change in contemporary China. Regardless of whether they represent a transition toward societal corporatism or an emerging civil society, associational activities indicate the restructuring of Chinese society through the breaking down of the vertical control structure and the development of horizontal social grouping. This process has contributed to an emerging realm of organized social life, increasing societal autonomy, and the development of differentiated social interests. In other words, the thriving associational activities illustrate a development in the state-society relationship that has closely paralleled the intellectual rethinking of the state-society relationship.

The retreat of the state, the growing independence of associations, and the expansion of the realm of autonomous social and economic life under-line the concepts of state-society dualism and societal autonomy, while the differentiation of social interests and the development of horizontal social groupings give plausibility to the concepts of social pluralism and civil society as applied to contemporary China. Associational activities have come to be regarded by Chinese scholars as a key component of the "big society" that corresponds to "small government." Ideally, the development of associations will "enhance society's ability for self-organization and self-management," and allow the government to transfer many of its social and economic management functions to associations.[94]

5
Reorganizing Rural Society: Village Self-Government

The recent development of village self-government represents another important change in the social organization of contemporary China that has caught the attention of scholars. Like the emergence of associational activities, village self-government offers an example of the state's deliberate withdrawal from grassroots social and economic life. The increased autonomy of local rural society and its reorganization into self-governing communities illustrate the overall trend in China toward greater societal autonomy. Although this is a relatively new phenomenon, several Western as well as Chinese scholars have written on the subject, based on field observations, analysis of Chinese sources, or a combination of both.

The regime has referred to both associational activities and village self-government as "grassroots democracy," which is said to be part of China's "socialist democracy." Chinese scholars, on the other hand, have regarded both as evidence of emerging societal autonomy and as part of the "big society" corresponding to the idea of a "small government."[1] However, the difference between these two types of organizations is quite obvious. Unlike associations, self-government organizations in rural communities were established by law to serve as grassroots government institutions. They directly replaced the previous government institutions, which had been extensions of local governments, and their development has relied mainly on promotion by the regime leadership.

Several issues are raised by the development of village self-government. First, how democratic is the procedure by which the village self-government organizations are created? Second, what is the relationship between the self-government organizations and ordinary villagers – to what extent do they represent and respond to the interests of the villagers? Third, what is the relationship between village self-government organizations and the local government – are the former truly autonomous? Fourth, what is the relationship between self-government organizations and village Communist Party organizations? Which of them makes decisions in the village? Finally, what has motivated the regime to promote village self-government?

The following discussions aim at offering a comprehensive review of available evidence in an attempt to analyze the factors that contributed to the emergence of village self-government, its current situation, the nature of the self-governing organizations, their internal and external functions and relationships, the distinction between "democracy" and "self-government," and the political significance of village self-government in the changing state-society relationship.

The Emergence of Villagers' Committees

Economic reform in rural areas started in 1978. By the early 1980s, most farmland had been contracted to individual peasant households, and as a result, rural economic and political relationships changed fundamentally. The commune system based on collective farming was abandoned, and the state's direct command model of control over the rural economy and population became ineffective. Though township government was established to replace the government functions of the communes, political institutions below the township level were in disarray and a power vacuum developed. This situation was recognized by the regime and well described by Chinese scholars and officials as well as by Western scholars who studied the issue.[2]

Prior to the reform, the state monopolized rural economic resources and peasants depended on the state for allocation of their material needs. An important feature of pre-reform collective farming was that part of the harvest was turned directly over to the state. The rest was distributed among the peasants by the state-controlled collectives. The rural reform turned the tables: the peasants became economically rather independent, and the state came to depend on them for grain products and tax revenues. Taxation now required peasant households to turn part of their income over to the state, rather than the state retaining part of the collective income being distributed to them, as had been the case before the reform. So instead of allocating material goods among villagers as they used to do before the reform, village cadres now had to go after villagers to demand tax payment. Such a change of relationship certainly contributed to the growing tension between peasants and cadres and the weakening position of village cadres, and made it more difficult to implement state taxation policies.[3] Tyrene White pointed out that the growing tension between villagers and village cadres after the rural economic reform largely resulted from the failure of the old political structure to cope with the changed socioeconomic circumstances. Consequently, institutional innovations were necessary to maintain social stability in rural areas.[4]

Economic independence also led to the peasants' growing concern over village affairs and the behaviour of village cadres, because villagers increasingly felt that these directly affected their self-interests. Villagers became dissatisfied that decisions on issues concerning their personal interests were made by a few government-appointed cadres behind closed doors. Abuses of power by cadres were likely to make villagers more angry than before. Meanwhile, a village cadre's income often compared rather unfavourably to that of those fellow villagers who had seized the opportunities opened up by the reform to get rich. Investing time in a cadre's job was no longer always considered worthwhile, and many cadres began to devote themselves to more profitable activities.[5]

To deal with this situation, the state tried "traditional methods" – moral education combined with disciplinary actions – to boost cadre morale, rectify cadre behaviour, and adjust the peasant-cadre relationship, but such methods failed to be effective on a large scale, as observed by Chinese scholars and officials in charge of rural work. Socialist education campaigns met with strong resistance at the grassroots; government work teams sent to villages were prevented from entering by villagers. It was obvious that these traditional methods of control were invalidated by the fundamentally changed social reality in rural communities. As a result, opening up the grassroots political system to peasant participation appeared to be a viable way to restore political order in rural areas.[6]

In this process of economic and political change, the central state played a crucial role in searching for ways to rebuild grassroots political institutions and to establish a mechanism of indirect state control over key policy areas. The central state effort can be observed in a series of legislative and policy-making actions. Article 111 of the 1982 Constitution called, for the first time, for the establishment of villagers' committees *(cunmin wei-yuanhui* or *cunweihui)* and defined them as "grassroots mass organizations of self-government" *(jiceng qunzhongxing zizhi zuzhi)*. Though no follow-up implementation measures were formulated at the time, writing village self-government into the constitution was significant in itself because it paved the way for future political and legislative development in favour of village self-government. In 1983, after the dissolution of the communes, the party's Central Committee and the State Council jointly issued a circular on the establishment of township government to replace the government function of the communes. The same circular also called for the development of village self-government in accordance with the constitution.

With this central state initiative, large-scale grassroots institutional change started in 1983. Communes were replaced by townships and production brigades were replaced by villagers' committees. In a few southern provinces, production brigades were replaced by townships and production teams were replaced by villagers' committees. By early 1985, nearly 950,000 villagers' committees were established throughout the country.[7] The change during this period was very fast but quite superficial: in reality, change was in name only. Local government dominated most villagers' committees and continued to appoint village cadres. Villagers' committees were not at all organizations of self-government.[8]

Nevertheless, the central leadership appeared determined to make village self-government a reality. In December 1987, after years of internal debate, the NPC passed the Organic Law of Villagers' Committees, which stipulated that villagers' committees were to be directly elected by villagers and were not to be agencies of the township government, and that the role of the township government was to provide guidance *(zhidao)* rather than leadership *(lingdao)* for villagers' committees.[9] *(Zhidao* means advising but not necessarily commanding, while *lingdao* means directly issuing orders.) The "trial implementation" in following years met with strong resistance from local officials and was further delayed by the post-Tiananmen political backlash. However, in 1990 Peng Zhen, a top regime leader generally known as a conservative, personally intervened in favour of implementing the Organic Law. The Central Committee issued a directive in December 1990 that effectively ended the debate and started large-scale implementation.[10]

Such strong central leadership initiative, especially from such a supposed leading conservative as Peng Zhen, raised the question of the regime's motivation. A common explanation is that the regime was convinced that rural social and economic changes had made village self-government the only way to restore law and order in rural areas so that the state could implement its rural policies, including taxation, grain acquisition, and family planning. In other words, it was a matter of political necessity. Daniel Kelliher, for example, suggested that the proponents of village self-government made only "instrumental" arguments for it, rather than arguing for the value of democracy itself. His review of the internal Chinese debate on village self-government suggested that the issue of democracy was raised not for its own sake, but as a measure of political expediency, for the purpose of restoring order in rural communities and guaranteeing effective implementation of central state policies.[11] There is certainly an element of truth in this explanation. Nevertheless, it is a little simplified and neglects some important ideological, institutional, and personal factors that also favoured the implementation of the Organic Law.

The concept of democracy has always been a component of official ideology. Such ideas as popular sovereignty, mass line, and "let the people be masters of their own house" have been incorporated into the PRC constitution. As McCormick pointed out, Leninism contained "hidden transcripts" of democracy, which created a criterion that the regime was frequently measured against and pressured to live up to.[12] One focus of the debate on political reform throughout the 1980s was how to realize the old idea of letting the people be masters of their own house. "Grassroots democracy" was a convenient solution proposed by the regime and is the ideological foundation of the Organic Law of Villagers' Committees. Contrary to Kelliher's suggestion, arguments for democracy as valuable in itself have been repeatedly made by regime leaders and senior government officials, to say nothing of academics. The regime leadership appears to be not only fully aware of the democratic implication of village self-government, but deliberately promoting it as a Chinese version of democracy.

For example, Peng Zhen stated that the purpose of village self-government was to "run democracy training class for eight hundred million peasants" and to "put the concept of democracy in everyone's mind."[13] At the passage of the Organic Law, a leading member of the NPC's Law Committee claimed that village self-government was significant as "an important component of socialist democratic politics" that embodied the democratic principles of "all power to the people" and "let the people be masters of their own house."[14] Doje Cering, minister of civil affairs, declared at a conference on village self-government held by his ministry in 1995 that village self-government was "an important part of construction of the socialist democratic political system with Chinese characteristics." Its far-reaching significance was to pave the way for further democratization.[15] It is hard to maintain that such remarks were made by regime leaders and government officials purely for political expediency and contain no ideological element.

It is true that the internal debate on village self-government appeared to focus on the political feasibility of village self-government, but to say that the issue of democracy was ignored is to miss a huge part of the debate. Democracy overshadowed the entire debate and put the opponents of village self-government in a weak, defensive position, because they could not openly declare that democracy was a bad thing. The two sides appeared to concentrate on the more practical issue of policy implementation precisely because the opponents never said they were against democracy. All they could argue instead was that peasants were culturally backward and therefore were not yet ready for such a good thing as democracy.

Institutionally, the law has been promoted by the central government but resisted by local officials, indicating a rift between the centre and the local state. Kelliher was quite correct when he pointed out that the main obstacle to the implementation of village self-government was the local party and government officials, who were afraid that they would lose control of a most valuable resource: the villagers.[16] The centre and local government do not simply differ on how to effectively implement state policies, but face a clash of interests concerning the amount of tax that should be levied upon the peasants. The centre's interest lies in maintaining long-term economic growth and political stability in rural areas so that they will serve as a moderate but steady source of revenue and grain products. For this reason, it has demanded that the total tax burden on peasants should not exceed 5 percent of their net income per capita.

Many local officials, on the other hand, are engaged in ambitious plans of local development that can benefit them politically or personally, and treat peasants as an immediate source of local revenue, thus aggravating the heavy tax burdens on peasants and causing political instability in rural areas. The centre has clearly been alarmed by this problem and the related issues of cadre corruption, rural lawlessness, and social instability. It has issued many directives to local officials, ordering them to reduce burdens on peasants, which have fallen on deaf ears to the frustration of the centre.[17] In recent years, incidents of peasant unrest have been frequently reported, most of which can be described as tax revolts against local government officials. From this perspective, it is unsurprising that local state organizations have resisted the implementation of the Organic Law. It is quite conceivable that the centre may be trying to empower villages against the encroachment of the local officials. In other words, the centre's promotion of village self-government may represent a sort of centre-grassroots political coalition-building against the local officials – to hold them more accountable not only to peasants but also to the centre.

At the personal level, many elders in the regime leadership started their political careers as rural revolutionaries, and it is possible that some of them genuinely believe that peasants should be masters in their own villages. For example, Peng Zhen was known in the 1960s as a "legalist" within the regime leadership and was criticized during the Cultural Revolution for advocating that everyone was equal before the law. Between 1982 and 1987, as the NPC chairman, he vigorously promoted village self-government and the drafting of the Organic Law, which turned out to be the last important law passed by the NPC before he stepped down in March 1988.[18] The Organic Law bore his signature; to oppose it was to oppose him personally.

In short, for the regime leadership, village self-government could potentially kill many birds with one stone, namely, develop grassroots democracy – window-dressing or not – rebuild rural political institutions, overcome rural lawlessness, combat cadre corruption, alleviate tension in the cadre-peasant relationship, check local state encroachment on peasants, and above all, facilitate central policy implementation.

The Current Situation

With persistent effort by the centre, large-scale implementation of the Organic Law began in the early 1990s, and to date has achieved initial success. Villagers' committees have been set up in all villages. After some restructuring, including the merging of some small, neighbouring villages into relatively large villages, there are now fewer than 800,000 villages in China, with an average population of about 1,000. Most villages have gone through two or three rounds of elections, and most provinces have passed legislation on the implementation of village self-government.[19] There is evidence that, in many areas, the quality of village elections is improving and the system of village self-government is being gradually consolidated. At present, the central government is engaged in an ambitious plan to set up one model self-governing village in every township throughout China.[20]

In the process of implementing village self-government, an important institutional development has occurred, namely the emergence of village representative assemblies (VRA: *cunmin daibiao huiyi* or *cundaihui*). Generally speaking, a VRA is made up of twenty to forty members, each of whom is elected by a group of ten to fifteen households. No VRA is necessary for villages with only a few dozen households. By 1994, at least half of China's villages had established VRAs.[21] VRAs appear to be necessary because the population of most Chinese villages is so large as to render "direct democracy" through villagers' councils *(cunmin huiyi)* – meetings of all adult villagers or a representative from each household – impractical and ineffective. A deeper reason, however, lies in the peasants' growing concern over village affairs and their consequent demand for a more effective way to articulate their interests and participate in the village decision-making process.[22]

The development of VRAs has raised two issues concerning the democratic process within the village: the choice between direct and indirect democracy, and the nature of the decision making itself. The original intention of the Organic Law was to let ordinary villagers decide on village affairs directly, but VRAs are obviously a form of indirect democracy, with no legal foundation in the Organic Law. One justification for VRAs is that they complement rather than replace villagers' councils, in that they only function as a decision-making body when villagers' councils are not in session, and crucial decisions are still made by villagers' councils.[23] However, since villagers' councils are rarely in session, VRAs have actually taken over the decision-making function of villagers' councils and reduced the latter's role to merely electing villagers' committee members. In some cases, even that role has been partially usurped by VRAs.[24]

On the other hand, the VRA system is undoubtedly more effective as a mechanism for interest articulation and democratic decision making. The system is conducive to broadly admitting all kinds of local elite – people representing various social interests that have emerged since the economic reform – into the political process, and to facilitate political accommodation and compromise, thus contributing to grassroots social stability. Anne F. Thurston cautioned against focusing solely on the election of village leaders, and pointed out that the newly emerged VRAs played an important role in democratic decision making, accommodating different interests, providing a mechanism of effective participation, and thus raising the democratic consciousness of villagers.[25] In other words, what appears to be less democratic may actually be more democratic. For this reason, the development of the VRA system can be regarded as indicating the institutional maturity of village self-government (Figure 5.1). The legalization of VRAs has been proposed in scholarly discussions, and a new law has recently been drafted making the establishment of VRAs obligatory.[26]

Initial success in implementing village self-government has been confirmed by both reports in the Chinese media and studies conducted by Chinese and Western scholars. Evidence from both sources indicates that in many Chinese villages, village leaders have been elected through open, fair, and competitive elections, and candidates often have to run election campaigns among villagers in order to get votes. Kevin O'Brien reported that such elections were "not limited to a few showcase villages." A Chinese official from the Ministry of Civil Affairs told a group of American observers at one such election that they were a common and regular practice in China.[27]

These reports suggest that in villages where leaders are thus elected and the VRA system is established, the decision-making process has become more transparent, and the village leaders are more accountable to villagers. Based on her analysis of the relationship between village elections and the behaviour of village cadres, Melanie Manion concluded that popular elections did affect cadre behaviour and made them more responsive to the demands put forward by their fellow villagers.[28] VRAs usually meet several times a year, or even once a month. Their powers include decision making

Figure 5.1

Village political organization

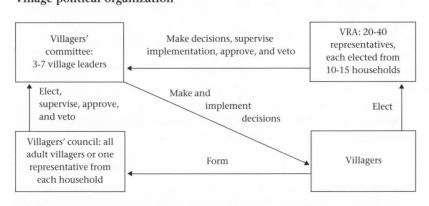

Note: Since it is difficult to hold villagers' council meetings, the functions of the villagers' council are largely played by the VRA, whose members are elected by specific constituencies among villagers.

on village affairs and supervising implementation of their decisions by villagers' committees. Some of them have been known to impeach corrupt members of villagers' committees and force them to resign between elections, and even to supervise village party branches and occasionally over-rule party branch decisions. In many places, the village revenue and expen-diture are made public once a month. A village in Shandong even carries live broadcast of the VRA meetings on the village cable TV network.[29]

Though at present such democratic villages appear to constitute a very small minority, their demonstrative effect should not be underestimated.[30] Kevin O'Brien observed that the relatively small number of the villages that were successful in democratic self-government were all well-to-do. He sug-gested that there was a correlation between property ownership and the desire for political participation, and that economic prosperity facilitated democratic self-government. Anne F. Thurston also noticed a relationship between democratic self-government and economic development.[31] Susan Lawrence, on the other hand, argued that her own case study had shown that a relatively poor village could develop democratic self-government because adverse economic circumstance could actually motivate the vil-lagers to support a more accountable institutional arrangement. She sug-gested that it was the development of self-government that eventually brought economic prosperity to the village. This argument, however, sup-ports rather than challenges O'Brien's conclusion about the correlation between economic prosperity and effective self-government.[32] In any case, the apparent association between democracy and affluence could make democracy attractive to peasants of poorer and less democratic villages.

The actual percentage of villages in China that regularly hold open and competitive elections is not available. O'Brien suggested such villages fell into two categories: those that are considered "up to standard" by the gov-ernment, which are mostly model "demonstration villages," and those that are considered "runaway" – taken over by societal forces independent of the state. According to Jiang Wandi, 82,266 villages were set up as dem-onstration villages between 1990 and 1995, roughly 10 percent of the vil-lages in China.[33] However we cannot assume that all of the government-designated demonstration villages are actually successful in democratic self-government. There are also indications of a growing number of run-away villages, which will be discussed below.

Anne F. Thurston observed that democratic villages also tended to be "pluralistic villages" – those with a number of powerful associations. The presence of grassroots civil society, in her opinion, contributed to grass-roots democracy, in that political power in such villages was dispersed among different social groups rather than concentrated in the hands of a few elite.[34] Jorgen Elklit suggested that the different degrees of openness in village elections could be due to the widely different local rules and regulations for the implementation of village self-government, which might indicate different degrees of enthusiasm on the part of the local officials who drafted them. Taking advantage of the vagueness of the Organic Law of Villagers' Committees, some local regulations for its implementation allowed the township government and party organizations to intervene in the elections and actually control the nomination procedure. In some places, secret ballot was not practised. Rules for campaigning also varied from place to place.[35]

On the whole, it appears that the experiment with village self-government has thus far had some visible impact on the political attitude and behaviour of both village cadres and ordinary villagers, and on the political relationships both inside and outside villages. First, it has been reported that in villages where free and fair elections were held, the peasants' attitude toward elections changed from initially sceptical to serious. Once they saw that these elections offered them a genuine opportunity to have a say on village affairs that affected them personally, they participated with enthusiasm.[36] Second, there are reports that democratic procedures have altered cadre behaviour and the cadre-peasant relationship. On the one hand, popularly elected cadres feel that they have the support of the villagers and therefore are in a strong position to carry out their work. On the other hand, they take care to stay close to the villagers because they know that the latter can withdraw their support in the next election. Ties between village cadres and their fellow villagers thus become closer as a result of popular elections.[37]

Third, the new cadre-peasant relationship is said to have contributed to economic development and the implementation of state policies. There are many reports on how popularly elected cadres are capable of mobilizing villagers to donate money for economically beneficial public projects. In contrast, traditional authoritarian decision making and the crude, commandist, work style are said to have failed to garner mass support for public projects and led to tension between peasants and the government. Popularly elected cadres are also said to be more capable of implementing unpopular state policies, including taxation, grain acquisition, and birth control. One reason for this, as Kelliher explained, is that now these unpopular policies can be implemented more evenly among villagers, rather than unfairly in favour of cadres and their relatives.[38]

Fourth, popular elections have strengthened the position of village cadres in relation to the local state. There have been reports that attempts by local governments to meddle with village elections and village affairs have met with indignation and protest from both villagers and popularly elected village leaders. One such incident involved a villagers' committee chair in Jiangsu Province who sued the county government for illegally interfering in his work and undermining his authority in the village.[39]

Local government officials have complained that popular elections have made villages and village cadres difficult to control. Now the local government must try to solicit support from village cadres in order to ensure smooth implementation of its decisions. When it decides to extract money and labour from peasants, it must rely on village cadres to convince the peasants that the extraction is necessary. Unreasonably large levies may be rejected by villagers through popularly elected cadres.[40] In a recent incident, two popularly elected village leaders – the chair and deputy chair of a village in Henan Province – led hundreds of their fellow villagers to the township government office to protest against high taxes levied by the local government. The two village leaders were reportedly detained by the police as a result of their actions on behalf of their constituency.[41]

Finally, popular elections are altering the relationship between village party branches and popularly elected political institutions in villages. Peasant resistance to grassroots party organizations is not a new problem. Before the passage of the Organic Law, there were reports that peasants in some villages openly declared that they did not want party members in their villagers' committees. There was even a popular movie made on the subject. A large-scale survey conducted by the "parties concerned" *(youguan fangmian)* at the end of 1980s revealed that 7.9 percent of village party branches were completely paralyzed. Another 59.5 percent were in a "so-so" state: they had aging leadership, no organizational development, and no appeal among villagers, were engaged in economic work only, and paid no attention to politics and ideology.[42]

The Organic Law has placed village party branches in an even more difficult position. Though "party leadership" is also a constitutional principle, the institution of popular elections has made it increasingly difficult for party branches to control village affairs without the support of popularly elected cadres. The chief problem in the relationship between the party branch and the villagers' committee is determining which has the power to make decisions.[43] In order to retain leadership, party branches in many villages have tried to intervene in elections in order to place their own people on the villagers' committees. The result is widespread concurrent office-holding: most chairs of villagers' committees are party branch secretaries or vice-secretaries.[44] The case study in Hainan Province indicated that 94 percent of the villagers' committee chairs were concurrently held by village party branch secretaries.

The Organic Law made it illegal for local government or grassroots party organizations to try to fix village elections, and such attempts may result in prison terms. For example, a village party secretary in Fujian Province is reported to have been sentenced to three years' imprisonment for fixing an election in his favour.[45] The proponents of village self-government strongly opposed this kind of illegal meddling in village elections. However, they accepted concurrent office-holding so long as the party branch followed normal election procedures. Some hope that once it becomes established that the party branch has to win popular elections in order to control village affairs, the village party organization itself will come to be controlled by villagers. There is an indication that things may be moving in that direction in some areas, where the party control in villages is gradually weakening.

Village elections are increasingly seen as a necessary mechanism in giving party branches the mandate to rule and placing them under the supervision of ordinary villagers; Niu Fengrui found this to be true in her case study of Hainan Province.[46] Lawrence reported in her case study that the VRA, whose members were mostly not party members, supervised the party branch, sometimes overruled decisions made by the party, and even took some disciplinary actions against corrupt party branch members.[47] It has also been reported that in some places, popular elections have affected the selection of village party secretaries: they can no longer be appointed by township party committees or elected solely by village party members. In some places, villagers even demand that party branch secretaries be popularly elected as well.[48]

In short, it appears that in areas where village self-government has been successfully implemented, grassroots political institutions have been rebuilt, order has been restored, tension between cadres and villagers has been alleviated, cadre corruption is under control, some autonomy vis-à-vis the local government has been established, and village party branches are subject to a degree of popular control.

In spite of these achievements, many problems remain that may hinder further implementation of village self-government. The biggest obstacle appears to be the effort made by many local party and government officials to dominate village affairs. The key to their domination is to place the "right" people in the village leadership. Therefore, villagers' committee elections have been the focus of contention between villagers and the local state. Various tactics, some illegal, have been used by local officials to manipulate elections, including creating "public opinion" pressure in favour of officially determined candidates, deleting the names of competing candidates from the ballot, using party-controlled organizations to coerce voters, holding elections among people who are close to the party instead of among all villagers, holding indirect rather than direct elections, and election by a show of hands rather than secret ballot.[49]

Chinese scholars have offered both cultural and "rational choice" explanations for the desire of such local officials to control the village leadership. They are said to hold a traditional paternalist and condescending attitude toward peasants, believing that peasants are culturally and politically backward, and will inevitably choose the wrong people, even bad people, if allowed to elect their own leaders, thus making it impossible to implement state policies. Local officials are also characterized as wanting to control village leadership for various self-interested purposes, for example, to maintain their own power or to extract extra money and labour from peasants. For example, a *Renmin Ribao* (People's daily) article accused selfish local officials of continuing to use overt and covert measures to extract extra money from peasants, in spite of repeated directives from the central government.[50]

As a result of the local state manipulation of village elections, many villagers' committees remain tightly controlled by local officials and offer little resistance to their encroachment on peasants. Within villages, the relationship between villagers' committees and village party branches has not always been smooth, nor has it consistently favoured the committees. Frequently, either there is tension between them, or villagers' committees end up executing decisions made by party branches rather than by VRAs.[51] A conservative backlash occurred in some successful demonstration villages, and local officials regained tight control after a period of democratic self-government. For example, a group of graduate students at Beijing University recently conducted a follow-up study of a few villages in Zhao County, Hebei Province, including Beiwang village, the demonstration village where Susan V. Lawrence had conducted her case study. They found that Jia Guosuo, the popular village chief who had successfully established democratic self-government when Lawrence did her study there, had already left. Selfish local officials had regained control, placed their cronies in charge of village affairs, and ruthlessly exploited villagers – a scenario that was somewhat foreseen in Lawrence's observation that the self-government was weakly institutionalized and depended too much on the popularity of one person.[52]

Although tight control by local party and government officials can be a big problem, lack of party/state control can also jeopardize democratic self-government. Opponents of village self-government have predicted the resurgence of traditional forces or the emergence of new societal forces that could take over control of rural communities from the state, resulting in runaway villages. The most fearsome traditional force is the powerful clans that dominated vast rural areas before the Communist revolution. One argument in favour of party branch intervention in village elections was that it was necessary to offset powerful local clans.[53] Ironically, one of the original purposes of village self-government was to check the resurgence of clans. The revival of clans has been reported in recent years, especially by conservative media within the party, indicating persistent inner-party opposition to village self-government.

For example, a report in the conservative party journal *Zhenli de Zhuiqiu* (The pursuit of truth) described clan domination in some rural areas in Hunan Province. In a village where there was a dominant clan, the clan chief often chose both the party branch secretary and the chair of the villagers' committee. If there was a balance of power between two clans, then one would hold the position of the party branch secretary and the other the chair of the villagers' committee. The clans were said to have openly challenged the local state "on sensitive issues such as political power distribution, economic benefits division, various tax matters, family planning, and legal matters." A *Renmin Ribao* (People's daily) article also noted the widespread revival of clans and declared that the government should guard against both the "infiltration of external capitalist culture" and the "revival of feudal culture."[54]

In addition to traditional clans, there are also reports of villages that have come to be dominated by "capable people" *(nengren)*, meaning those private entrepreneurs who have become very rich. Traditional clans are said to be generally more powerful in underdeveloped areas while "capable people" are more powerful in prosperous areas. This seems to indicate that the political status of the newly emerging business people – the new bourgeoisie – is elevated by their economic success.[55] In both cases, a village may "run away" from party-state control.

A well-known example of the latter is Daqiu Village in Tianjin's Jinghai County, where a peasant entrepreneur achieved great success in business and subsequently became board chairman of the village enterprise and the party secretary of the village. This multimillionaire and his family controlled the political and economic life of the entire village, which he ruled with an iron hand. His men would attack, detain, or beat to death anyone who dared to oppose him. He even ordered some villagers to attack police officers investigating murders committed by his relatives. When he was finally brought to justice and sentenced to 20 years' imprisonment in 1993, his crimes included not only harbouring criminals, bribery, unlawful detention of people, and obstructing law enforcement, but also "unlawful control of people."[56]

By analyzing the internal and external relationships of a village, Kevin O'Brien developed a typology of Chinese villages based on two variables: the degree of voluntary popular participation in open and fair village elections, and the effectiveness of the village leadership in implementing unpopular state rural policies. Among those villages with high popular participation, some are demonstration villages, where popularly elected village leaders effectively implement state policies, and others are runaway villages, where popularly elected village leaders resist the implementation of state policies. Among those with low popular participation, some are authoritarian villages controlled by local officials, and others are paralyzed villages where political institutions have become totally ineffective. O'Brien's discussion also referred to "a second pattern" of authoritarian villages, which were controlled by local elites seeking to establish "independent kingdoms."[57] Daqiu Village appears be an example of this type. X.L. Ding suggested that many of China's rural areas today are controlled by powerful clans, criminal gangs, and private businesses.[58]

It is obvious that loss of control by the state does not necessarily lead to democratic self-government. Autonomy does not always entail democracy; it sometimes leads to authoritarian self-rule by powerful societal players such as clan chiefs or big businessmen. Such villages, though effectively self-governed, are tightly controlled by a small number of local elite. In terms of their relationship with the state, these are runaway villages of the authoritarian, not the democratic, kind. While this phenomenon needs to be further explored in order to achieve a better understanding of political change in rural China, it does illustrate increasing societal autonomy and the dramatic retreat of the state from grassroots rural society.

It also appears that leaders of runaway villages are as capable as local party and government officials at manipulating village elections. One kind of election irregularity typically involves local entrepreneurs, who buy votes to get themselves elected. A *Renmin Ribao* (People's daily) article reported massive purchasing of votes by rich entrepreneurs and said that this kind of "electoral bribery" has been on the rise in both village and township elections. Leaders of powerful clans, like some local officials, also fix elections. It is reported that in clan-dominated villages, villagers who are not members of powerful clans "dare not become cadres."[59]

For the state, the big problem with runaway villages – whether authoritarian or democratic – is not election irregularities, but their resistance to state rural policies. In spite of the effort by proponents of village self-government to publicize allegedly effective implementation of state policies in self-governing villages, there have been reports of policy implementation failure due to resistance from powerful clans or popularly elected village cadres. For example, the failure of birth control in rural areas in the 1980s was well known and generally blamed on rural reform and the resulting paralysis of rural political institutions. It appears that the implementation of village self-government in the 1990s has so far been unable to improve the birth control situation. In some cases, the local state effort to implement birth control policy was violently resisted by members of the powerful local elite, such as clan chiefs.[60]

The central state leadership is clearly quite nervous about these developments, and the state may conceivably try to reestablish some direct control mechanism to bring such villages back on track. The party's resolution at the fourth plenary session of the fourteenth Central Committee focused on "party building," especially the rebuilding of party organizations at the grassroots, "so as to give full scope to the healthy trends and suppress the evil ones, [and] preserve the advanced nature and purity of the ranks."[61] This resolution was followed by a series of speeches by party and state leaders emphasizing party building in rural grassroots. At the end of 1994, a decision was reached to "overhaul and consolidate" all of the party's 800,000 village branches within three years, and to allow party chiefs at the county level to select village party branch secretaries.[62] This recent emphasis on the party's role in villages highlighted the confines of village self-government: the party's position is not to be challenged. Democratic decision making is limited to village affairs and how to, not whether to, implement state policies.

To sum up, China's village self-government can be viewed as an effort by the state to rebuild rural grassroots political institutions in the new socio-economic circumstances of the reform era, and to establish a mechanism of indirect state control over key policy areas. Its implementation, however, presents a complicated picture of successes and failures, achievements and problems, harmony and conflicts. In addition to up-to-standard demonstration villages, there are also authoritarian villages controlled by local officials, popularly controlled runaway villages, authoritarian runaway villages controlled by powerful non-state players, and paralyzed villages. In paralyzed villages, cadres do their jobs only nominally or have left their jobs altogether, political institutions are totally ineffective, the political community has more or less dissolved, and a sort of state of nature has prevailed, a condition typically found in poor areas weakly controlled by the state.[63]

Both Chinese and Western scholars analyzing peasant behaviour in relation to village self-government have often featured "the rational peasant." This is the self-interested individual making rational choices about participating in a new system based on the calculation of risks versus gains. The peasants can become concerned with village affairs once they see their own interests are at stake. They may participate when they see clear benefits in doing so, or they may abstain when they decide that the gains are not enough to offset risks. This is the fundamental motivation for their participation in, or abstention from, village politics. Therefore, it has been suggested that the successful implementation of village self-government hinges on taking the interests of villagers into account and making them realize that participation will be to their advantage.[64]

Theoretical Considerations
Village self-government has raised a few theoretical issues concerning its nature, the internal and external relationships of self-governing villages,

and the implications of village self-government for the state-society relationship. Villagers' committees are constitutionally defined as "grassroots mass organizations of self-government." The term "mass organizations" indicates a specific understanding of the nature of village self-government, by grouping villagers' committees with associations. Both are labelled "mass organizations" and viewed as "bridges" or "transmission belts" connecting the state with a certain category of people, in this case peasants.[65] In the late 1980s, when early forms of VRA appeared, they were categorized with the various unofficial associations that emerged in large numbers during the same period.[66]

There is an apparent justification for this categorization. Both village self-government and associations have been promoted by the state to deal with the same issue, namely, the power vacuums created by the economic reform. The rationale behind both is the need for a new mechanism of indirect state control over an area of social and economic life that has been removed from the direct control of the state. In other words, both illustrate the erosion of the work unit system as a form of social organization within the state's vertical control structure, the development of new structures and organizational forms to partially replace it, and the growing societal autonomy in this process. In this sense village self-government, like associational activities, represents a new social reality that parallels the intellectual circles' rethinking of the state-society relationship discussed in Chapters 2 and 3.

In addition to their similar raison d'être, villagers' committees and some official associations also have a similar dual nature and function. They have an ambiguous relationship with the state and are regarded as both official – being the state-designated organization for a certain group of people – and unofficial – not being a formal part of the state system. Consequently, they suffer from a functional conflict between the implementation of state policies and the representation of constituency interests.[67]

In spite of these similarities, villagers' committees are obviously very different from associations. Villagers' committees are grassroots government organizations, not merely mass organizations, though the Chinese state officially ends at the township level. Villagers' committees can therefore be considered part of the formal political structure, albeit a marginal part, while associations are part of the informal structure, even though some of them are quite official in nature. As quasi-government organizations, villagers' committees are sociogeographically based: there can be only one in each village. The rules governing the creation of villagers' committees are part of the Organic Law system, which provides the legal foundation and specifications for the organization of different levels of government. This obviously puts villagers' committees into a different legal category from associations.[68]

Unlike associations, the official status of a villagers' committee results not only from the controlling effort by local party and government organizations (justified by their legally assigned roles of leadership and guidance respectively), but from the fact that it is actually government at the village level. A villagers' committee has both external and internal functions. Externally, it is responsible for articulating villagers' interests and for implementing state policies. Internally, it is responsible for day-to-day decision making on issues concerning social, economic, and cultural life within the village, and for implementing decisions made by the VRA or the villagers' council. In its external relationship, it appears to serve as an intermediary between the state and society, like an association, but its relationship with villagers is in itself a kind of state-society relationship at the grassroots level.

Consequently, analytical concepts such as corporatism and civil society are not quite suitable for villagers' self-governing organizations. The more appropriate concepts are "grassroots self-government" *(jiceng zizhi)* or "grassroots democracy" *(jiceng minzhu)*. However, self-government should not be equated with democracy, even though the two concepts are closely related. Democracy requires self-rule, and the potential for democracy in a specific issue area is limited by the degree of autonomy in that area, but self-government does not necessarily entail democracy. In fact, a degree of village self-government existed in China in imperial times. Similar local self-rule was also found in medieval Europe. In both cases, it was authoritarian rule by local elite. Since the founding of the PRC, the concept of self-government *(zizhi)* has been applied without democratic implication to regions and localities populated mostly by ethnic minorities. In contemporary China, however, democratic self-government in villages stands a chance of being realized, both because of the deliberate state effort to create democratic institutions in villages and because rural society is increasingly commercialized and engulfed by modern values.[69]

In practical terms, "self-government" refers to a village's external relationship with the local state. "Grassroots democracy" refers to the internal relationship between villagers and village leaders. These two spatial contexts are allowed different degrees of autonomy and therefore have different potentials for democracy. Where implementation of state policies is concerned, village self-government is very limited, and grassroots democracy too is limited to the problem of fair and even implementation among villagers rather than whether the state policies should be implemented at all. On issues concerning social, economic, and cultural life within a village, there can be much more self-government, and thus the possibility of much greater grassroots democracy.

A narrow focus on a village government's external functions and relationships may result in a "state perspective": viewing village self-government solely as a mechanism of policy implementation and interest representation vis-à-vis the state, and overlooking its internal functions and relationships. The internal affairs of a village are an area in which the villagers' committee and the VRA have important decision-making functions, which largely explains why many people are willing to participate in village politics and why some have even tried to buy votes in order to get elected. Similarly, lack of theoretical distinction between democracy and self-government may lead to the neglect of the possible emergence of authoritarian self-government, as it has already occurred in some of China's villages.

Conclusion

The frequently reported peasant tax revolts against local officials in recent years have highlighted both the great difficulty in and the urgent need of developing genuine grassroots democracy in China's vast rural areas, not merely in a small number of demonstration villages. However, in spite of the difficulty, the current rather limited development of village self-government remains a significant phenomenon in the changing state-society relationship. In a general sense, it indicates a major retreat of the Chinese state from rural society and an effort to thoroughly reorganize the rural society into grassroots self-governing communities.

More specifically, village self-government has several implications. First of all, it indicates the further deepening of the rural reform, which now has moved from the realm of economy to the realm of politics.[70] Economic reform in rural areas has removed a huge part of the Chinese population from the direct control of the state and led to the emergence of an "unofficial" realm of social and economic life. Within this realm, social differentiation has occurred as a result of commercialization and industrialization. Large numbers of former peasants have turned themselves into commercialized farmers, individual entrepreneurs, capitalists, and industrial employees. This has laid the foundation for political change in rural communities. In this sense, the development of village self-government and grassroots democracy is a necessary continuation of the rural economic reform, representing a search for a form of political organization that is suitable for the changed socioeconomic reality in rural communities and conducive to political stability and economic development.[71]

Second, village self-government may provide the necessary institutional guarantee of the social and economic autonomy rural residents have come to enjoy as a result of the economic reform. Instead of an attempt to reimpose the state upon villagers, as some may have suspected, the implementation of village self-government formalizes the withdrawal of the state from rural communities. Chinese scholars have suggested that both associations and grassroots self-government are part of the restructuring of the state-society relationship aiming at "small government and big society" – a reform Marxist position accepted by the regime. Wang Juntao, a well-known political dissident, expressed the view that these were part of what he termed the "grey democracy" emerging in China.[72] By officially establishing political institutions that allow villagers themselves to make decisions on issues concerning much of their own life, the state has actually promised to maintain the changed state-society relationship that resulted from the rural economic reform, though its consolidation depends on whether village self-government can be successfully institutionalized.

Third, the practice of democratic self-government may indeed serve as a "democracy training class for eight hundred million peasants," as Peng Zhen, one of the chief designers of village self-government, proposed more than ten years ago. One generally recognized difficulty with democratization in China is the lack of democratic elements in traditional Chinese culture and political practice, which, in recent years, has become the main excuse for the regime to delay democratization. If China is to democratize, this kind of "training class" is necessary and beneficial. Successful practice of grassroots democratic self-government will allow people to gain experience with democratic procedures and make it difficult for the regime to continue using "backward culture" to argue against democratization. Once people become accustomed to democratic procedures at the grassroots, they may come to see that such procedures can be applied to higher levels as well.

The long-term significance of village self-government may be that it could serve as a starting point for a gradual process of democratization, as suggested by Doje Cering, minister of civil affairs.[73] This idea seems to find support in a recent "unlawful" direct popular election of a township mayor in Sichuan Province. It was reported that the election was organized by reform-minded officials and monitored by some academics from Beijing, who wanted to upgrade grassroots democratic elections from the village level to the township level. Some central government officials initially expressed the opinion that the election violated the current law on elections. A few weeks later, however, the central government indicated its acceptance of the election result but signalled that such elections should not be extended to other townships at this stage.[74]

Marc Blecher regarded grassroots democratic participation as an important political development on the grounds that it contradicted the authoritarianism of the larger state. Chinese scholars also suggested that village self-government was justified by the Marxist idea of the withering away of the state, during which society gains an increasingly higher level of autonomy. Village self-government was said to be a beginning for this long process.[75] The fact that the regime has chosen to develop grassroots democracy and self-government as key elements of rural political reform – whether for political expediency or for other reasons – indicates that it has maintained the idea of putting democracy into some degree of practice. While there is no guarantee at this point that village self-government will be successfully institutionalized throughout the country, there is reason to believe that, like rural economic reform, grassroots democracy and self-government, once widely established, may trigger a process of political change that goes beyond what was expected by those who originally started the process.

6
Cultural Distinction and Psychological Independence

The changing relationship between the state and society in contemporary China is indicated by not only intellectual and organizational changes, but also an increasingly pronounced cultural distinction between the state and society, indicated by people's growing alienation from orthodox political, ideological, and cultural values and feeling of independence from the state. The cultural differentiation of society from the state has become an important dimension of this transitional process.

This differentiation can be viewed hypothetically as a by-product of socio-economic change and the consequent increase of societal autonomy and individual freedom. It can also be regarded as a reflection of the dualism in the state-society relationship – the cultural dimension of the growing societal freedom that is described and justified by the theory of dualism. The primary social effect of the economic reform has been increasing economic freedom of the individual, which has resulted in a growing feeling of individual independence. Meanwhile, the opening of China to the outside world has introduced Western ideas and cultural values on a large scale. While the political leadership in China has pledged to uphold the orthodox ideology and cultural values, Chinese society, especially the younger generation, appears to be more receptive of new ideas and values from the West. The resulting cultural gap between the state and society reflects, in a sense, their growing dualism. Chinese society is being freed from the state both socioeconomically and culturo-psychologically.

In *The Civic Culture*, Gabriel Almond and Sidney Verba defined political culture as referring to several psychological orientations toward political objects, such as "cognitive orientation," "affective orientation," and "evaluational orientation." The objects of these orientations included the general political system, its various elements and aspects, and "the self as political actor." Specific elements of political culture outlined by Almond and Verba were knowledge, beliefs, feelings, attitudes, values, opinions, and judgments. To distinguish political culture from individual political psychology, they pointed out that "the political culture of a nation is the particular distribution of patterns of orientation toward political objects among the members of the nation," and that it served as an essential link between "micro-politics" and "macro-politics" – "between individual political psychology and the behaviour of political systems and subsystems."[1] In other words, political culture is the mass-level aggregation of the political psychology of individuals.

Almond and G. Bingham Powell Jr. explained the role of political culture in relation to the political system. They pointed out that political culture was part of the domestic environment which the political system was embedded in and constantly interacted with. In other words, political culture is the fundamental social reality in the context of which a political system operates. The importance of political culture is that it affects people's political behaviour and their idea of political legitimacy. A change in the values, beliefs, and attitudes of the masses can result in an erosion of legitimacy and subsequent pressure for a change in a political system.[2]

Change of political values, beliefs, and attitudes in China, especially among the younger generation, has been noticed and extensively discussed by both Western and Chinese academics. Western scholars, however, have disagreed on whether there is significant cultural change in China and how important it is in China's changing state-society relationship. Lucian Pye, for example, insisted that the political upheavals in recent years had only demonstrated repeated patterns and the continuity of the traditional culture. Nevertheless, he also noticed that an "identity problem" was "at the core" of China's current "legitimacy difficulties," indicating a degree of change in the political culture in contemporary China, since both political identity and political legitimacy are important elements of political culture.[3]

Other Western sinologists discussed the change in Chinese political culture in more explicit terms. For example, Lowell Dittmer analyzed the increasingly deepening "ideological secularization" and suggested that it was partially responsible for the declining concern for both ideals and the public interest and the growing attention to the material interests of private individuals. The regime's deliberate demolition of the "the cult of Mao" as a necessary measure in the late 1970s eventually undermined the credibility of the orthodox ideology and deprived the regime itself of "a powerful instrument" of social control.[4]

Perry Link also suggested that the current ideological and moral crisis and the prevalence of the "money-first ethos" was related to a "morality vacuum" created by the decline of communism and the subsequent lack of a "publicly accepted set of moral values to define proper behaviour." In his opinion, what China needs are "values and institutions that can help restructure a civil society."[5] Link and his colleagues explored the development of an "unofficial culture" in Chinese society, demonstrated in different aspects of social and individual life. They maintained that a gap had developed between official and unofficial culture, and that the growing cultural alienation of society from the state had contributed greatly to the tension between them.[6]

Some scholars noticed the emergence of survey research in China and made use of the many Chinese samples that became available.[7] Stanley Rosen, for example, considered the Chinese samples flawed but usable. The large number of surveys conducted by Chinese scholars, in his opinion, provided "a fascinating picture of society in transition." Rosen focused his attention on the value change among youth revealed in Chinese surveys. The younger generation were found to be politically, ideologically, and culturally alienated from the regime. The results of these surveys generally indicated growing Western influence and a "de-collectivization of morality," a cultural tendency with profound political implications.[8]

Significant cultural shift was also revealed by Godwin C. Chu and Yanan Ju's survey conducted in the late 1980s in the greater Shanghai area, where traditional Chinese culture was found to be crumbling before advancing Western culture. The authors attributed this to Maoist rule, especially the experience of the Cultural Revolution, which had severely damaged traditional culture, leaving it vulnerable to Western cultural inroads and the rise of individualism and materialism.[9]

One might argue that the significance of Chu and Ju's survey is limited, since it was conducted in a region that was more exposed to Western culture than most other regions in China. Moreover, the national sample from Andrew Nathan and Tianjian Shi's "civic culture" survey, conducted in 1990, seemed to indicate that traditional political culture still prevailed among the general population. Their sample suggested that ordinary Chinese had a relatively low level of awareness of government impact on their lives and a low degree of tolerance for sharply different opinions. Nathan and Shi believed that these were potential impediments to democratization, because people might be unmotivated to engage in politics and might favour the repression of unpopular ideas. However, the survey also revealed a sharp difference between the more educated people and the rest of the population in terms of both the awareness of government impact on their lives and political tolerance.[10]

Peter R. Moody cautioned that Nathan and Shi's findings from the sample might be skewed by its timing, and might reflect the conservative backlash from the Tiananmen incident and its impact on the population.[11] Shi's prior survey on political participation in Beijing in 1988 had provided evidence of value change – political alienation and the decline of collectivism among the younger generation – resulting in the change of people's political behaviour, even though he argued that "institutional setting" was a primary factor in determining not only people's political behaviour but also social norms and values.[12]

Alfred L. Chan and Paul Nesbitt-Larking's analysis of the Min Qi sample – a nationwide political culture survey conducted by a group of Chinese scholars – also suggested that a significant section of Chinese society, especially the younger generation, had developed a "critical citizenship," an awareness of the distinction between the party-state and the national community as different objects of political identification and support. This, Chan and Nesbitt-Larking believed, was an important cultural element of an emerging civil society. Their analysis supported Rosen's view that there was growing political and ideological alienation in China.[13]

The same opinion was expressed by X.L. Ding, who described the Chinese debate on the "crisis of faith" and the decline of the official ideology among young people. He pointed out that the better-educated part of the population had developed a kind of patriotism that viewed the party-state not as the embodiment but as the impediment of the nation. Merle Goldman and co-authors also pointed out that a keen awareness of the distinction between the party-state and the national community played a significant role in the mentality of the intellectuals and students involved in the 1989 pro-democracy movement, as demonstrated by their slogan: "We love our country, but we hate our government."[14]

Scholarly Discussions in China

In the past ten years or so, many Chinese scholars have also discussed the value change in Chinese society, forming a large body of literature that covers a wide range of issues. Two among these that are directly relevant here are political and ideological alienation, as indicated by a growing awareness of the political distinction between the state and society and by the "crisis of faith," and cultural alienation, indicated by the rise of individualism and materialism.

As the issue was originally raised by some prominent regime intellectuals in the early 1980s, "political alienation" referred to the distance between the government and the people it was supposed to serve, and expressed a feeling of estrangement from the current regime rather than a fundamental challenge to the official ideology. The politically alienated scholars remained faithful to Marxist ideology and accused the regime of failing to live up to its own ideals. Bill Brugger and David Kelly suggested that the ideological debates in the late 1970s and throughout the 1980s eroded the Leninist orthodoxy and split the Chinese Marxists into three groups: orthodox Leninists, revisionists, and humanists. The last group was said to have offered a genuinely critical Marxism by advocating democracy as the only way to combat political alienation and to restore the "humanist essence" of Marxism. The 1983-4 debate on humanism and alienation, in Brugger and Kelly's opinion, was the last chance for the survival of Marxism in China. It became a turning point because when Marxist humanism was rejected by the regime, the Marxist humanists turned against it and called for an end to one-party rule.[15]

Subsequently, the topic of political alienation became a "forbidden zone" in China's intellectual discourse. Those who openly promoted the idea were penalized. Well-known examples of penalization include Wang Ruoshui's polemic argument for Marxist humanism, Liu Binyan's discussion of "two kinds of loyalty" *(liangzhong zhongcheng)*, and Bai Hua's screenplay, *Ku Nian* (Unrequited love), which described the painful experience of a scholar whose patriotism remained strong even though he was politically persecuted by the Maoist regime. These writings indicated that political alienation in China was manifested by an increasing awareness of the distinction between the nation and the party-state as different objects of political identification and support. The fact that leading intellectuals have repeatedly brought up the issue and that the demonstrating students clearly expressed their awareness of this important political distinction indicates that political alienation is probably quite strong among a significant section of the population.

Ideological alienation, on the other hand, was from its beginning related to the "crisis of faith" among the younger generation. This crisis was in essence the loss of faith not just in the current regime, but in the orthodox ideology that provided the fundamental rationale for the entire political system. In this sense, ideological alienation represents a deepening of political alienation. Alienation from the orthodox cultural values of collectivism and idealism can in turn be seen as a logical consequence of ideological alienation, because in contemporary China, these cultural values are largely sustained by the official ideology. While these are closely related aspects of cultural change, analysis of their differences aims at a thorough understanding of the overall transformation of political culture.

Ideological alienation among young people has alarmed the regime to a degree, and some discussions have been allowed. The well-known debate on the Pan Xiao letter in the early 1980s demonstrated the depth of the crisis of faith among the younger generation. This powerful expression of disillusionment with Communist propaganda was published in *Zhongguo Qingnian* (China youth) under the pseudonym "Pan Xiao" in May 1980. The letter drew an overwhelming response from readers and started a nationwide debate. By the end of 1980, *Zhongguo Qingnian* had received more than 60,000 letters in response to, and mostly in support of, the Pan Xiao letter, many of which were signed by dozens, or even over a hundred people.[16] Since then, many surveys have been conducted by Chinese scholars on the ideological orientations of young people in China. Some of these surveys will be reviewed in the following section of this chapter.

The change of cultural values appears to be treated more as an academic issue in China and has been the subject of prolonged discussions and debates. Many have noticed the rising individualism and materialism and the decline of collectivism and idealism in Chinese society. The Chinese people today, especially young people, are said to be much more self-interested than older people, and to attach more importance to material benefits and less importance to spiritual elements such as personal loyalty, social status, prestige, and even family ties in interpersonal relations. Similarly, they are said to emphasize material gains for the present over ideals for the future. In short, contemporary Chinese culture is reported to be increasingly individualistic, materialistic, and hedonistic.[17]

In addition to descriptive accounts, Chinese scholars have critiqued or justified the perceived cultural change. Some have been alarmed, seeing evidence of "moral decline" or even "moral collapse" *(daode bengkui)* resulting from a negative side-effect of the market economy, or a backlash from the hypocrisy and extremism of the Mao era highly politicized collectivism, or harmful Western influence. They have painted a dark picture of a materialist and commercialized Chinese society, in which greedy, selfish people are everywhere engaged in cutthroat competition and single-minded pursuit of material wealth, often at the expense of others. As a result, interpersonal relationships are rapidly deteriorating. Since the primary principle of the market economy is "free competition and the survival of the fittest," collectivist values are abandoned, and people are turned into "economic animals."[18]

Others, however, have responded positively to the cultural change, pointing out that changing values inevitably accompany rapid socioeconomic change. Various justifications have been provided for the emerging individualism and materialism. Economically, individualism is said to be a positive value arising from the market economy, which requires individual participants in the market to be free, equal, and independent. Since China's economic modernization means a transition from the traditional statist economy to market economy, a corresponding value change is both necessary and inevitable.[19] Politically, individual freedom and independence have come to be viewed as values inherent in modern democratic politics. Many have expressed the idea that the principle of majority rule must be balanced by respect for individual freedom and rights, which is an equally important principle of democracy.[20]

In addition to economic and political reasoning, the proponents of

Marxist humanism have provided a moral and ideological justification for individualism. They have demanded a return to the "humanist essence" of the original Marxism, which, they believe, condemns the dehumanization in modern society and calls for the restoration of the human values through the complete emancipation of the individual in "a commonwealth of free people," where "the freedom of each and every individual is a precondition of freedom for all," as Marx suggested in the *Communist Manifesto*.[21]

However, the humanists are obviously less materialist than the proponents of the free market. The apparent agreement between them on the value of the individual seems to have fallen apart in the recent Chinese debate on economic efficiency versus social justice, which revealed a conflict between the pursuit of profits and the pursuit of human values. One outcome of that debate is the emergence of a relatively balanced view, representing an attempt to patch up the basic difference. This view recognizes both the merits and the demerits of the free market, and proposes that commercialism needs to be tempered with humanism in order to maintain a healthy balance between economic efficiency and social justice, material benefit and spiritual well-being, profit-seeking for oneself and the satisfaction of human needs for all. This does not represent a return to the traditional collectivism, but is rather an attempt to reconstruct the community on the basis of individualism.[22]

Underlying these different perspectives is a clear and general recognition by mainstream Chinese scholars that cultural change is taking place in China today, and that traditional values are being seriously challenged by emerging new values.

Based on these scholarly discussions, the rest of this chapter will examine two closely related areas of empirical evidence from (mostly) Chinese surveys, in an attempt to establish that change in the political culture represents an important dimension of change in the state-society relationship. These two areas are: (1) political alienation, as indicated by growing alienation from both the current regime and the official ideology, and by an awareness of the distinction between the nation and the state; and (2) the rise of individualism and materialism, and a growing feeling of independence among ordinary Chinese.

Main Sources of Data

1. The Min Qi survey was the first national survey on Chinese political culture. It was conducted in 1987, when China was eight years into the economic reform and the political atmosphere was relatively liberal and relaxed. Though it is a little dated, it still offers a rare and important data set for the study of Chinese political culture. The 119 tables in Min's book contain a large amount of valuable material, much of which remains to be

explored. The book's greatest advantage is that it provides a lot of statistical details, making it possible to break down and reassemble many of the statistics for further analysis.[23]

The major problem with the Min Qi survey is that people with higher education, cadres, and party members were oversampled, while the rural population was undersampled. However, this can be largely remedied by breaking down responses by education level, political status, or urban/rural cohort when there is a significant variation on one of these bases.

2. The CASS conducted a thirteen-city survey on political culture in early 1989. The CASS survey is a purely urban sample, and the published materials do not contain as many statistical details as the Min Qi survey. It is, however, useful as a complement.[24]

3. The China Youth Research Centre conducted a national survey in 1995 on the values held by Chinese youth. The survey is said to have covered over a hundred cities and counties in twelve provinces. The survey report, however, provides only a few statistical details.[25]

4. Some local Chinese samples as well as several Western sources are explored for supporting evidence, including Rosen's discussions of Chinese surveys, Chu and Ju's Shanghai sample, Shi's Beijing sample, and Nathan and Shi's "civic culture" sample.[26]

In general, the data reviewed and analyzed below are collected from limited available sources, which represent the embryonic state of survey research in China. Therefore the conclusions drawn from these data can only be regarded as tentative and suggestive. A related problem with evaluating cultural change in China using contemporary survey data is the lack of longitudinal data to make historical comparisons, and hence the difficulty of determining whether there is actually a change over time. To remedy this problem, the following analysis emphasizes the evidence of generational difference within each sample. This approach conforms with the "socialization hypothesis" proposed by Ronald Inglehart, who suggested that a person tends to hold on to the values acquired in his or her formative years. Therefore, cultural change in a society can be observed through its "generational effects."[27] In the Chinese context, this means that cultural change should be indicated by greater alienation from orthodox values and stronger feelings of independence from the state among the younger generation.

Political Alienation
Evidence of political alienation in contemporary China is found in several areas, including growing awareness of the distinction between the nation and the state, declining support for the current regime, and alienation from the official ideology.

The Chinese are known to have a strong identification with their national community and a strong sense of commitment to their nation. This is well illustrated in Table 6.1, which shows that the powerful commitment to the well-being of the national community is consistent in all age groups, and only slightly affected by political status and place of residence. The Chinese word *guojia* has two meanings: the national community or the state. The statement in Table 6.1 is an old Chinese maxim *(guojia xingwang, pifu you ze)*, in which *guojia* clearly refers to the national community, and the response to it is overwhelming support.

Table 6.2 combines the responses to three different statements and further confirms that the respondents have a high degree of commitment to the national community. In the second and third statements, the meaning of *guojia* is a little ambiguous and may be confused for the political state instead of the national community, which may have contributed to the decrease in the percentage of positive answers. In addition to the ambiguity of the term *guojia*, the difference between "to betray" and "not to love" probably also affected the response to statement 3. To betray one's country is certainly more difficult than simply not to love it.[28]

On the whole, the responses to these three statements demonstrate strong support for the national community. Traditionally, the lack of distinction between nation and state has helped the party to demand loyalty and support in the name of the nation. The orthodox view of patriotism

Table 6.1

Response to the statement: "The fate of the country is everyone's responsibility."

	Agree %	Disagree %	Number
Cadres	98.29	1.71	350
Others	93.19	6.81	1,381
Party members	96.43	3.57	448
Non-members	93.63	6.37	1,241
25 and younger	94.60	5.40	556
26-35	94.42	5.58	484
36-45	93.37	6.63	360
46-55	95.36	4.64	237
56 and older	91.30	8.70	92
Urban	95.03	4.97	684
Suburban	95.75	4.25	588
Rural	90.91	9.09	440
Total	94.22	5.78	1,731

Source: Min Qi, *Zhongguo Zhengzhi Wenhua* (Chinese political culture) (Kunming: Yunnan People's Press, 1989), 27-8.

has emphasized that the party represents the Chinese nation and that it is unpatriotic not to support the party.[29]

In recent years, however, there has been an indication of a growing awareness among ordinary Chinese of the distinction between the national community and the party-state as different objects of political identification and support. Evidence of such a differentiation of political objects is found in many Chinese surveys on political attitudes. For example, a series of surveys of high school and college students conducted in different areas during the 1980s indicated repeatedly that the support rate for the Communist Party and the official ideology was no higher than 30 percent, and that the students had a strong feeling of contempt for cadres. Meanwhile, the surveys suggested that the students remained strongly patriotic in spite of their disillusionment with the party and the official ideology. This indicates that they had developed a kind of patriotism that was independent of the party leadership.[30]

Evidence of the same tendency among the general population is found in both the 1987 Min Qi sample and the 1989 CASS sample. Based on their analysis of the Min Qi sample, Chan and Nesbitt-Larking suggested that the Chinese people, especially the younger generation, have developed the ability to distinguish the party-state from the national community as a different object of political identification and support.[31] This "critical citizenship" indicates a degree of political alienation from the current regime and a growing awareness of the political and cultural distinction between the state and society. As a result, the high degree of support for the nation has not translated into strong support for the current regime.

The Communist Party, the present government, and government officials are three important components of the party-state. In contrast to the strong

Table 6.2

Commitment to the national community

	Positive %	Negative %	Number
1 "The fate of the country is everyone's responsibility."	94.22	5.78	1,731
2 "If the country disappoints you, you have reason to betray it."	85.69	14.31	1,705
3 "If the country disappoints you, you have reason not to love it."	74.95	25.05	1,712
Mean percentage	84.95	15.04	

Note: Agreement with statement 1 and disagreement with statements 2 and 3 are regarded as an expression of positive commitment.
Source: Min Qi, *Zhongguo Zhengzhi Wenhua* (Chinese political culture) (Kunming: Yunnan People's Press, 1989), 23-8.

support for the national community, Table 6.3 indicates the widespread negative attitude toward these key components of the party-state. What is more, this negative attitude is significantly related to the political status of the respondents. People who are not cadres or party members tend to be much more negative than cadres and party members, except in the evaluation of the Communist Party, which is the most negatively evaluated among the three. Different degrees of support for the national community and the party cadres were also revealed in the Shanghai survey conducted by Chu and Ju, in which the support rate was 74.5 percent for the former and 50.3 percent for the latter.[32]

The percentages given in Table 6.3 are the mean percentages of the responses to a number of different statements. The five statements for the evaluation of government asked the respondents to express their opinions of the government, their feelings and attitudes toward the government, and whether they were satisfied with government policies and performance. For the evaluation of cadres, the respondents were asked to agree or disagree with ten statements – both positive and negative – describing various types of cadre behaviour. For the evaluation of the party, the respondents were asked to respond positively or negatively to nine statements concerning the party itself, its objectives and policy orientation, the behaviour of party members, and the attractiveness of party membership.

One might argue that a support rate of 50 percent is actually quite high, considering the fact that governments of many Western democracies often have an approval rating of lower than 50 percent. However, the Chinese are usually more reluctant than Westerners to express disapproval of their own government in front of strangers, because in China, criticism of government

Table 6.3

Evaluation of the regime

	Evaluation of government		Evaluation of cadres		Evaluation of the party	
	Positive %	Negative %	Positive %	Negative %	Positive %	Negative %
Cadres	64.97	28.45	61.09	37.91	41.98	47.84
Others	53.08	37.62	45.33	53.42	41.03	45.19
Party members	64.88	29.53	n/a	n/a	n/a	n/a
Non-members	55.20	32.88	n/a	n/a	n/a	n/a
Mean percentage	58.01	31.75	49.32	50.51	41.25	45.80
Number of items	5		10		9	

Source: Min Qi, *Zhongguo Zhengzhi Wenhua* (Chinese political culture) (Kunming: Yunnan People's Press, 1989), 68-77, 85-7, 98-101.

used to, and may still, have unhappy consequences for individuals. That fear of repercussion has simply become a habit for many and must be factored into the analysis of Chinese survey results.

In addition to correlating with political status, the degree of alienation from the party-state also correlates significantly with age. Evidence of this is found in Table 6.4, which shows that the younger generation is more alienated from the party-state than the older generation.

In Table 6.4, age consistency in the political commitment to the national community falls apart when the respondents are asked to express their support for the government. While overall support for the government is much lower than the support for the national community, the younger generation is found to be especially alienated. We can also infer from Table 6.4 that the younger generation is more aware of the distinction between the national community and the party-state than the older generation.

Increased political alienation among youth was also confirmed by the thirteen-city survey conducted by the CASS in early 1989. The statement in Table 6.5 expresses an extremely negative view of politics, which is directly opposed to the positive and moralistic view of politics endorsed in traditional culture. This explains the low percentage of overall endorsement for it. Nevertheless, Table 6.5 shows that younger respondents have a much worse attitude toward politics than older respondents. Nearly three times as many in the youngest age cohort as in the oldest age cohort agreed with the statement. Tianjian Shi's Beijing survey also found that the younger respondents were more hostile than the older respondents toward the political establishment.[33]

Table 6.4

Evaluation of government compared with commitment to national community

	Commitment to national community		Evaluation of government	
	Positive %	Negative %	Positive %	Negative %
25 and younger	85.64	14.36	54.58	34.94
26-35	84.31	15.69	56.26	32.32
36-45	84.22	15.78	59.96	30.74
46-55	86.27	13.73	63.83	26.53
56 and older	82.42	17.58	69.04	23.50
Average	84.95	15.04	58.01	31.75
Number of items	3		5	

Source: Min Qi, *Zhongguo Zhengzhi Wenhua* (Chinese political culture) (Kunming: Yunnan People's Press, 1989), 23-8, 68-73.

Another indication of political alienation is the loss of faith in the official ideology, especially among the younger generation. Some of the local surveys among university students reported by Rosen indicated both political and ideological alienation.[34] Table 6.6 presents some evidence of the decreasing commitment to the official ideology among the general population.

The question in Table 6.6 asks the respondents to express their ideological orientation toward socialism, rather than their commitment to the country. If the question had been: "Are you proud of living in China?" the responses would have been very different. Comparing Table 6.6 to Tables 6.1 and 6.2, it is clear that while the support for the country (*guojia*) as the national community is strong, the support for the "socialist country"

Table 6.5

Agreement with the statement: "Politics means a few people fighting for power and personal gains."

Age	%	Number
15-19	33.2	207
20-9	28.5	694
30-9	22.0	506
40-9	13.6	295
50 and older	12.3	294
Total	22.8	1,995

Source: Zhang Mingdui, *Zhongguo "Zhengzhiren"* (China's "political person") (Beijing: Chinese Academy of Social Science Press, 1994), 20. The total sample size and age breakdown are provided on p. 11 and p. 64 of the same book.

Table 6.6

Answer to the question: "Are you proud of living in a socialist country?"

	Yes %	I don't care %	No %	Number
Cadres	66.57	21.90	11.53	347
Others	51.02	31.44	17.54	1,374
Party members	69.98	16.93	13.09	443
Non-members	48.51	34.03	17.46	1,237
25 and younger	51.71	30.81	17.48	555
26-35	45.79	35.11	19.07	487
36-45	60.50	25.77	13.73	357
46-55	62.61	23.91	13.48	230
56 and older	67.39	20.65	11.96	92
Total	54.15	29.52	16.32	1,721

Source: Min Qi, *Zhongguo Zhengzhi Wenhua* (Chinese political culture) (Kunming: Yunnan People's Press, 1989), 33-4.

(shehuizhuyi guojia) is much weaker. Also notable in Table 6.6 is that the choice "I don't care" is actually a negative response, because it expresses indifference toward a key component of the official ideology.

Table 6.6 also shows that people's attachment to socialism is significantly correlated with age and political status. While overall support for socialism is rather low among the respondents, ordinary people are much less proud of socialism than cadres and party members. Young people are particularly alienated from socialism. On the whole, the table demonstrates that a significant section of the population have withdrawn their support for the official ideology.

This result from the Min Qi sample has been confirmed by a survey on young people's ideological orientations conducted in Beijing, Shanghai, and Zhejiang in 1995. When asked if they believed in Communism, 40 percent of the 1,767 respondents said yes, 36 percent said no, and 15 percent answered "I don't know." Moreover, 76 percent of the respondents agreed with the statement that "many different values should be allowed to coexist."[35]

Evidence of ideological alienation is also found in surveys on people's understanding of democracy, which has been a hot issue and a crucial point of contention between orthodoxy and the counterculture. For example, a 1986 survey of Beijing University students found that 204 of the 257 respondents (79.4 percent) considered the United States the most democratic country in the world.[36] Four surveys conducted in 1989 – one before and three after the Tiananmen incident – among university students in

Table 6.7

Support for "democratic centralism"

Which statement* best describes your understanding of democracy? (Choose one only)	Democracy is guided by the centre. %	Number
Cadres	39.72	293
Others	21.07	1,049
Party members	37.79	389
Non-members	19.91	939
25 and younger	18.76	485
26-35	21.98	364
36-45	30.58	242
46-55	35.18	199
56 and older	37.35	83
Total	24.98	1,373

* The other seven statements are included in Table 6.8.
Source: Min Qi, *Zhongguo Zhengzhi Wenhua* (Chinese political culture) (Kunming: Yunnan People's Press, 1989), 181-2.

Beijing, Tianjin, Xi'an, and Jiangsu found that the support for "bourgeois democracy" was 53 percent, 66 percent, 62 percent, and 53.5 percent respectively.[37] These surveys focused on a small social group – university students – and may have been affected by the traumatic events of the time. Some evidence from the Min Qi sample may help us get a more balanced picture in this respect.

During the survey, the respondents were asked to choose one of eight statements that best described their understanding of democracy. The first – "democracy is guided by the centre" – is an important component of the orthodox view of democracy. Table 6.7 confirms what is found in Table 6.6: the younger generation and ordinary people have much less attachment for official doctrines than older people, cadres, and party members. Twice as many respondents over fifty-five as those twenty-five and under chose "democracy is guided by the centre" as the best description of democracy. Table 6.8 shows the average responses to all the choices on democracy in the same survey.

Apart from statement 1, age variation was significant in the responses to statements 2, 6, and 7 as well. Twenty-one percent of the respondents under twenty-six chose "broadly solicit people's opinions," in comparison with 12 percent of those over fifty-five. "People can elect political leaders" was chosen by 8.7 percent of the respondents under twenty-six, in comparison with 3.6 percent of those over fifty-five. Thirteen percent of those under twenty-six chose "people have effective participation in managing society," in comparison with 8.4 percent of those over fifty-five. In general, younger respondents appear to place more emphasis on effective participation

Table 6.8

Understanding of democracy

Which statement best describes your understanding of democracy?
(Choose one only)   %

1	Democracy is guided by the centre.	24.98
2	The government broadly solicits people's opinions.	19.45
3	People become masters of their own houses.	11.58
4	The minority is subordinate to the majority.	5.17
5	Decisions are made in the interests of the people.	10.92
6	People can elect political leaders.	6.55
7	People have effective participation in managing society.	10.85
8	Power is limited and divided.	3.35
9	Other	0.87
10	I don't know.	6.26
	Number	1,373

Source: Min Qi, *Zhongguo Zhengzhi Wenhua* (Chinese political culture) (Kunming: Yunnan People's Press, 1989), 181-2.

through democratic procedures and are less committed to Leninist democracy than older respondents.

To sum up, the evidence discussed in this section suggests that (1) a significant number of people in China today are politically and ideologically alienated from the current regime, (2) political alienation coincides with a growing awareness of the distinction between the national community and the party-state as different objects of political identification and support, and (3) both political alienation and the ability to distinguish the national community from the party-state are related to age. Younger respondents demonstrated a greater degree of political alienation and a greater ability to distinguish the party-state from the national community as a different political entity.

This distinction between the national community and the party-state is highly significant for our purpose. First, it indicates the failure of the official patriotism propaganda, which has always insisted that the Communist Party embodies the spirit of the Chinese nation, and that patriotism therefore primarily means love for the Communist Party and support for the government. The existing survey evidence clearly supports X.L. Ding's claim that there are now two different kinds of patriotism in China. Orthodox patriotism calls for loyalty to the party-state, while the patriotism of the counterculture condemns the party-state for bringing disaster to the nation.[38] Second, and more importantly, this ability indicates a cognitive differentiation of society from the state, which parallels the intellectual conception of the state-society relationship discussed in Chapters 2 and 3. It shows that many people in China today clearly perceive the Chinese state as a separate entity from Chinese society. They are aware that identification with the latter does not necessarily mean support for the former.

Rise of Individualism and Materialism

As Dittmer pointed out, the rise of individualism and materialism in China is closely related to the decline of official ideology, which has always upheld the values of collectivism and idealism.[39] The connection between the change in cultural values and the changing political attitude of the general public is illustrated by the popular response to the regime's call for "socialist spiritual civilization." The regime's intention was to counteract rising materialism in society – the tendency to "think of money in doing everything" *(yiqie xiang qian kan)* – and to restore faith in the orthodox political and social values. However, the public responded with cynicism: "The material is in short supply, so use the spiritual as a substitute" *(wuzhi bugou, jingshen laicou).*[40]

Though comparative data for age cohorts are relatively insufficient in this area, scholarly discussions have suggested that the decline of collectivism and idealism and the rise of individualism and materialism are especially conspicuous among the younger generation. In their survey in the greater Shanghai region, Chu and Ju concluded that young people are more exposed to and receptive of Western cultural values, and hence are more individualistic and materialistic than old people. They were more likely to choose "living happily" than "contributing to society" as the meaning of life, and to prefer "enjoy life" to "work hard" as a lifestyle choice.[41]

The most easily noted aspect of cultural change in Chinese youth is their increasing preoccupation with the individual's immediate material well-being, which is in sharp contrast with the traditional emphasis on the moral and spiritual commitment to the state, the collective, and the future. A significant portion of the younger generation appears to be alienated not only from the regime, but also from the orthodox and traditional values. The counterculture in China today is largely the youth culture.

This situation is well illustrated in Tables 6.9 and 6.10, which present some of the results available from the China Youth Research Centre's 1994 survey on the values of Chinese youth. The first two items in Table 6.9 indicate that less than half of the respondents accept the two key components of the orthodox values: collectivism and idealism. Items 3 to 5 further illustrate the deep penetration of individualist and materialist values among the urban youth. Item 6, on the other hand, shows that individualism and materialism do not necessarily lead to greediness and the lack of generosity. Most of the respondents still consider the "spirit of giving" a positive value.

Table 6.10 compares urban and rural youth, and shows that even though the rural respondents were less receptive to individualist and materialist values than urban respondents, less than 60 percent of rural respondents

Table 6.9

Urban youth's response to individualism and materialism

		Agree %	Not sure %	Disagree %
1	Ideals are more important than money.	49.22	23.07	27.71
2	Collective affairs are more important than individual affairs.	47.49	33.01	19.50
3	People are born selfish.	41.59	16.54	41.87
4	One should seek pleasure here and now.	31.36	26.77	n/a
5	A good name means nothing; money means everything.	24.41	n/a	n/a
6	Fools talk about the spirit of giving.	15.24	22.52	62.23

Note: Among the six statements, 1 and 2 are expressions of orthodox values, while 3 to 6 are expressions of the opposite.
Source: China Youth Research Centre Project Group, "1994-1995 Zhongguo Qingnian shehui fazhan yanjiu baogao" (Research report on the Chinese youth's social development, 1994-1995), *Zhongguo Qingnian Yanjiu* (China youth research) no. 5 (1995): 8.

endorsed collectivism and idealism. The rise of individualism and materialism is also confirmed by the 1995 survey on youth's ideological orientation. When asked to indicate what they believed in most, 34 percent of 1,767 respondents chose themselves and 17 percent chose money.[42]

The decline of traditional values is also indicated by the acceptance of Western culture, because in China, Western culture is generally perceived as representing modernity, or the antithesis of traditional Chinese culture.

Table 6.11 indicates the degree of tolerance, not acceptance, of Western cultural inroads. This may explain the unusually high percentages. However, we can assume that a higher degree of tolerance implies a higher degree of acceptance. The table shows clear variation among different education levels and age groups, and between urban and rural respondents. Education appears to be the most significant factor in the degree of acceptance of Western culture. Those with college education are almost twice as tolerant of Western culture as those who are illiterate or with elementary education. The variation among age cohorts and between the urban and rural respondents may be largely due to their different educational levels. We can infer from Table 6.11 that among the Chinese population, urban youth with college education are most accepting of Western culture. A similar conclusion was drawn by Nathan and Shi in their "civic culture" survey on Chinese people's political tolerance, and by Chu and Ju in their survey on Shanghai people's different degrees of exposure to, and acceptance of, Western cultural values.[43]

This conclusion is also supported by a number of local surveys. For example, a survey of 500 Shanghai families conducted by the Shanghai Family Education Society in early 1994 showed that a little over one-third of the parents hoped that their children would go and live abroad, while several surveys conducted in the late 1980s among university students in Beijing and Shanghai found an overwhelming majority of the respondents – more than 80 percent – desired to go and study in Western countries.[44]

A further sign of rising individualism is found in people's growing feeling of independence from the state. At the individual level, this feeling

Table 6.10

Urban/rural differences among youth

Percentage who agree with the following statements:	Urban %	Rural %
Ideals are more important than money.	49.22	59.28
Collective affairs are more important than individual affairs.	47.49	58.34

Source: China Youth Research Centre Project Group, "1994-1995 Zhongguo Qingnian shehui fazhan yanjiu baogao" (Research report on the Chinese youth's social development, 1994-1995), *Zhongguo Qingnian Yanjiu* (China youth research) no. 5 (1995): 8.

indicates a psychological change. At the mass, aggregate level, it indicates a transformation of political culture from a pre-reform-era culture of individual dependence to a culture of individual independence. Tables 6.12 and 6.13 provide some evidence of the growing feeling of independence among the Chinese people.

The statement in Table 6.12 is a traditional expression of gratefulness for the party-state propagated for decades by the official media. It both describes the actual condition of dependence that existed in pre-reform China and expresses an individual's psychological dependence on the party-state. The table demonstrates that, in spite of decades of propaganda, overall support for the statement is low, due mainly to the lack of support among young and middle-aged people. While older people still maintain a relatively strong emotional attachment to the state, the younger generation displays a much stronger feeling of independence from the state.

This feeling is also reflected in the perceived limit of state power vis-à-vis individual citizens. Those who feel themselves independent of the state tend to view the state as having no business in the private life of individuals. Evidence of this perception is presented in Table 6.13, which shows that younger respondents are more conscious of the necessary limit of state power and more sensitive about their personal freedom than older respondents.

Finally, the decline of traditional values among the younger generation is indicated by the increasing popularity of premarital sex, "unlawful"

Table 6.11

Attitudes toward the impact of Western thought on China

	Tolerant %	Intolerant %	Number
25 and younger	74.09	10.12	494
26-35	79.33	5.67	353
36-45	76.29	11.64	232
46-55	70.71	11.62	198
56 and older	62.82	16.67	78
Illiterate	47.72	27.27	44
Elementary	43.51	18.32	131
Junior high	72.50	13.33	460
Senior high	77.17	9.45	381
College	86.86	2.35	426
Urban	82.98	6.53	658
Suburban	75.00	9.48	348
Rural	59.00	15.93	339
Total	75.49	9.26	1,365

Source: Min Qi, *Zhongguo Zhengzhi Wenhua* (Chinese political culture) (Kunming: Yunnan People's Press, 1989), 128-9.

cohabitation, and the growing tolerance of such unconventional behaviour by the general public. Traditionally, such pleasure-seeking behaviour is regarded as a "decadent bourgeois lifestyle" contrary to the orthodox values, which uphold strong commitment to "revolutionary ideals." A 1996 survey of 2,580 Shanghai couples found that 69 percent of them had sex before they were married.[45] Living together before marriage – defended by its supporters as "trial marriage" *(shihun)* – has become so widespread that the authorities of some cities, such as Tianjin and Wuhan, have decided to impose a fine of 1,000 to 2,000 yuan on cohabiting unmarried couples. However, a nationwide survey conducted in the early 1990s found that 38 percent of the 1,731 respondents considered such behaviour acceptable, 46 percent opposed it, and 16 percent declined to comment.[46]

Conclusion

The empirical evidence presented in the above two sections indicates that significant cultural change is taking place in contemporary China. There is indeed a growing gap between the orthodox culture and mass culture, as has been suggested by the scholarly discussions.

Politically, an increasing number of Chinese people today have developed an awareness of the distinction between the state and society as different objects of political identification and have come to view the state as a political entity that is separate from society. Underlying this awareness of the state-society distinction is a widespread "crisis of faith" in the orthodox ideology, and the rise of individualism and materialism, which seriously challenges the traditional and orthodox cultural values. These different aspects of cultural change indicate the overall tendency toward cultural differentiation of society from the state.

The growth of social and economic freedom in Chinese society today

Table 6.12

Response to the statement: "I owe everything I have to the government."

	Agree %	Disagree %	Number
25 and younger	45.98	54.02	548
26-35	50.42	49.58	484
36-45	51.40	48.60	358
46-55	58.36	41.64	233
56 and older	70.00	30.00	90
Total	51.31	48.69	1,713

Source: Min Qi, *Zhongguo Zhengzhi Wenhua* (Chinese political culture) (Kunming: Yunnan People's Press, 1989), 70-1.

is accompanied by the rise of individualism and materialism. The development of societal autonomy is paralleled by a transformation from the culture of individual dependence of the pre-reform era to a culture of individual independence. The changing state-society relationship in China today is marked by an ongoing struggle between the orthodoxy and the counterculture. To a certain extent, Chinese society is increasingly defined by the counterculture rather than the orthodoxy. B. Michael Frolic suggested that the development of modern citizenship requires not only "rational, self-directing individuals" who have broken free from traditional communitarian values, but that such individuals must "elevate their private interests to a consideration of the greater public good." In other words, they must be able to reconstruct community on the basis of rational individualism. The rise of individualism in China has indicated the beginning of this "long journey from subject to citizen."[47]

The existing evidence also indicates that a generation gap exists in all areas of political culture. The younger generation is on the cutting edge of the advancing counterculture, leading the older generation in political and ideological alienation, rising individualism and materialism, and psychological independence from the state. Age difference is meaningful in two ways. First, it implies a correlation between the different aspects of cultural change, since the same generation gap has occurred simultaneously in all of them. The part of the population that is the least supportive of the party-state – the younger generation – also has the least attachment to the orthodox ideological and cultural values. More importantly, in the absence of longitudinal comparative data, this generation gap serves as an important indicator of cultural change. The fact that the rejection of the orthodox culture is particularly strong among the younger generation and that the

Table 6.13

Response to the statement: "Government should not interfere with the private life of individuals."

	Agree %	Disagree %	Number
25 and younger	69.73	30.27	555
26-35	71.93	28.07	488
36-45	69.92	30.08	359
46-55	59.32	40.68	236
56 and older	56.04	43.96	91
Total	68.25	31.75	1,729

Source: Min Qi, *Zhongguo Zhengzhi Wenhua* (Chinese political culture) (Kunming: Yunnan People's Press, 1989), 186.

counterculture is largely the youth culture indicates that society is under-going a rapid cultural transformation, which has manifested itself in con-spicuous differences between older and younger generations.

Among the various aspects of the cultural change, the rise of individualism has challenged the traditional values most fundamentally. Unlike in the United States, where liberal individualism is the orthodoxy, both the tradi-tional and the Communist orthodoxy in China have upheld communitar-ian values; liberal individualism is the counterculture. For our purposes, the ascendance of individualism is significant in that it not only indicates a growing cultural distinction of society from the state, but also constitutes the cultural and psychological reality underlying the rethinking of democ-racy occurring in intellectual circles.

A collectivist view of "the people" justifies the orthodox notion of democracy, which emphasizes unity of interests and support for the highly centralized power of the state. In the same way, liberal individualism pro-vides a rationale for a pluralist view of society, independence of society from the state, and democracy understood as a process of accommodation of diversified social interests and a system of checks and balances on state power. In this sense, the intellectual circles' new understanding of democ-racy has corresponded to the cultural dimension of change in the state-society relationship – the growing individualism in China.

7
Conclusion:
Theory and Reality

In Chapters 2 and 3, I analyzed the significant qualitative change in the intellectual conception of democracy. The core components of this conception are the theory of dualism, which distinguishes state and society, and the theory of social pluralism, which recognizes the emergence and equal rights of diverse social group interests. Democracy is now understood, in its early stage, to be the freedom of society from the state, and, in its advanced form, to be societal control of the state. Democracy is also viewed as a process of accommodation, coordination, and compromise among interests in a pluralistic society. In Chapters 4, 5, and 6, I discussed the transformation of social and cultural reality that has paralleled this remarkable conceptual evolution. The formal intellectual change appears to be a self-conscious attempt to respond to the changing reality, justify it theoretically, and to an extent even prescribe a "right" course for its development.

The traditional unity of state and society has been challenged by this multidimensional process of intellectual, socio-organizational, and cultural change. The conceptual evolution of democracy provides a theoretical basis for the contraction of the state and the expansion of an autonomous realm of social and economic life, as indicated by the emphasis on "small government and big society." The theory of civil society combines the theories of dualism and social pluralism and focuses attention on the reorganization of society into autonomous and horizontal social groupings, as demonstrated in the development of mass associations and village self-government. These theoretical and social developments are also contemporaneous with the cultural appreciation of people's feeling of independence from state authority. Intellectual attention to social pluralism leads to exploration of the sensitive issue of political pluralism; formal recognition of the legitimacy and equality of the different social interests that are emerging from economic decentralization and marketization facilitates a focus on the need for mechanisms within the political system that represent and articulate the interests of diverse social groups.

These theoretical developments stem from a process of ideological change that started in the late 1970s, when the orthodox Leninist democracy began to metamorphose into its current watered-down version. The original orthodox view of democracy upheld by the Leninist regime in pre-reform China, and once supported by the scholars, has its origin in both Leninism and the traditional culture. As Andrew Nathan pointed out, some of its key elements, such as dictatorship and centralism, came directly from Leninism. Others, such as the emphasis on unity rather than plurality and the collective instead of the individual, can be traced to political reformers such as Liang Qichao and Sun Yat-sen in the early Republican era. Both Liang and Sun expressed the opinion that democracy was a mechanism for collecting power from the individual and concentrating it in the state in order to make the state powerful. They both assumed that the interests of the people, the nation, and the state were unified. Sun Yat-sen, for example, argued that democracy, which was the recognition of the sovereign power of the people, would contribute to the building of a strong nation-state rather than promoting individual rights and freedoms. He suggested that Chinese people were like "a plate of loose sand," because they enjoyed "excessive individual liberty" but lacked proper discipline and a sense of commitment to the public good. The purpose of democracy, in his opinion, was to "break down individual liberty" and to "weld our state into firm unity."[1]

Following this intellectual tradition and embracing Leninism, the orthodox view of democracy has always emphasized a vanguard party's highly centralized rule on behalf of the basic and unified interests of "the people" and dictatorship over "enemy classes." The assumed fundamental unity of interests, both among the people and between the state and society, justifies a powerful state having effective control over society. Until the end of the 1970s, this was the theoretical framework within which Chinese debates on democracy were conducted. The regime was criticized by many scholars not for having a wrong idea of democracy, but for failing to live up to its own democratic ideals.[2]

In the early 1980s, this understanding of democracy began to erode. While the "four cardinal principles" were upheld, enemy classes were declared extinct by the regime, and "the people" subsequently became close to an all-inclusive term. Dictatorship lost much of its rationale and the state's functional focus consequently shifted to management of society. Centralism was discredited, and "contradictions among the people" replaced class struggle as the main social dynamic for progress. While these theoretical developments paved the way for a new understanding of democracy, they have been no more than a modification, not an abandonment, of key elements of the orthodoxy. This limited effort to cope with the changing reality by modifying the theory has resulted in a watered-down or "reform" version of the orthodoxy. The difficulty faced by the reform leadership is finding a theoretical justification for market reform without abandoning the Leninist justification for one-party rule. For this purpose, the reformist regime proposed the idea of a "preliminary stage of social- ism" in the late 1980s and the idea of a "socialist market economy" in the early 1990s.

Recently, President Jiang Zemin proposed the idea of "three representa- tives": the Communist Party should represent "advanced productive forces, advanced culture, and the fundamental interests of the people." This appears to be an effort to give further flexibility to the official ideology, and as such, the idea is reportedly under attack from the die-hard orthodox Leninists. The conservatives argue that the idea is contrary to the Leninist idea that the Communist Party must be the "vanguard of the proletariat" and represent only the "fundamental interests of the people." The "three representatives" view, on the contrary, emphasizes "advanced productive forces," which means science, technology, and economic development, and "advanced culture," which implicitly justifies greater openness to modern Western culture. The regime theoreticians, on the other hand, argue that "three representatives" justifies "large-scale policy adjustment" so that the party can "meet new challenges in a new situation." An aid to Jiang Zemin reportedly admitted that advanced productive forces and advanced culture are now represented more by the educated and the propertied classes rather than the industrial working class.[3]

The new scholarly understanding of democracy as described and ana- lyzed in Chapters 2 and 3, on the other hand, marks a qualitative change and a clear break from orthodox Leninism, which it now views as a justifi- cation of authoritarianism – understood as the domination of society by an unlimited state power.[4] This new understanding indicates the conceptual differentiation of society from the state, emphasizing societal autonomy, economic freedom, and the recognition of diverse and equal social inter- ests. Democracy is consequently understood as the control of a limited state by an independent society and the accommodation and coordination of diverse social interests in the political process.

This new intellectual understanding of democracy is similar to Western liberal democracy in several important ways. The liberal ideas of individual freedom, minority rights, and limited government have been largely incor- porated in the new Chinese understanding. The need for some kind of political pluralism to respond to the emerging social pluralism has also been suggested, without explicitly endorsing the Western model of multi- party competition for political leadership. Consultation rather than com- petition has become the preferred procedure for political decision making.

Unlike in contemporary Western liberalism, individual freedom in the new intellectual democracy is largely defined negatively, emphasizing freedom from state intervention instead of the positive capacity for individual development. In the same way, the equality advocated by many Chinese scholars is very much the application of equal rules to all players in the market, largely ignoring the actual inequality between the rich and the poor. The intellectual conception of democracy has also focused more on social and economic freedom than on political freedom. The emphasis is on the need to develop the socioeconomic and cultural infrastructure for democracy rather than on immediate democratization, hence the scholarly focus on the development of civil society instead of a transformation of political authority. In this sense, the new intellectual understanding of democracy shares some common ground with Sun Yat-sen's notion of "tutelage" as a preparation for a "constitutional government." Sun's tutelage included both "psychological reconstruction" and "material reconstruction," meaning cultural transformation and economic development, to pave the way for a transition to constitutional government. For many Chinese intellectuals, the development of civil society is the necessary socioeconomic and cultural tutelage for democratization.

Each in its own way, the different views of democracy existing in contemporary China are correlated with different social and political realities. As a main component of the pre-reform-era official ideology, the orthodox view of democracy helped prescribe the political reality of that era, which was the domination of society by the Leninist party-state. Since the beginning of the economic reform, both this official ideology and the consequent political reality have eroded, and are being challenged by new ideas and an emerging new reality. The transformed view of Leninism adopted by the current regime represents its effort to cope with the emerging new reality by deploying limited theoretical modifications. The intellectual rethinking of democracy analyzed in Chapters 2 and 3, on the other hand, is an enthusiastic and positive response to the new reality of the reform era. Through the theories of dualism, social pluralism, and civil society, the new understanding of democracy both describes and justifies the withdrawal of the state from large areas of social life, growing societal autonomy, differentiation of social interests, the emergence of horizontal social groupings, and the development of grassroots self-government.

The economic reform has resulted in the development of a large non-state sector economy and the gradual weakening of the state's direct control of social and economic life. This has in turn led to the gradual breaking down of the vertical control system and significant change in the way society is organized, especially in areas related to market economic activities. New structures and organizational forms have evolved in two important developments: the emergence of horizontal social groupings through the growth of associational activities, and the development of autonomous quasi-government organizations – village self-government – in rural communities.

Both of these types of organizations are part of the transformation of the old organizational structure and the movement toward greater societal autonomy. As B. Michael Frolic suggested, they are manifestations of an emerging civil society in China.[5]

The intellectual and organizational change is accompanied by profound cultural change in Chinese society. The intellectual rethinking of democracy is underscored by the decline of collectivism and the rise of individualism. The development of societal autonomy is accompanied by a movement from the pre-reform-era culture of dependence toward a culture of independence. The social and economic freedom gained by individuals is paralleled by their growing feeling of independence from the state. The evidence presented in Chapter 6 indicates a gap between the orthodox culture and mass culture. Cultural differentiation of society from the state is demonstrated by widespread alienation from the orthodox political, ideological, and cultural values.

The broad trends in social and cultural development have closely paralleled the intellectual rethinking of the state-society relationship. The new concepts developed in the scholarly debates directly describe and theorize the emerging social reality of the reform era. The idea of state-society dualism portrays the retreating state and an expanding realm of social and economic life outside state domination. "Small government and big society" justifies societal autonomy, grassroots self-government, and the independence of economic entities. The theory of civil society addresses the organization of society into autonomous and horizontal social groupings. The differentiation of social interests in the process of economic decentralization and marketization is depicted by the concept of social pluralism, which argues for the equality of different interests in society. The idea of economic freedom characterizes individuals as independent players in the free market.

Meanwhile, the relationship between intellectual and social development is by no means a one-way street. The intellectual debates not only reflect and describe the society, but in a way have also helped shape it. Economic reform in China has been a revolution from the top, initiated and implemented by the political elite with the help of the intellectual elite. While there is frequent tension and sharp disagreement between the regime and the scholars, there is also clear evidence of close collaboration and frequent exchange of ideas between them in the launch of crucial reform projects. Scholarly input has added key reform ideas to the regime's policy-making process.

One well-known example was the marathon Conference on the Party's Theoretical Work held between January and April 1979, during which leading intellectuals played a crucial role in fundamentally changing the regime's policy orientation. The subsequent formation of Hu Yaobang's network of intellectuals and Zhao Ziyang's think tanks directly contributed to the development of various reform policies. The current Jiang Zemin regime has followed this tradition and has actively sought advice from scholars in key policy areas. In fact, since the beginning of the economic reform, all important issues concerning the reform have been subject to heated scholarly discussions and debates. This includes topics such as rural reform, urban reform, the establishment of village self-government, the development of a corporatist structure to replace direct state control of enterprises, state-owned enterprise reform, housing reform, reform of financial institutions, and legal system reform, not to mention the frequent debates on issues concerning political reform. These debates have clearly contributed to the policy-making process: crucial reform ideas are often proposed by scholars first and adopted by the regime later. Many research institutions have been established in Beijing and provincial capitals to serve as government think tanks at different levels. The Chinese response to the Hong Kong Court of Final Appeal's ruling on the right of abode, and more recently, to Taiwan's presidential election, also revealed the growing influence of scholars in key policy areas. An interesting subject of study would be the political relationship between scholars and the regime leadership, to see how they interact and how their interactions affect the formulation of public policies.

However, frequent interaction between the political and intellectual elite does not necessarily mean that the old model of the relationship between ideology and social reality suggested by Schurmann is still valid today. As society becomes increasingly autonomous, ideological concepts become less influential in shaping social reality. Their relationship with social reality has undergone an important change. During the Maoist era, the official ideology was a determining factor in the creation of the social reality. In contemporary China, the emerging ideological concepts are more descriptive than prescriptive. They are related to the emerging social reality not just by attempting to shape it but more by describing and justifying it. Thus, what can be observed is interrelationship and more or less simultaneous transformation without a clear causal direction.

The significance of such an interrelated and multidimensional development in contemporary China is that it indicates the familiar process of change known as modernization. Unlike the experience of the West in the eighteenth and nineteenth centuries, China's modernization process has been squeezed into a relatively short period, due to the strong influence of the already modernized Western world. Brantly Womack used the term "compressed intellectual modernization" to describe the fast appropriation of Western ideas by Chinese scholars.[6] In the same way, the past two decades in China can be described as "compressed socioeconomic modernization." A late-modernizing society like China has to achieve in two or three generations what the West accomplished in about 200 years. In this accelerated modernization process, an autonomous bourgeois society is rapidly emerging and becoming increasingly influential. Traditional cultural values are quickly eroding. Most ironically, Marxism, which is supposed to be part of the official ideology and the ideology of the proletariat, is being revised into a justification of the emerging bourgeoisie.

Barrington Moore Jr. observed that the presence of a strong bourgeoisie – the modern business middle class – was the crucial factor in the development of modern democracy in Western Europe and North America.[7] In several East Asian "post-Confucian societies" in the past few decades, democratization followed a period of robust development of an industrial economy and the emergence of a strong middle class, in spite of their deep-rooted authoritarian political and cultural traditions. Robert A. Scalapino, for example, suggested that South Korea and Taiwan have abandoned some of their traditional political culture in the process of democratization.[8] In 1989, some believed that China's political reform process had been violently short-circuited, but few would dispute that China is now in the midst of a very important transition.[9] Scalapino pointed out that, while democracy is not an immediate prospect for a post-Leninist society like China, what is taking place now is a transition toward "authoritarian pluralism," in which the economy is becoming marketized and a civil society has emerged and gained limited autonomy from the state.[10] This scenario of neo-authoritarianism was also predicted by Richard Baum, who described it as a market economy under a strong "tutelary" government, following the "quasi-pluralistic free-market vision" of Zhao Ziyang and inspired by the experiences of East Asian NICs.[11] Frolic also expressed the view that what is emerging from the current transition can be described as "soft authoritarianism."[12]

Seminal to this transition has been a remarkable change in the formal intellectual conception of democracy. Increasingly, democracy is understood in terms of the control of a limited state by an independent society and the accommodation and coordination of diverse social interests in a political process predicated in the dualism of state and society. This evolving pluralism constitutes a significant departure from both traditional political culture and the Leninist concept of democracy. The significance of the intellectual rethinking of democracy in contemporary China is that it may possibly indicate both the emergence of a bourgeois society as a result of the economic reform, and the development of a modern bourgeois ideology – a Chinese-style liberalism – to provide a rationale for the new social reality. In this sense, it presents a fundamental challenge to the traditional ideology and Leninist democracy.

Notes

Note: Author names and original-language titles of articles cited from online news agencies are not always available. A title in parentheses indicates a translation.

Chapter 1: Introduction

1   Andrew J. Nathan, *Chinese Democracy* (New York: Alfred A. Knopf, 1985), 228.

2   See, for example, Yuan Ming, (Democracy must be promoted in order to realize four modernizations), *Wen Hui Bao* (Wen Hui Daily), 10 January 1979, 1, cited from Joint Publications Research Service (JPRS) 73201 no. 507, 11 April 1979, 2.

3   Franz Schurmann, *Ideology and Organization in Communist China* (Berkeley: University of California Press, 1968), 38-9, 68-9, 102-4, 105-11, 479-80, 496.

4   Ibid., 54, 86, 518-19.

5   Stuart R. Schram, "The Cultural Revolution in Historical Perspective," in *Authority, Participation and Cultural Change in China,* ed. S.R. Schram (Cambridge: Cambridge University Press, 1977), 23-5, 30-1.

6   Stuart R. Schram, *Mao Zedong: A Preliminary Reassessment* (Hong Kong: Chinese University Press, 1983), 79-80; Stuart R. Schram, "Decentralization in a Unitary State: Theory and Practice, 1940-1984," in *The Scope of State Power in China,* ed. Stuart R. Schram (Hong Kong: Chinese University Press, 1985), 84-5; Stuart R. Schram, "Party Leader or True Ruler? Foundations and Significance of Mao Zedong's Personal Power," in *Foundations and Limits of State Power in China,* ed. Stuart R. Schram (Hong Kong: Chinese University Press, 1987), 214.

7   Maurice Meisner, *Mao's China and After* (New York: Free Press, 1999), 185, 345-7.

8   Mao Tse-tung, *On the Correct Handling of Contradictions among the People* (Beijing: Foreign Languages Press, 1957), 8-9.

9   Deng Xiaoping, "Shixian sige xiandaihua bixu jianchi sixiang jiben yuanze" (The four cardinal principles must be upheld in order to realize the four modernizations), *Zhongguo Zhengzhi* (Chinese politics) no. 5 (1987): 23.

10 Nathan, *Chinese Democracy,* 124, 228; and Andrew J. Nathan, *China's Crisis: Dilemmas of Reform and Prospects for Democracy* (New York: Columbia University Press, 1990), 172.

11 Brantly Womack, "In Search of Democracy: Public Authority and Popular Power in China," in *Contemporary Chinese Politics in Historical Perspective,* ed. Brantly Womack (New York: Cambridge University Press, 1991), 59-60, 65, 68, 73, 85.

12 Robert Ware, "What Good Is Democracy? The Alternatives in China and the West," in *Comparative Political Philosophy,* eds. Anthony J. Parel and Ronald C. Keith (New Delhi: Sage Publications, 1992), 115-40.

13 See, for example, Gu Shicheng, "Zhubu jianshe gaodu minzhu de shehuizhuyi zhengzhi zhidu" (Gradually establish a highly democratic socialist political system), *Faxue Zazhi* (Journal of legal science) no. 1 (1982): 7-10; Qiu Zhen and Yu Chi, "Shilun woguode guoti

he zhengti" (A tentative theorizing on China's form of state and form of government), *Xuexi yu Yanjiu* (Learn and study) no. 7 (1982): 14-19; Zhu Qinjun, "Lun guojiade minzhu zhineng jiqi zai zhengzhi tizhi gaige zhongde xiaoying" (On democracy as a function of the state and its effect in political system reform), *Anhuisheng Dangxiao Xiaokan* (Journal of Anhui Provincial Party School) no. 1 (1987): 75-8, 84; Xu Bin, "Zhengzhi tizhi gaige yu zhengti lilunde gengxin – guanyu guoti zhengti, minzhu jizhong guanxide zai renshi" (Political system reform and the renewal of the theory of political system: Rethink the form of state, the form of government, and the relationship between democracy and centralism), *Zhejiang Xuekan* (Zhejiang journal of learning) no. 5 (1987): 30-3; Ju Xingjiu and Li Guangzhi, "Minzhu zhengzhi lilun shi zhengzhi tizhi gaige de lilun yiju" (The theory of democratic politics is the theoretical basis for political system reform), *Lilun Tantao* (Theoretical exploration) no. 4 (1988): 25-8; Yu Haocheng, "Guanyu woguo zhengzhi tizhi gaige he fazhi jianshe de jige wenti" (A few questions on China's political system reform and legal system construction), *Wen Hui Bao*, 14 January 1989, 4.

14 See, for example, Chen Zhonghua and Ma Runqing, "Lun guojiade guanli zhineng" (On the management function of the state), *Guizhou Shehui Kexue* (Social sciences in Guizhou) no. 3 (1982): 1-7; Li Detian and Yuan Minwu, "Dui guojia zhineng de zairenshi" (Rethink the function of the state), *Lilun Yuekan* (Theory monthly) no. 4 (1986): 21-5; Situ Yan, "Zhongguo zhengzhi tizhi gaige de beijing yu qianjing" (Background and prospect of China's political system reform), *Zhengzhixue Yanjiu* (Political science research) no. 1 (1987): 1-6; Lang Yihuai, "Zhongguo shinian zhengzhi gaige de jiben zouxiang" (Basic directions in China's ten years of political reform), *Shehuizhuyi Yanjiu* (Socialist studies) no. 1 (1989): 11, 20-4.

15 See, for example, Zhou Yongchuang, "Guanyu bu shuyu jieji douzheng fanwei de shehui maodun" (On social contradictions that do not belong to the realm of class struggle), *Shehui Kexue* (Social sciences) no. 8 (1982): 28-9; Lei Yun, "Lun tuidong woguo shehui fazhan de zhongyao maodun" (On important contradictions that promote China's social development), *Shehui Kexue* (Social sciences) no. 8 (1982): 41-2; The Writing Group of the Scientific Socialism Teaching and Research Office of the CPC Central Committee Party School, "Lun shehuizhuyi shehui de maodun" (Contradictions of socialist society), *Guangming Ribao* (Guangming daily), 31 October 1983, 3. See also Lang, "Zhongguo shinian zhengzhi gaige."

16 See for example, Wu Cheng, "Tantan jiaqiang shehuizhuyi minzhu he fazhi" (On strengthening socialist democracy and the legal system), *Faxue Zazhi* (Journal of legal science) no. 1 (1982): 11-13; Qiu and Yu, "Shilun woguode guoti he zhengti"; Liao Gailong, "Quanmian jianshe shehuizhuyi de daolu" (Road to all-round construction of socialism), *Yunnan Shehui Kexue* (Social sciences in Yunnan) no. 2 (1982): 1-8; Li and Yuan, "Dui guojia zhineng de zairenshi"; Xu Hongwu and Li Jingde, "Zhengzhi tizhi gaige shi jingji tizhi gaige de baozheng" (Political system reform is the guarantee of economic system reform), *Guangming Ribao* (Guangming daily), 30 June 1986, 3; Chen Xianglin and Liu Xijun, "Jingji tizhi gaige huhuanzhe zhengzhi tizhi gaige" (Economic system reform calls for political system reform), *Lilun Tantao* (Theoretical exploration) no. 1 (1987): 48-54; Xu, "Zhengzhi tizhi"; Gao Fang, "Zhengzhi tizhi gaige zhide sikao de jige wenti" (A few questions in political system reform that we should think about), *Jiaoxue yu Yanjiu* (Teaching and research) no. 6 (1987): 20-5; Liu Xiaojun et al., "Zhengzhi tizhi gaige: lishi yu xianshi de sikao" (Political system reform: Reflections on the past and the present), *Tianfu Xinlun* (New ideas from Sichuan) no. 1 (1988): 1-8; Zhang Zhanbing, "Quanli guofen jizhong: zhengzhi tizhi gaige de jiaodian" (Overly centralized power: Focus of political system reform), *Tianjin Shehui Kexue* (Social sciences in Tianjin) no. 3 (1988): 27-9.

17 A comprehensive analysis of the relationship between the orthodox ideology and the pre-reform organizational structure is found in Schurmann, *Ideology and Organization*. For a discussion of the functions of a work unit, see Kenneth Lieberthal, *Governing China: From Revolution through Reform* (New York: W.W. Norton and Company, 1995), 179. See also Shi, *Political Participation*, 13-17, 159.

18 See Gordon White, *Riding the Tiger: The Politics of Economic Reform in Post-Mao China* (Stanford: Stanford University Press, 1993), 200-1. See also Marc Blecher, "The Contradictions

128   *Notes to pages 10-16*

of Grass-roots Participation and Undemocratic Statism in Maoist China and Their Fate,"
in *Contemporary Chinese Politics in Historical Perspective*, ed. Brantly Womack (New York:
Cambridge University Press, 1991), 134-5.

19 See Pan Debing, "Woguo xianxing tizhi jiegou yu shehui wenti" (China's present system
structure and its social problems), *Zhengzhixue Yanjiu* (Political science research) no. 1
(1986): 22-5; Lu Xueyi, "Hainan sheng zhengzhi yu shehui tizhi gaige de shijian" (The
reform of political and social systems in the Hainan Province), in *"Xiao zhengfu da shehui"
de lilun yu shijian* (Theory and practice of "small government and big society"), eds. Ru
Xin et al. (Beijing: Social Science Literature Publishing House, 1998), 20-4.

20 Tianjian Shi, *Political Participation in Beijing* (Cambridge, MA: Harvard University Press,
1997), 17-21. See also Victor C. Falkenheim, "Citizen and Group Politics in China," in
Citizens and Groups in Contemporary China, ed. Victor C. Falkenheim (Ann Arbor: University of Michigan Center for Chinese Studies, 1987), 4-6.

21 Lowell Dittmer, "Ideology and Organization in Post-Mao China," in *Perspectives on Development in Mainland China*, ed. King-yuh Chang (Boulder, CO: Westview Press, 1985), 53,
56-7.

22 Peter R. Moody Jr., *Chinese Politics after Mao* (New York: Praeger, 1983), 2-3, 79-80.

23 *China News Digest*, 15 February 1998.

24 Sun Liping, "Guojia yu shehui de jiegou fenhua" (Structural differentiation of state and
society), *Zhongguo Shehui Kexue Jikan* (Chinese social science quarterly) no. 1 (November
1992): 72-3; Wang Ying, Zhe Xiaoye, and Sun Bingyao, "Shetuan fazhan yu zhuzhi tixi
conggou" (Development of associations and the rebuilding of organizational systems),
Guanli Shijie (Management world) no. 2 (1992): 193-5. See also Xie Weihe, "Shehui ziyuan
liudong yu shehui fenhua: Zhongguo shimin shehui de keguan jichu" (The movement of
social resources and social differentiation: Objective foundation for China's civil society),
Zhongguo Shehui Kexue Jikan (Chinese social science quarterly) no. 4 (Summer 1993): 6-7.

25 See Vivienne Shue, "China: Transition Postponed?" *Problems of Communism* 41, 1-2
(1992): 158; B. Michael Frolic, "State-Led Civil Society," in *Civil Society in China*, eds. Timothy Brook and B. Michael Frolic (Armonk, NY: M.E. Sharpe, 1997), 52; and Robert A.
Scalapino, "Modernization and Revolution in Asia," *Problems of Communism* 41, 1-2
(1992): 181. See also Richard Baum's discussion of neo-authoritarianism in his "China
after Deng," *The China Quarterly* no. 145 (March 1996): 161.

Chapter 2: Pre-Tiananmen Intellectual Rethinking of State and Society

1 Benedict Stavis, *China's Political Reforms: An Interim Report* (New York: Praeger, 1988).

2 See notes 13, 14, 15, and 16 to Chapter 1.

3 Li Kejing, "Woguode zhengzhi tizhi gaige yu zhengzhixuede fazhan – Zhongguo shehui
kexue zazhishe zhaokai de 'zhengzhi tizhi gaige' xueshu zuotanhui zongshu" (China's
political system reform and development of political science – A summary of the conference on political system reform organized by the Chinese Journal of Social Sciences),
Zhongguo Shehui Kexue (Chinese social sciences) no. 4 (1986): 3-14.

4 Li Ping, Shen Jian, and Ding Wang, "1987 nian gaige shehui xingli diaocha baogao"
(Report on the 1987 survey on the social psychology of reform), *Jingji Ribao* (Economic
daily), 24 October 1987, 2, and 27 October 1987, 2. See also Lei Dongsheng, "Shehui
xieshang duihua zhidu zhi wojian" (My opinion on the system of social consultation and
dialogue), *Hubei Shehui Kexue* (Social sciences in Hubei) no. 4 (1988): 51.

5 Su Shaozhi, "Zhengzhi tizhi gaige yu fandui fengjianzhuyi yingxiang" (Political system
reform and the fight against the influence of feudalism), *Renmin Ribao* (People's daily), 15
August 1986, 8. See also "Shaoshu yao fucong duoshu, duoshu yao baohu shaoshu –
minzhu jianshe zhongde yige wenti" (The minority should be subordinate to the majority, and the majority should protect the minority: An issue in the development of
democracy), *Guangming Ribao* (Guangming daily), 7 October 1986, 1; Qin Xiaoying, "Shehuizhuyi minzhu yeying baokuo 'shaoshu yuanze'" (Socialist democracy should also
include the 'minority principle'), *Qiushi* (Seeking truth) no. 8 (1988): 20-3.

6 Zheng Chengliang, "Shangpin jingji, minzhuzhengzhi de fazhan yu faxuede chonggou"
(Development of a commodity economy and democratic politics, and the rebuilding of

jurisprudence), *Zhengzhi yu Falu* (Politics and law) no. 1 (1989): 10-12; Yang Haikun, "Shehuizhuyi chujijieduan liyiqunti lun" (Interest groups in the preliminary stage of socialism), *Zhengzhi yu Falu* (Politics and law) no. 2 (1989): 1-5.

7 Lin Yunong, "Lun shehuizhuyi minzhu fazhan yu jingji tizhi gaige de tongbu guanxi" (On the parallel development of socialist democracy and economic system reform), *Zhongguo Shehui Kexue* (Chinese social sciences) no. 5 (1986): 9-10.

8 Wu Zhilun, "Bixu jianli zhengzhijia yu putong qunzhong de youji lianxi" (An organic relationship must be built up between politicians and ordinary people), *Zhengzhixue Yan-jiu* (Political science research) no. 1 (1988): 24-9. See also Zhang Qian, "Shehuizhuyi zhengzhi tizhi yu duoyuanhua" (Socialist political system and pluralization), *Lilun Xingxi Bao* (Theoretical information news), 26 September 1988, 4.

9 Wang Jue, "Minzhu zhengzhi de xinfeng" (New style of democratic politics), *Hongqi* (Red flag) no. 8 (1988): 29. The difference between collective and group interests was discussed in Ronald C. Keith, "Legislating Women's and Children's 'Rights and Interests' in the PRC," *The China Quarterly* no. 149 (March 1997): 37.

10 Merle Goldman, "The Intellectuals in the Deng Xiaoping Era," in *State and Society in China: The Consequences of the Reform,* ed. Arthur L. Rosenbaum, 193-218 (Boulder, CO: Westview Press, 1992); Merle Goldman, *Sowing the Seeds of Democracy in China* (Cambridge, MA: Harvard University Press, 1994); Merle Goldman, "Politically-Engaged Intellectuals in the Deng-Jiang Era: A Changing Relationship with the Party-State," *The China Quarterly* 145 (March 1996): 35-52; Xue Liang Ding, *The Decline of Communism in China: Legitimacy Crisis 1977-1989* (Cambridge: Cambridge University Press, 1994).

11 Zheng Shiping, "Lun Zhongguo zhengzhi tizhi jichu de gaige" (On reforming the foundation of China's political system), *Zhengzhixue Yanjiu* (Political science research) no. 1 (1986): 29.

12 Yan Jiaqi's 1986 article, "Division of State Power in Four Directions" was republished in a collection of his works titled *Toward a Democratic China* (Honolulu: University of Hawaii Press, 1992), 108-17.

13 Su Shaozhi, *Democratization and Reform* (Nottingham, England: Spokesman, 1988), 179. This collection of his works includes the 1986 article titled "Rethink Socialism," which first appeared in *World Economic Herald,* 24 November 1986.

14 Rong Jian, "Lun Makeside minzhu sixiang" (On Marx's democratic ideas), *Zhengzhixue Yanjiu* (Political science research) no. 3 (1987): 6-7; Rong Jian, "Makesizhuyi guojia xueshuo yu zhengzhi tizhi gaige" (Marxist theory of the state and political system reform), *Guangzhou Yanjiu* (Guangzhou research) no. 2 (1987): 25, 27.

15 Rong Jian, "Cong zhengzhi he jingji de eryuanhua kan jingji gaige he zhengzhi gaige de guanxi" (The relationship between political reform and economic reform from the perspective of dualism of politics and economy), *Zhengzhixue Yanjiu* (Political science research) no. 6 (1987): 13.

16 Rong, "Cong zhengzhi he jingji," 14.

17 Shu-Yun Ma, "The Chinese Discourse on Civil Society," *The China Quarterly* 137 (March 1994): 180-93.

18 He Baogang, "The Ideas of Civil Society in Mainland China and Taiwan," *Issues and Studies* 31, 6 (1995): 24-64.

19 Chen Shi, "Jingji gaige yu zhengzhi ziyou" (Economic reform and political freedom), *Gongren Ribao* (Worker's daily), 15 August 1986, 3.

20 See Lin, "Lun shehuizhuyi minzhu fazhan," 38.

21 Liu Junning, "Shehui quanli, zhengzhi quanli, jingji quanli" (Social power, political power, economic power), *Gaige* (Reform) no. 4 (1988): 161.

22 See Lin, "Lun shehuizhuyi minzhu fazhan," 38. See also Xing Fensi, "Xianjieduan Zhongguo shehui gaige de ruogan lilun wenti" (A few theoretical problems concerning China's social reform at the present stage), *Shehui Kexue Zhanxian* (Social science front) no. 1 (1988): 14.

23 He Peiyu, "Lun minzhu zhengzhi de shehui jingji jichu" (On social, economic foundations for democracy), *Tansuo: Zheshiban* (Exploration: Philosophy and social science edition) no. 1 (1988): 24.

24   Zhou Jianming, "Cong shenfen guanxi dao qiyue guanxi zhuanbian zhi wojian" (My opinion on the transition from status relationship to contractual relationship), *Zhengzhi yu Falu* (Politics and law) no. 6 (1986): 9-11.

25   Liao Xun, "Lun 'da shehui, xiao zhengfu'" (On big society, small government), *Zhongguo Xingzheng Guanli* (Chinese administrative management) no. 8 (1988): 4-6.

26   Barry Sautman, "Sirens of the Strongman: Neo-authoritarianism in Recent Chinese Political Theory," *The China Quarterly* 129 (March 1992): 72-102.

27   Wu Jiaxiang, "Xinquanweizhuyi shuping" (Explaining neo-authoritarianism), *Shijie Jingji Daobao* (World economic herald), 16 January 1989, 12; Wu Jiaxiang and Zhang Bingjiu, "Jijinde minzhu haishi wenjiande minzhu – Wu Jiaxiang and Zhang Bingjiu duihualu" (Radical democracy or stable democracy: A dialogue between Wu Jiaxiang and Zhang Bingjiu), *Guangming Ribao* (Guangming daily), 31 March 1989, 3.

28   Tang Daiwang, "Shehuizhuyi chujijieduan de guojia zhineng" (The function of the state at the preliminary stage of socialism), *Zhengzhixue Yanjiu* (Political science research) no. 6 (1988): 16-18. See also Zheng, "Lun Zhongguo zhengzhi tizhi"; Yan, "Division"; Cai Tuo, "Zhengfu zhineng xintan" (A new exploration of government functions), *Tianjin Shehui Kexue* (Social sciences in Tianjin) no. 1 (1988): 25-7; Wu Yue, "Shehui guanli zhineng yu zhengfu jigou gaige" (Social management function and the reform of government institutions), *Qinghai Shehui Kexue* (Social sciences in Qinghai) no. 4 (1988): 4-7.

29   See Cai, "Zhengfu zhineng xintan." Wu Yue expresses a similar view in "Shehui guanli zhineng."

30   See Tang, "Shehuizhuyi chujijieduan."

31   Gao Changyun and Shi Yuan, "'Xiao zhengfu da shehui' de Hainan mushi – yizhong zhengzhixue de sikao" (The Hainan model of "small government and big society": A political science reflection), *Hainan Kaifa Bao* (Hainan development news), 23 September 1988, 3.

32   Liao, "Lun 'da shehui, xiao zhengfu.'"

33   See Gao and Shi, "'Xiao zhengfu da shehui.'"

34   Han Zhulin, "Xiao zhengfu, da shehui – guanyu zhengfu jigou gaige mubiao mushi de tantao" (Small government and big society: Explore the model for the reform of government institutions), *Shehui Kexue* (Social sciences) no. 3 (1989): 31.

35   See Ma, "Chinese Discourse," 182-4.

36   See Li, "Woguode zhengzhi tizhi gaige," 14.

37   See, for example, Shen Rendao and Yang Ming, "Liyi jituan de gainian he fenlei" (The concept and typology of interest groups), *Zhengzhixue Yanjiu* (Political science research) no. 3 (1986): 19-22.

38   Gu Jialing and Wu Zhilun, "Zhengzhi tizhi gaige de mubiao xuanze" (The choice of target for political system reform), *Zhengzhixue Yanjiu* (Political science research) no. 6 (1987): 10.

39   Wang Huning, "Zhongguo zhengzhi-xingzheng tizhi gaige de jingji fenxi" (An economic analysis of China's political-administrative system reform), *Shehui Kexue Zhanxian* (Social science front) no. 2 (1988): 115; Zheng Yongnian, "Jingji fazhan yu minzhu zhengzhi" (Economic development and democratic politics), *Guangming Ribao* (Guangming daily), 13 February 1989, 3; Min Qi, "Guanyu zhuanxingqi de Zhongguo zhengzhi" (Chinese politics in the transition period), *Xuexi yu Tansuo* (Study and exploration) no. 4 (1988): 78. See also Bai Wei, "Luelun jingji gaige yu zhengzhi xiandaihua" (On economic reform and political modernization), *Rencai yu Xiandaihua* (Human resources and modernization) no. 1, (1986): 20; Liu, "Shehui quanli," 164; Huang Shaohui, "Lun shehui xieshang duihua zhidu" (On the system of social consultation and dialogue), *Guangming Ribao* (Guangming daily), 7 December 1987, 3; Chi Dao and Ji Ning, "Shehui xieshang duihua 'xin' zai nali?" (What is 'new' about social consultation and dialogue?), *Liaowang* (Outlook) no. 16 (1988): 18; Zu Xuguang, "Xietiao maodun shi minzhu dangpai canzheng de yige zhongyao fangmian" (Coordinating contradictions is an important aspect in the democratic parties' participation in politics), *Renmin Zhengxie Bao* (The people's political consultation news), 17 June 1988, 3.

40   See Li, Shen, and Ding, "1987 nian," 42; Bai, "Luelun jingji gaige," 30; Jiang Nanyang, "Shehuizhuyi gaige zhongde 'hunluan' zhuangtai jiqi duice" (The state of 'confusion' in socialist reform and the way to handle it), *Tansuo: Zhesheban* (Exploration: Philosophy

and social science edition) no. 4, 1987, 30. See also Zu, "Xietiao maodun," 3; Wang Jun-chang, "Shehui gaige lilun chutan" (An initial exploration of the theory of social reform), *Zhejiang Xuekan* (Zhejiang journal of learning) no. 3 (1988): 10.

41 See Min, "Guanyu zhuanxingqi," 78.

42 See Bai, "Luelun jingji gaige," 21. See also Wang Huning, "Jianli yizhong xinde zhengzhi fazhan guan" (Form a new concept of political development), *Zhongguo Qingnian Bao* (China youth news), 19 August 1988, 3.

43 See Situ Yan, "Zhongguo zhengzhi tizhi gaige de beijing yu qianjing" (Background and prospect of China's political system reform), *Zhengzhixue Yanjiu* (Political science research) no. 1 (1987): 5-6; Bai, "Luelun jingji gaige," 21, 23. Wang, "Jianli yizhong"; Xu Yong, "Zhengzhi xiandaihua: shijie yu Zhongguo" (Political modernization: World and China), *Shehuizhuyi Yanjiu* (Socialist studies) no. 4 (1988): 8-13.

44 See Situ, "Zhongguo zhengzhi," 6; Gu and Wu, "Zhengzhi tizhi gaige," 1-3; Zhou Zhong-shu, "Zhengque renshi zhengzhi tizhi gaige de jinqi mubiao" (Correctly understand the short-term target of the political system reform), *Xuexi yu Jianshe* (Learning and construc-tion) no. 5 (1988): 27; Wang Yaohua, "Tan zhengzhi tizhi gaige de changqi mubiao he jinqi mubiao" (On the long-term and short-term targets of the political system reform), *Lilunjie* (Theoretical circles) no. 5/6 (1988): 18-19. This position appeared to be supported by the regime. See Huang Hai, "Jinxing zhengzhi tizhi gaige de qiangda sixiang wuqi" (A powerful ideological weapon for the political system reform), *Renmin Ribao* (People's daily), 27 July 1987, 5; Chi Fulin, "Zhengzhi tizhi gaige dadao shenme mudi, baokuo naxie neirong?" (What are the objectives and substances of the political system reform?), *Liaowang* (Outlook) no. 8 (1987): 9-11.

45 See Chi and Ji, "Shehui xieshang duihua," 18.

46 See Huang, "Lun shehui."

47 See Min, "Guanyu zhuanxingqi," 79.

48 Wang Renbo, "Guanyu fenquan mushi de jiazhi sikao" (Evaluative reflections on the model of separation of powers), *Tansuo: Zhesheban* (Exploration: Philosophy and social science edition) no. 4 (1988): 34, 36.

49 Lu Zhen, "Shi nian fansi: gaige de si da wuqu" (Rethink the past ten years: Four big errors in the reform), *Shulin* (Books) no. 4 (1989): 4.

50 Chen Ziming, "Gaige zhongde zhengzhi yu jingji" (Politics and economy in the reform), *Zhengzhixue Yanjiu* (Political science research) no. 1 (1987): 7-9.

51 See Zheng, "Jingji fazhan."

52 See Chi and Ji, "Shehui xieshang duihua," 18; Xiao Rong, "Guanyu guojia minzhu zhidu de jianshe" (On the building of the state's democratic system), *Guangming Ribao* (Guang-ming daily), 26 January 1989, 3.

53 Kevin J. O'Brien, "China's National People's Congress Reform and Its Limits," *Legislative Studies Quarterly* 13, 3 (1988): 343-74; Kevin J. O'Brien, *Reform without Liberalization* (New York: Cambridge University Press, 1991).

54 See Huang Shaohui, "Lun zhengzhi xietiao" (On political coordination), *Sichuan Shifan Daxue Xuebao: Sheke Ban* (Journal of Sichuan Normal University: Social science edition) no. 4 (1988): 5; Li Mingyao, "'Liyi fenhua yu liyi xietiao,' 'zhengzhi minzhu yu zhengzhi wending' xueshu taolunhui zongshu" (A summary of the conference on "interest differ-entiation and interest coordination" and "political democracy and political stability"), *Zhengzhixue Yanjiu* (Political science research) no. 2 (1989): 35.

55 See, for example, Arend Lijphart, *Democracy in Plural Societies* (New Haven: Yale University Press, 1977); Giuseppe Di Palma, *To Craft Democracies* (Berkeley, CA: University of Cali-fornia Press, 1990); Samuel P. Huntington, *The Third Wave* (Norman, OK: University of Oklahoma Press, 1991); and Georg Sorensen, *Democracy and Democratization* (Boulder, CO: Westview Press, 1993).

56 Zhao Chengxing, "Zhongguo minzhu zhengzhi lilun chutan – quanguo shouci minzhu zhengzhi jianshe yantaohui zongshu" (An initial theoretical exploration of the building of democratic politics in China: A summary of the first nationwide conference on the building of democratic politics), *Lilun Xingxi Bao* (Theoretical information news), 7 November 1988, 1.

Chapter 3: Post-Tiananmen Discussions

1 See Merle Goldman, *Sowing the Seeds of Democracy in China* (Cambridge, MA: Harvard University Press, 1994), 332-7.

2 Sun Guohua, "Minzhu jianshe bixu naru fazhi guidao" (The building of democracy must be in accordance with the rule of law), *Zhongguo Faxue* (Chinese legal science) no. 5 (1990): 9.

3 Chen Zhen, "Minzhu shi renlei jingbu he wenming de jiejing" (Democracy is the crystallization of human progress and civilization) *Zhongguo Faxue* (Chinese legal science) no. 5 (1990): 11-12.

4 Zhu Changping, "Lun gongmin zhengzhi canyu de zhiduhua" (On institutionalization of citizens' political participation), *Ningxia Shehui Kexue* (Social sciences in Ningxia) no. 4 (1990): 15-17.

5 Chen Binhui, "Guojiade guanli zhineng xintan" (New exploration into the management function of the state), *Fujian Xuekan* (Fujian journal of learning) no. 3 (1991): 65, 69-71.

6 Li Jing, "Minzhu wenhua yu Zhongguode minzhu jianshe" (Democratic culture and China's democratic construction), *Shehui Kexue* (Social sciences) no. 9 (1991): 15-18.

7 Wang Puli, "Lun minzhujizhongzhi de shizhi" (On the essence of democratic centralism), *Guangming Ribao* (Guangming daily), 7 October 1991, 3.

8 Liu Zuoxiang, "Yanjiu quanli zhiyue wenti de lilun jiazhi he shijian yiyi" (The theoretical value and practical significance of studying the issue of restriction of power), *Zhengzhi yu Falu* (Politics and law) no. 1 (1992): 7-10.

9 Rong Yiren, "Jianchi ba shijian zuowei jianyan zhenli de weiyi biaozhun" (Insist on taking practice as the sole criterion of truth), *Renmin Ribao* (People's daily), 15 June 1992, 5.

10 "Lun jiefang sixiang" (On the liberation of the mind), *Renmin Ribao* (People's daily) editorial, 4 July 1992, 1.

11 Chen Shi, "Zhengfu zhineng bixu zhuanbian" (The role of government must be changed), *Gongren Ribao* (Worker's daily), 15 May 1992, 3; Goldman, *Sowing the Seeds,* 159, 163, 171.

12 Li Peng, "Jiji tuijing xianji jigou gaige" (Actively promoting institutional reform at the county level), *Renmin Ribao* (People's daily), 7 July 1992, 1; Lu Xueyi, "Hainan sheng zhengzhi yu shehui tizhi gaige de shijian" (The reform of political and social systems in the Hainan Province), in *"Xiao zhengfu da shehui" de lilun yu shijian* (Theory and practice of "small government and big society"), eds. Ru Xin et al. (Beijing: Social Science Literature Publishing House, 1998), 16, 20-1.

13 "Yao qieshi zhuanbian zhengfu zhineng" (The role of government should be truly changed), *Renmin Ribao* (People's daily) editorial, 5 August 1992, 1.

14 Zhang Jingli, "Jiefang hongguan" (Macro-level liberation), *Renmin Ribao* (People's daily), 8 August 1992, 3.

15 Shi Xuehua, "Lun shehui zhuanxing yu zhengfu zhineng zhuanbian" (On the social transition and changing the role of the government), *Tianjin Shehui Kexue* (Social sciences in Tianjin) no. 2 (1995): 21-3; Yan Qin, "Guanyu zhengzhi tizhi gaige de ruogan sikao" (Reflections on political system reform), *Shehui-Shanghai* (Society-Shanghai) no. 9 (1992): 11-13; Cai Tuo, "Shichang jingji yu zhengzhi fazhan" (Market economy and political development), *Tianjin Ribao* (Tianjin daily), 9 February 1993, 6.

16 See Cai, "Shichang jingji." See also Yu Keping, "Shehuizhuyi shimin shehui: yige xinde yanjiu keti" (Socialist civil society: A new subject of research), *Tianjin Shehui Kexue* (Social sciences in Tianjin) no. 4 (1993): 45-8; Xie Qingkui, "Zhengfu zhineng zhuanbian de hanyi" (The meaning of government role change), *Jingji Ribao* (Economic daily), 13 May 1993, 7.

17 See, for example, Fan Yongfu, "Xiang Gang de shehui zizhi he zixun xitong jiqi dui neidi jigou gaige de qishi" (Society's self-management and consultation system in Hong Kong and its implications for the institutional reform in the mainland), *Hainan Tequ Bao* (Hainan SEZ news), 26 October 1993, 3.

18 Wang Jianqin, "Dangqian woguo zhengfu jigou gaige weishenme nanyi tuijing?" (Why is it difficult to carry out government institutional reforms?), *Qiyejia Bao* (Entrepreneur's news), 6 January 1994, 3.

19 See Shi, "Lun shehui zhuanxing," 24-6.

20 Yin Guanghua, "Zhengfu zhineng zhuanbian de san da nandian" (Three big difficulties in changing the role of government), *Jingji Ribao* (Economic daily), 15 April 1993, 7.

21 He Zengke, "Shimin shehui gainian de lishi yanbian" (Historical evolution of the concept of civil society), *Zhongguo Shehui Kexue* (Chinese social sciences) no. 5 (1994): 67-81.

22 Deng Zhenglai and Jing Yuejing, "Jiangou Zhongguo de shimin shehui" (Building civil society in China), *Zhongguo Shehui Kexue Jikan* (Chinese social science quarterly) no. 1 (November 1992), 61.

23 Ibid., 64.

24 Ibid., 59.

25 Ibid., 66.

26 See Jing Yuejing, "'Shimin shehui yu Zhongguo xiandaihua' xueshu taolunhui shuyao" (A summary of the conference on civil society and China's modernization), *Zhongguo Shehui Kexue Jikan* (Chinese social science quarterly) no. 5, (Autumn 1993): 197-202.

27 Guo Dingping, "Woguo shimin shehui de fazhan yu zhengzhi zhuanxing" (Development of civil society and political transformation in China), *Shehui Kexue* (Social sciences) no. 12 (1994): 52-5, 60.

28 Lu Pinyue, "Zhongguo lishi jingcheng yu shimin shehui zhi jiangou" (China's historical progress and the development of civil society), *Zhongguo Shehui Kexue Jikan* (Chinese social science quarterly) no. 8 (Summer 1994): 174.

29 Deng and Jing, "Jiangou Zhongguo de shimin shehui," 66.

30 See He Zengke, "Guanyu shimin shehui gainian de jidian sikao" (Some reflections on the concept of civil society), *Xiandai yu Chuantong* (Modernity and tradition) no. 4 (1994): 44-5. See also Lu, "Zhongguo lishi," 178.

31 Liu Wujun, "Shimin shehui yu xiandai fa de jingshen" (Civil society and the spirit of modern law), *Faxue* (Legal science) no. 8, 1995, 30. See also Xie Hui, "Quanli yu quanli de gongneng beifang" (The opposite functions of rights and power), *Ningbo Daxue Xuebao — Renwen Kexue Ban* (The journal of Ningbo University: Human sciences edition) no. 2 (1995): 96-104.

32 See Lu, "Zhongguo lishi jingcheng," 178.

33 Sun Liping, "Guojia yu shehui de jiegou fenhua" (Structural differentiation of state and society), *Zhongguo Shehui Kexue Jikan* (Chinese social science quarterly) no. 1 (November 1992): 69-76; Xu Guodong, "Shimin shehui yu shimin fa" (Civil society and civil law), *Faxue Yanjiu* (Studies in law) no. 4 (1994): 3-9.

34 Jing Yuejing, "Shimin shehui yanjiu jiqi yiyi" (The study of civil society and its significance), *Xiandai yu Chuantong* (Modernity and tradition) no. 4 (1994): 32. See also Guo, "Woguo shimin shehui," 54-5, 60; Yu, "Shehuizhuyi shimin shehui," 48; Zhang Chengfu, "Xingzheng minzhu lun" (On administrative democracy), *Zhongguo Xingzheng Guanli* (Chinese administrative management) no. 6 (1993): 23-7.

35 Guo Daohui, "Renquan, shehui quanli yu fading quanli" (Human rights, social rights, and legal rights), *Zhongguo Shehui Kexue Jikan* (Chinese social sciences quarterly) no. 3 (Spring 1993): 37-49.

36 Guo Daohui, "Shehuizhuyi ziyou – dangdai shehuizhuyi fade jingshen" (Socialist freedom: The spirit of law in contemporary socialism," *Faxue* (Legal science) no. 10 (1994): 2-6.

37 Guo Daohui, "Fazhi guojia yu fazhi shehui" (Rule of law state and rule of law society), *Zhengzhi yu Falu* (Politics and law) no. 1 (1995): 17-20.

38 Ma Changshan, "Cong shimin shehui lilun chufa dui fa benzhi de zai renshi" (Rethink the essence of law according to the theory of civil society), *Faxue Yanjiu* (Studies in law) no. 1 (1995): 41-8.

39 See Xu, "Shimin shehui," 3-9. Xu's article was named by the editorial board of *Faxue Yanjiu* (Studies in law) as one of the best articles published in *Faxue Yanjiu* since 1978.

40 See Xie Pengcheng, "Lun dangdai Zhongguo de falu quanwei" (On the authority of law in contemporary China), *Zhongguo Faxue* (Chinese legal science) no. 6 (1995): 3-13. See also Liu, "Shimin shehui," 28-30.

41 See, for example, Cui Peiting, "Jianli shehuizhuyi shichang jingji tizhi yaoqiu shenhua zhengzhi tizhi gaige" (Building socialist market economy requires further political system reform), *Lilun Yanjiu* (Theoretical studies) no. 2 (1993): 2-4.

42   Gong Zhihui, "Zhengzhi tizhi gaige zhongde zhengzhi wending" (Political stability in political system reform), *Shehuizhuyi Yanjiu* (Socialist studies) no. 5 (1993): 15-19. See also Cai, "Shichang jingji," 6; Bao Xinjian, "Jiji tuijing shehuizhuyi zhengzhi xiandaihua" (Actively promote socialist political modernization), *Guangming Ribao* (Guangming daily), 14 December 1992, 3.

43   Wang Song and Sun Li, "Lun jingji liyi duoyuanhua yu zhengzhi yitihua" (On pluralism of economic interests and political integration), *Zhongguo Xingzheng Guanli* (Chinese administrative management) no. 7 (1993): 24-7; Guo Dingping, "Cong duoyuan shehui tanji zhengzhi gongshi" (Political common understanding in plural society), *Shehui Kexue* (Social sciences) no. 8 (1993): 28-31.

44   Shi Xianmin, "Zhongguo shehui zhuanxingqi de jiegou fenhua yu shuang eryuan shehui jiegou" (Structural differentiation in China's transitional stage and double dualist social structure), *Zhongguo Shehui Kexue Jikan* (Chinese social science quarterly) no. 5 (Autumn 1993): 55-65; Li Jingpeng, "Dangdai Zhongguo shehui liyi jiegou de bianhua yu zhengzhi fazhan" (Changes in the structure of social interests and political development in contemporary China), *Tianjin Shehui Kexue* (Social sciences in Tianjin) no. 3 (1994): 31-7.

45   Sun Xiaoxia, "Lun falu yu shehui liyi" (On law and social interests), *Zhongguo Faxue* (Chinese legal science) no. 4 (1995): 52-60.

46   Ronald C. Keith, *China's Struggle for the Rule of Law* (New York: St. Martin's Press, 1994); Ronald C. Keith, "The New Relevance of 'Rights and Interests': China's Changing Human Rights Theories," *China Information* 10, 2 (1995): 38-61; Ronald C. Keith, "Legislating Women's and Children's 'Rights and Interests' in the PRC," *The China Quarterly* no. 149 (March 1997): 29-55.

47   See Gu Benhua, "Shichang jingji tiaojianxia quanli jiegou de zouxiang" (The way the structure of power changes under the condition of market economy), *Hunan Shifan Daxue Shehui Kexue Xuebao* (Hunan Normal University social science journal) no. 2 (1994): 17-21. See also Yan, "Guanyu zhengzhi," 13-14; and Deng and Jing, "Jiangou Zhongguo de shimin shehui," 61.

48   Jia Dongqiao, "Shichang jingji dui woguo zhengzhi de yingxiang qiantan" (A brief discussion of the impact of market economy on Chinese politics), *Shehui Kexue* (Social sciences) no. 10 (1993): 12, 25-8; Wang Jiangang, "Duodang hezuo yu shehui zhengzhi wending" (Multiparty cooperation and social, political stability), *Zhongguo Qingnian Zhengzhi Xueyuan Xuebao* (The journal of the China Youth Political Institute) no. 6 (1993): 41-5, 49.

49   Wang Song, "Jingji liyi duoyuanhua yu dangdai Zhongguo zhengzhi fazhan" (Pluralism of economic interests and political development in contemporary China), *Tansuo yu Zhengming* (Exploration and debate) no. 10 (1994): 39-41; Zhou Yezhong, "Lun minzhu yu liyi, liyi jituan" (On democracy, interests, and interest groups), *Xuexi yu Yanjiu* (Learn and study) no. 2 (1995): 70-6.

50   Wang Huning, *Minzhu Zhengzhi* (Democratic politics) (Hong Kong: Joint Publishing [H.K.] Company, 1993), 64-8.

51   Brantly Womack, "Party-state democracy: a theoretical exploration," *Issues and Studies* 25, 3 (1989): 37-57.

52   Discussed in Zhang Hailing, "Kua shiji de da lunzhan" (A great cross-century debate), *Huaxia Wenzhai* (CND Chinese magazine) Supplementary Issue no. 202 (10 January 2000). Reprint from *Yazhou Zhoukan* (Asia weekly) no. 40 (10 October 1999).

53   Ibid. See also in the same issue of *Huaxia Wenzhai*: Zhu Xueqin, "1998: ziyouzhuyi de yanshuo" (1998: Liberal opinions), and Gan Yang, "Ziyouzhuyi: guizu de haishi pingmin de?" (Liberalism: For upper class or common people?). Both articles are reprinted from *Dushu* (Read books) no. 1 (1999). See also "Faguo meiti zhi zhongguo dalu chuxian 'xin zuopai' fengchao" (French media reports the emergence of 'new left' in the Chinese mainland), *Zhongguo Shibao* (China times), 12 July 2000.

54   Zhou Duo, "Yao jianjin minzhu, buyao jiduan zhuyi" (We need gradual democratization, not extremism), *Huaxia Wenzhai* (CND Chinese magazine) no. 482 (23 June 2000).

55   See Jing, "'Shimin shehui yu Zhongguo xiandaihua,'" 197-202.

56   Merle Goldman, "Politically-Engaged Intellectuals in the Deng-Jiang Era: A Changing Relationship with the Party-State," *The China Quarterly* no. 145 (March 1996), 49.
57   Ibid., 51.
58   This impression is based on my own conversations with a number of young Chinese scholars.

Chapter 4: Emerging Civil Society

1   Niu Fengrui, "Hainan de cunmin zizhi zhidu jianshe" (Building the system of villagers' self-government in Hainan), in *"Xiao zhengfu da shehui" de lilun yu shijian* (Theory and practice of "small government and big society"), eds. Ru Xin et al. (Beijing: Social Science Literature Publishing House, 1998), 314-45. Niu is a researcher at the CASS Institute of Sociology.
2   B. Michael Frolic, "State-Led Civil Society," in *Civil Society in China,* eds. Timothy Brook and B. Michael Frolic (Armonk, NY: M.E. Sharpe, 1997), 63.
3   Hu Xiaoming, "Shehui tuanti wenti zhongzhong" (Various problems with associations), *Beijing Ribao* (Beijing daily), 20 November 1990, 3; She Dehu, "Youguan woguo shehui tuanti wenti de sikao" (Reflections on the problems concerning associations), *Qiushi* (Seeking truth) no. 17 (1991): 15.
4   Guo Dingping, "Lun Zhongguo tese de tuanti zhengzhi" (On Chinese-style group politics), *Zhengzhi yu Falu* (Politics and law) no. 3 (1995): 24. Some of these figures were obviously from a 1993 *China Daily* report and were cited by other authors as well. See also Jonathan Unger and Anita Chan, "Corporatism in China: A Developmental State in an East Asian Context," in *China After Socialism,* eds. Barrett L. McCormick and Jonathan Unger (Armonk, NY: M.E. Sharpe, 1996), 105.
5   See Gordon White, "Prospects for Civil Society in China: A Case Study of Xiaoshan City," *The Australian Journal of Chinese Affairs* no. 29 (January 1993): 63, 71. The Chinese scholars who participated in the study include Wang Ying, Sun Bingyao, and Zhe Xiaoye, who published several papers on the study in Chinese academic journals.
6   Sun Bingyao, "Xiangzhen shetuan yu Zhongguo jiceng shehui" (Township-level associations and Chinese society at the grassroots), *Zhongguo Shehui Kexue Jikan* (Chinese social science quarterly) no. 9 (Autumn 1994): 26.
7   Xie Weihe, "Shehui ziyuan liudong yu shehui fenhua: Zhongguo shimin shehui de keguan jichu" (The movement of social resources and social differentiation: Objective foundations for China's civil society), *Zhongguo Shehui Kexue Jikan* (Chinese social science quarterly) no. 4 (Summer 1993): 6-7.
8   Sun Liping, "Guojia yu shehui de jiegou fenhua" (Structural differentiation of state and society), *Zhongguo Shehui Kexue Jikan* (Chinese social science quarterly) no. 1 (November 1992): 72-3.
9   Wang Ying, Zhe Xiaoye, and Sun Bingyao, "Shetuan fazhan yu zuzhi tixi conggou" (Development of associations and the rebuilding of organizational systems), *Guanli Shijie* (Management world) no. 2 (1992): 193-5. See also White, "Prospects for Civil Society," 72.
10 Sun Bingyao, "Zhongguo shehui tuanti guan-min erchongxing wenti" (The dual nature of China's associations), *Zhongguo Shehui Kexue Jikan* (Chinese social science quarterly) no. 6 (February 1994): 18. See also White, "Prospects for Civil Society," 72; Wang, Zhe, and Sun, "Shetuan fazhan," 196.
11 See Sun, "Zhongguo shehui tuanti," 18; Sun, "Xiangzhen shetuan," 25-6.
12 Xue Liang Ding, *The Decline of Communism in China: Legitimacy Crisis, 1977-1989* (Cambridge: Cambridge University Press, 1994), 66-76.
13 See Sun, "Zhongguo shehui tuanti," 18. See also White, "Prospects for Civil Society," 77.
14 See Sun, "Zhongguo shehui tuanti," 18.
15 See Jonathan Unger, "'Bridges': Private Business, the Chinese Government and the Rise of New Associations," *The China Quarterly* no. 147 (September 1996): 797.
16 See White, "Prospects for Civil Society," 77. See also Sun, "Zhongguo shehui tuanti," 18.
17 See Wang, Zhe, and Sun, "Shetuan fazhan," 189.
18 Ma Changshan, "Luelun woguo shehui tuanti de falu diwei ji danhua qi xingzhenhua

qingxiang" (On the legal status of China's associations and on reducing their tendency to become administrative entities), *Zhengzhi yu Falu* (Politics and law) no. 3 (1992): 37.

19   See Guo, "Lun Zhongguo tese," 25. See also Wang Ying, "Zhongguo de shehui zhongjian-ceng: Shetuan fazhan yu zhuzhi tixi conggou" (The intermediary level of Chinese society: Development of associations and the rebuilding of the organizational system), *Zhongguo Shehui Kexue Jikan* (Chinese social science quarterly) no. 6 (February 1994): 25.

20   See White, "Prospects for Civil Society," 75-6. See also Wang, "Zhongguode shehui zhongjianceng," 25, 29; Wang, Zhe, and Sun, "Shetuan fazhan," 190.

21   See Wang, "Zhongguo de shehui zhongjianceng," 25, 32. See also Sun, "Zhongguo shehui tuanti," 19.

22   See White, "Prospects for Civil Society," 73-7.

23   See Wang, "Zhongguo de shehui zhongjianceng," 26.

24   Ibid., 34. See also Unger, "'Bridges,'" 798-9; Christopher E. Nevitt, "Private Business Associations in China: Evidence of Civil Society or Local State Power?" *The China Journal* no. 36 (July 1996): 28, 30, 42.

25   See Guo, "Lun Zhongguo tese," 27.

26   See Sun, "Xiangzhen shetuan," 26.

27   See Unger and Chan, "Corporatism in China," 118.

28   Xue Muqiao, "Jianli he fazhan zizhi hangye zuzhi" (Establish and develop autonomous industry organizations), *Renmin Ribao* (People's daily), 10 October 1988, 5 (cited from *Foreign Broadcast Information Service Daily Reports on China [FBIS-CHI] 88-201*, 18 October 1988, 34-5).

29   *Jingji Ribao* (Economic daily), 12 October 1992, 2. Cited from Unger and Chan, "Corporatism in China," 109.

30   Ronald C. Keith, "Legislating Women's and Children's 'Rights and Interests' in the PRC," *The China Quarterly* no. 149 (March 1997), 52.

31   See Sun, "Zhongguo shehui tuanti," 17, 20-1, 23.

32   See Guo, "Lun Zhongguo tese," 26-8. See also Wang, "Zhongguo de shehui zhongjian-ceng," 25-6.

33   See Wang, ibid., 26.

34   See Ma, "Luelun woguo shehui," 36-7.

35   Willy Wo-lap Lam, "Worker Unrest Said Threatening Social Stability," *South China Morning Post*, 6 December 1995, 19 (cited from *FBIS-CHI-95-234*, 6 December 1995, 22); Cao Min, (Workers learn to protect their rights), *China Daily*, 24 January 1996, 1 (cited from *FBIS-CHI-96-017*, 25 January 1996, 10); Trish Saywell, "On the Edge," *Far Eastern Economic Review*, 25 February 1999, 46-8.

36   Ge Xiangxian, Guo Yuanfa, and Song Jishui, "Gonghui yao zhenzheng daibiao zhigong liyi" (The labour union should truly represent workers' interests), *Liaowang* (Outlook) no. 17 (1988): 12-14; Zhao Yongjin and Cao Zheng, "Zhigong quanyi de weishi" (Champion of workers' rights and interests), *Liaowang* (Outlook) no. 17 (1988): 16-17. An excellent discussion of the trade union is also found in Anita Chan's "Revolution or Corporatism? Workers and Trade Unions in Post-Mao China," *The Australian Journal of Chinese Affairs* no. 29 (January 1993): 31-61.

37   *China Labour Bulletin* (Hong Kong) no. 3 (May 1994): 8-9. Cited from Unger and Chan, "Corporatism in China," 122.

38   See Unger and Chan, "Corporatism in China," 110.

39   (Trade unions urged to protect worker interests), *Xinhua News Agency*, 30 July 1995, cited from *FBIS-CHI-95-146* (31 July 1995), 32-3.

40   See Unger, "'Bridges,'" 811-12.

41   See Nevitt, "Private Business Associations," 31, 33. The quoted passage is from pp. 36-7. See also Unger, "'Bridges,'" 811-12.

42   See Sun, "Xiangzhen shetuan," 29.

43   Li Chunling, "Hainan shehui zhongjie zuzhi de peiyu ji fazhan" (The nurturing and development of intermediate social organization in Hainan), in *"Xiao zhengfu da shehui" de lilun yu shijian* (Theory and practice of "small government and big society"), eds. Ru

Xin et al. (Beijing: Social Science Literature Publishing House, 1998), 302-7. Li is a researcher at the Institute of Sociology, CASS, and Ru is a vice-president of the CASS.
44 See Chan, "Revolution or Corporatism?" 45, 55, 57; Unger and Chan, "Corporatism in China," 128-9. See also Sun, "Zhongguo shehui tuanti," 23.
45 See Nevitt, "Private Business Associations," 31, 33. See also Unger, "'Bridges,'" 799-800.
46 See Nevitt, "Private Business Associations," 39-40; Unger and Chan, "Corporatism in China," 114-15.
47 See Unger and Chan, "Corporatism in China," 114-15; Unger, "'Bridges,'" 815-17.
48 See Unger, "'Bridges,'" 803, 816. See also Nevitt, "Private Business Associations," 29.
49 See Sun, "Zhongguo shehui tuanti," 22. See also Wang, "Zhongguo de shehui zhongjian-ceng," 25, 29.
50 See Sun, "Xiangzhen shetuan," 27.
51 See Kristen Parris, "Private Entrepreneurs as Citizens: from Leninism to Corporatism," *China Information* 10, 3/4 (1995-6): 20.
52 See Unger, "'Bridges,'" 800, 803. See also Unger and Chan, "Corporatism in China," 115; Nevitt, "Private Business Associations," 31; White, "Prospects for Civil Society," 74-5.
53 See Sun, "Xiangzhen shetuan," 33.
54 See Ding, *Decline of Communism*, 72.
55 See She, "Youguan woguo shehui tuanti," 18.
56 Yu Qian, "Zhongguo jieshefa heri chutai lai?" (When will we have a Chinese law on associations?), *Shehui Baozhang Bao* (Social insurance news), 31 March 1989, 1.
57 See Hu, "Shehui tuanti wenti zhongzhong," 3.
58 See Sun, "Xiangzhen shetuan," 26. The Hainan figures are from Li, "Hainan shehui zhongjie zuzhi," 283-4.
59 See Ding, *Decline of Communism*, 66-76.
60 See Sun, "Zhongguo shehui tuanti," 19; Wang, Zhe, and Sun, "Shetuan fazhan," 190. See also Wang, "Zhongguo de shehui zhongjianceng," 29; Sun, "Zhongguo shehui tuanti," 19. According to Sun, most associations in Xiaoshan were only "loosely tied" to their supervisory organizations.
61 See Ding, *Decline of Communism*, 72, 74-6.
62 See Sha Chun, (Mainland center banned for violating taboo in investigating hot topics), *Ming Pao*, 12 September 1994, A2 (cited from *FBIS-CHI-94-179*, 15 September 1994, 41-2).
63 See Willy Wo-lap Lam, "Scholars Vow to Promote Social Change," *South China Morning Post*, 7 June 1994, 11 (cited from *FBIS-CHI-94-109*, 7 June 1994, 32-3). Vivien Pik-kwan Chan, "Critical Chat Served with Tea in Beijing Bookstore," *South China Morning Post* (Internet edition), 5 February 1999.
64 See Sun, "Zhongguo shehui tuanti," 19.
65 See Unger, "'Bridges,'" 812.
66 See Yu, "Zhongguo jieshefa heri chutai lai?"
67 Kung Shuang-yin, (China Confucius Foundation sues Ministry of Culture for illegal administrative interferences), *Ta Kung Pao*, 20 January 1996, A2 (cited from *FBIS-CHI-96-035*, 21 February 1996, 18).
68 Willy Wo-lap Lam, "PRC: Party Circular Warns of Spread of Illegal Trade Unions," *South China Morning Post*, 4 June 1996, 1 (cited from *FBIS-CHI-96-109*, 5 June 1996, 20).
69 "Zhongguo nongcun paoli fankang yundong zaiqi" (The resurgence of violent resistance movements in China's rural areas), *Duowei Xinwenshe* (Duowei news agency), 12 September 2000.
70 Vivien Pik-kwan Chan, "PRC: Book on Muslims' Sex Lives Sparks Outrage," *South China Morning Post*, 31 January 1996, 10 (cited from *FBIS-CHI-96-021*, 31 January 1996, 12). For the CPC and State Council circular, see *FBIS-CHI-94-223*, 5 December 1994, 41. The commentator's article appeared in *Renmin Ribao* (People's daily), 3 December 1994, 1 (cited from *FBIS-CHI-94-235*, 7 December 1994, 17-18).
71 "A CND Interview with Tong Yi," *China News Digest*, 9 August 1997. The interview was conducted by CND reporter Fang Wu on 26 July 1997.

72   Elizabeth Lowe, "China's House Churches" (paper presented at the conference on Modernization, the Church and the East Asian Experience held by the Boston Theological
Institute, March 1996).

73   Vivien Pik-kwan Chan, "100 Zhong Gong Offices Shut Down," *South China Morning Post*
(Internet edition), 1 February 2000.

74   Elisabeth Rosenthal, "While Defending Crackdown, China Admits Appeal of Sect," *New
York Times* (Internet edition), 5 November 1999.

75   See the July to December 1998 issues as well as no. 410 (5 February 1999) of *Huaxia Wenzhai* (CND Chinese magazine).

76   "Hunan Incident Symptomatic of Social Upheaval," *China News Digest,* 20 January 1999.
See also news reports in *Huaxia Wenzhai* (CND Chinese Magazine) no. 396 (30 October
1998).

77   Martin K. Whyte, "Urban China: A Civil Society in the Making?" in *State and Society in
China: The Consequences of the Reform,* ed. Arthur L. Rosenbaum (Boulder, CO: Westview
Press, 1992), 77-101.

78   Gordon White, *Riding the Tiger: The Politics of Economic Reform in Post-Mao China* (Stanford: Stanford University Press, 1993), 37, 203, 217-19, 226-8; White, "Prospects for Civil
Society," 63-87.

79   Barrett L. McCormick, Su Shaozhi, and Xiao Xiaoming, "The 1989 Democracy Movement: A Review of the Prospects for Civil Society in China," *Pacific Affairs* 65, 2 (1992):
182-202.

80   See Frederic Wakeman Jr., "The Civil Society and Public Sphere Debate," *Modern China* 19,
2 (1993): 109-10; Gu Xin, "A Civil Society and Public Sphere in Post-Mao China? An
Overview of Western Publications," *China Information* 8, 3 (1993-4): 38. See also White,
"Prospects for Civil Society," 64-8.

81   White, "Prospects for Civil Society," 66-7.

82   Heath B. Chamberlain, "On the Search for Civil Society in China," *Modern China* 19, 2
(1993): 199-215.

83   Tony Saich, "The Search for Civil Society and Democracy in China," *Current History* 93,
584 (1994): 260-4.

84   Dorothy J. Solinger, "Urban Entrepreneurs and the State: The Merger of State and Society," in *State and Society in China: The Consequences of the Reform,* ed. Arthur L. Rosenbaum
(Boulder, CO: Westview Press, 1992), 121-41.

85   Jean C. Oi, "The Role of the Local State in China's Transitional Economy," *The China
Quarterly* no. 144 (December 1995): 1132-49.

86   Unger and Chan, "Corporatism in China," 95-129; Chan, "Revolution or Corporatism,"
31-61; Unger, "'Bridges,'" 795-819.

87   Nevitt, "Private Business Associations," 25-43; Parris, "Private Entrepreneurs," 1-28.

88   Schmitter defined corporatism as "a system of interest representation in which the con-
stituent units are organized into a limited number of singular, compulsory, noncompeti-
tive, hierarchically ordered and functionally differentiated categories, recognised or
licensed (if not created) by the state and granted a deliberate representational monopoly
within their respective categories in exchange for observing certain controls on their
selection of leaders and articulation of demands and supports." See Philippe C. Schmitter,
"Still the Century of Corporatism?" in *The New Corporatism,* eds. Fredrick B. Pike and
Thomas Stritch (London: University of Notre Dame Press, 1974), 93-4.

89   Ibid., 86, 93-6, 102-5. A in-depth discussion of the distinction between state corporatism
and societal corporatism is also found in Leo Panitch, "The Development of Corporatism
in Liberal Democracies," *Comparative Political Studies* 10 (April 1977): 61-90.

90   Schmitter, "Still the Century?" 93-4, 96, 103-5.

91   Kenneth Lieberthal, *Governing China: From Revolution through Reform* (New York: W.W.
Norton and Company, 1995), 172-3.

92   See Unger and Chan, "Corporatism in China," 113.

93   Frolic, "State-Led Civil Society," 49, 58; Unger, "'Bridges,'" 818-19.

94   See Li, "Hainan shehui zhongjie zuzhi," 274. See also Jing Yuejing, "'Shimin shehui yu
Zhongguo xiandaihua' xueshu taolunhui shuyao" (A summary of the conference on civil

society and China's modernization), *Zhongguo Shehui Kexue Jikan* (Chinese social science quarterly) no. 5 (Autumn 1993): 200.

Chapter 5: Reorganizing Rural Society

1 See Niu Fengrui, "Hainan de cunmin zizhi zhidu jianshe" (Building the system of villagers' self-government in Hainan), in *"Xiao zhengfu da shehui" de lilun yu shijian* (Theory and practice of "small government and big society"), eds. Ru Xin et al. (Beijing: Social Science Literature Publishing House, 1998), 314-45.
2 Zhang Weiqing, "Jiaqiang nongcun minzhu jianshe, miqie dangqun ganqun guanxi" (Strengthening rural democratic construction, establishing close ties between the party and the masses and between cadres and the masses), *Qiushi* (Seeking truth) no. 4 (1991): 36 (Zhang is head of the Propaganda Department of the Shanxi Provincial Party Committee); Liu Zhenwei, "Cunji zuzhi jianshe tantao" (Explore the construction of village-level organization), *Zhongguo Xingzheng Guanli* (Chinese administrative management) no. 1 (1988): 37 (Liu is a member of the CPC Central Secretariat's Rural Policy Research Office); Zhong Zhushan, "Nongcun jiceng dang zuzhi xianzhuang tanxi" (An analysis of the current condition of rural grassroots party organization), *Liaowang* (Outlook) no. 1 (1990): 12-13. See also Kevin J. O'Brien, "Implementing Political Reform in China's Villages," *The Australian Journal of Chinese Affairs* no. 32 (July 1994): 35; Daniel Kelliher, "The Chinese Debate over Village Self-government," *The China Journal* no. 37 (January 1997): 66-7.
3 Gao Jie, "Cunmin weiyuanhui zuzhi jianshe de beijing, xianzhuang he zhengce daoxiang" (The organizational development of villagers' committees: Its background, current situation, and policy orientation), *Faxue Yanjiu* (Studies in law) no. 2 (1994): 13 (Gao is a member of the Hangzhou University Law Faculty); Tang Jinsu, "Cunmin huiyi yu cunmin daibiao huiyi" (Village assembly and village council), *Zhengzhi yu Falu* (Politics and law) no. 2 (1995): 12 (Tang is a member of the Bureau of the Grassroots Government under the Ministry of Civil Affairs); Tang Jinsu and Dong Chengmei, "Cunmin weiyuanhui zuzhifa (shixing) guanche shishi qingkuang diaocha baogao" (A findings report on the implementation of the Organic Law of Villagers' Committees [Trial Implementation]), *Zhongguo Faxue* (Chinese legal science) no. 2 (1992): 9 (Dong is a member of the People's University Law Faculty). See also Susan V. Lawrence, "Democracy, Chinese Style," *The Australian Journal of Chinese Affairs* no. 32 (July 1994): 62.
4 Tyrene White, "Rural Politics in the 1990s: Rebuilding Grassroots Institutions," *Current History* 91, 566 (1992): 274-5.
5 See Kelliher, "Chinese Debate," 67, 72; O'Brien, "Implementing Political Reform," 51-2.
6 See Tang, "Cunmin huiyi," 12. See also White, "Rural Politics," 276.
7 Jiang Wandi, "Grassroots Democracy Taking Root," *Beijing Review* 39, 11 (1996): 11. See also Gao, "Cunmin weiyuanhui," 11.
8 Tang Jinsu, "Woguo cunmin weiyuanhui jianshe zhuangkuang yu zhanwang" (The current condition and the prospects of China's village committees), *Zhengzhi yu Falu* (Politics and law) no. 6 (1992): 42; Wang Zhenhai and Han Xijiang, "Dangqian cunmin weiyuanhui zuzhi jianshe chulun" (Our opinions on current organization building of villagers' committees), *Zhengzhi yu Falu* (Politics and law) no. 5 (1988): 8. See also Kelliher, "Chinese Debate," 64.
9 See Chen Hefu, "Woguo minzhu zhengzhi jianshe de jianshi jichu" (Solid foundation for China's construction of democratic politics), *Zhengzhixue Yanjiu* (Political science research) no. 6 (1989): 50-1.
10 See White, "Rural Politics," 276. See also Tang and Dong, "Cunmin weiyuanhui zuzhifa," 7.
11 Kelliher, "Chinese Debate," 66-7, 85. See also O'Brien, "Implementing Political Reform," 35-6.
12 Barrett L. McCormick, "China's Leninist Parliament and Public Sphere: A Comparative Analysis," in *China after Socialism*, eds. Barrett L. McCormick and Jonathan Unger (Armonk, NY: M.E. Sharpe, 1996), 51-2.
13 (Civil Affairs Minister affirms village autonomy), *Xinhua News Agency,* 20 November 1995 (cited from *FBIS-CHI-95-223,* 20 November 1995, 29).

14   "Shixing jiceng minzhu qunzhong shi zhubu you qunzhong ziji ban" (Implement grass-roots democracy to gradually allow the masses to handle their own affairs), *Renmin Ribao* (People's daily), 5 December 1987, 3.
15   See Jiang, "Grassroots Democracy," 12. See also (Civil Affairs Minister affirms village autonomy), *FBIS-CHI-95-223*, 20 November 1995, 29.
16   See Kelliher, "Chinese Debate," 78.
17   See White, "Rural Politics," 275.
18   See Kelliher, "Chinese Debate," 64.
19   See Tang and Dong, "Cunmin weiyuanhui zuzhifa," 7; Tang Jinsu, "Jiaqiang nongcun jiceng minzhu zhengzhi jianshe" (Strengthening construction of rural democratic politics), *Zhengzhi yu Falu* (Politics and law) no. 4 (1994): 22. See also (Civil Affairs Minister), 28; Jiang, "Grassroots Democracy," 11.
20   Commentator's article, (Take effective measures to strengthen building of villagers' committees), *Renmin Ribao* (People's daily), 21 November 1995, 4 (cited from *FBIS-CHI-95-250*, 29 December 1995, 18).
21   Gao Jie, "Lun woguo cunmin daibiao huiyi zhidu" (On China's villagers' representative assembly system), *Faxue Yanjiu* (Studies in law) no. 2 (1995): 18. See also Tang, "Cunmin huiyi," 13.
22   See Gao, "Lun woguo cunmin," 17. See also Tang, "Cunmin huiyi," 11-12; Tang and Dong, "Cunmin weiyuanhui zuzhifa," 7.
23   See Gao, "Lun woguo cunmin," 19.
24   See Lawrence, "Democracy, Chinese Style," 63.
25   Anne F. Thurston, *Muddling toward Democracy* (Washington, DC: United States Institute of Peace, 1998), 18, 39, 41. See also O'Brien, "Implementing Political Reform," 44.
26   See Tang Jinsu, "Cunmin huiyi," 12; Gao, "Lun woguo cunmin," 20; Jorgen Elklit, "The Chinese Village Committee Electoral System," *China Information* 11, 4 (1997): 12.
27   See O'Brien, "Implementing Political Reform," 44. See also (PRC: Democratic Elections Come to Villages), *Xinhua News Agency*, 30 May 1996 (cited from *FBIS-CHI-96-109*, 5 June 1996, 35-6); Thurston, *Muddling toward Democracy*, 27-38; Jiang, "Grassroots Democracy," 14; Shui Tian, "Daguancun li xuan cunzhang – Jilin nongmin 'haixuan' diaocha ji" (Electing the village chief in Daguan Village: An investigative report on the "sea elections" among peasants in Jilin Province), *Huaxia Wenzhai* (CND Chinese magazine) no. 389 (11 September 1998).
28   Melanie Manion, "The Electoral Connection in the Chinese Countryside," *American Political Science Review* 90, 4 (1996): 736-48.
29   See O'Brien, "Implementing Political Reform," 43-4; Lawrence, "Democracy, Chinese Style," 64-6; Cui Zhiyuan, "Yanjiu dangdai zhongguo zhengzhi de xindongxiang" (A new trend in the study of contemporary Chinese politics), *Jingji Shehui Tizhi Bijiao* (Comparison of economic and social systems) no. 5 (1995): 3. See also Tang, "Woguo cunmin weiyuanhui jianshe," 43; Tang and Dong, "Cunmin weiyuanhui zuzhifa," 8; Zhang, "Jiaqiang nongcun minzhu jianshe," 37-8.
30   See O'Brien, "Implementing Political Reform," 40-1.
31   See ibid., 47; Thurston, *Muddling toward Democracy*, 21-3, 33-5.
32   See Lawrence, "Democracy, Chinese Style," 61-8.
33   See Jiang, "Grassroots Democracy," 12.
34   See Thurston, *Muddling toward Democracy*, 38, 41.
35   Elklit, "Chinese Village Committee," 3-10.
36   See Jiang, "Grassroots Democracy," 12.
37   See Kelliher, "Chinese Debate," 73-4; O'Brien, "Implementing Political Reform," 45. See also Manion, "Electoral Connection," 737, 742-3.
38   See Tang, "Woguo cunmin weiyuanhui jianshe," 43; Tang and Dong, "Cunmin weiyuanhui zuzhifa," 11; O'Brien, "Implementing Political Reform," 46; Jiang, "Grassroots Democracy," 12-13; Kelliher, "Chinese Debate," 71-3.
39   See O'Brien, "Implementing Political Reform," 45; Jiang, "Grassroots Democracy," 14.
40   See Kelliher, "Chinese Debate," 78-9; Jiang, "Grassroots Democracy," 13; O'Brien, "Implementing Political Reform," 46-7.

41 "Village Officials Held in Tax Protest," *South China Morning Post* (Internet edition), 3 November 1999.

42 See Zhong, "Nongcun jiceng," 12-13. See also Zhou Zuohan, "Guanyu cunmin weiyuanhui jianshe de jidian sikao" (A few reflections on the construction of villagers' committees), *Hunan Shifan Daxue Shehui Kexue Xuebao* (Hunan Normal University social science journal) no. 5 (1987): 20.

43 See Liu, "Cunji zuzhi jianshe tantao," 38.

44 See Kelliher, "Chinese Debate," 82-3. See also Lawrence, "Democracy, Chinese Style," 63; Niu, "Hainan de cunmin," 326.

45 C. Daniel Yang, "China: Democracy at Grassroots," *China News Digest,* 14 January 1996.

46 See Kelliher, "Chinese Debate," 84; Niu, "Hainan de cunmin," 327-8.

47 See Lawrence, "Democracy, Chinese Style," 65-6.

48 Teng Pi-yun, (CPC's control over rural areas weakens, replaced by traditional forces or 'capable people') *Lien Ho Pao* (United Daily News) (Hong Kong), 18 July 1995, 8 (cited from *FBIS-CHI-95-163,* 23 August 1995, 163).

49 Ma Changshan, "Cunmin zizhi zuzhi jianshe de shidai yiyi jiqi shijian fancha" (The organizational construction of village self-government: Its historical significance and its contrast with reality), *Zhengzhi yu Falu* (Politics and law) no. 2 (1994): 19-20. See also Tang and Dong, "Cunmin weiyuanhui zuzhifa," 10.

50 See Tang, "Woguo cunmin weiyuanhui jianshe," 44. See also Ma, "Cunmin zizhi zuzhi," 20; Tang and Dong, "Cunmin weiyuanhui zuzhifa," 10; Xia Jun, (Guard against "rebound" of peasant burdens), *Renmin Ribao* (People's daily), 25 August 1994, 2 (cited from *FBIS-CHI-94-190,* 30 September 1994, 33).

51 See Ma, "Cunmin zizhi zuzhi," 21.

52 Yang Zili, "Nongcun diaocha jishi" (Rural research notes), *Huaxia Wenzhai* (CND Chinese magazine) no. 413 (26 February 1999); Lawrence, "Democracy, Chinese Style," 68.

53 See Niu, "Hainan de cunmin," 327. See also O'Brien, "Implementing Political Reform," 36.

54 (Clan influence on rural politics increases), *Zhenli de Zhuiqiu* (The pursuit of truth), 11 June 1995, 31-3 (cited from *FBIS-CHI-95-180,* 18 September 1995, 14-15); Wang Hongzhi, "Guarding against revival of clan culture," *Renmin Ribao* (People's daily), 10 February 1996, 5 (cited from *FBIS-CHI-96-035,* 21 February 1996, 20). Wang is a research fellow from the Chinese University of Politics and Law.

55 See Teng, (CPC's control).

56 "Former Entrepreneur Sentenced to 20 Years," *Beijing Review* 36, 37 (1993), 7. See also Thurston, *Muddling toward Democracy,* 24-5.

57 See O'Brien, "Implementing Political Reform," 41-2, 50-8.

58 See Didi Tatlow, "Mainland Academic Says Party 'Eliminated' at Grass Roots," *Hong Kong Standard,* 1 October 1994 (cited from *FBIS-CHI-94-191,* 3 October 1994, 40). (Ding is quoted in this report.)

59 Research Office under the Central Organization Department, (Guard against 'electoral bribery' in rural areas), *Renmin Ribao* (People's daily), 21 May 1996, 11 (cited from *FBIS-CHI-96-116,* 14 June 1996, 18); Bian Qingguo, (Declining role of village committees in population control work), *Renkou yu Jingji* (Population and economy) no. 92 (25 September 1995), 33-5 (cited from *FBIS-CHI-96-032,* 15 February 1996, 16). See also (Clan influence on rural politics increases), *FBIS-CHI-95-180,* 18 September 1995, 14.

60 See Bian, (Declining role), 15-16. See also "Clan Influence," 15; O'Brien, "Implementing Political Reform," 57-8.

61 "CPC Decision on Party Building," *Beijing Review* 37, 44 (1994): 10. See also *FBIS-CHI-94-189,* 29 September 1994, 23-4.

62 "CPC to 'Overhaul' Grass-root Party Branches," *FBIS-CHI-94-250,* 29 December 1994, 33.

63 See O'Brien, "Implementing Political Reform," 51-3. Descriptions of paralyzed villages are also found in Bian, (Declining role), 16, and in Thurston, *Muddling toward Democracy,* 21-3.

64 See O'Brien, "Implementing Political Reform," 59.

65 See Zhou, "Guanyu cunmin weiyuanhui," 21; (Jiang Chunyun on grass-roots political

power), *Xinhua News Agency,* 21 November 1995 (cited from *FBIS-CHI-95-242,* 18 December 1995, 20).
66   See, for example, Zhao Zhongsan, "Jiceng minzhu zhengzhi jianshe de yizhong hao xingshi" (A good form of constructing grassroots democratic politics), *Qiushi* (Seeking truth) no. 2 (1988): 40; Li Wenshan, "Jiceng minzhu jianshe de xin xingshi" (A new form of grassroots democratic construction), *Xinhua Wenzhai* (New China digest) no. 4 (1989): 13.
67   See Chen, "Woguo minzhu zhengzhi," 50-1.
68   Wang Zhenhai, "Lun cun de shequ tezheng yu quanli jiegou" (On community characteristics and power structures of a village), *Zhengzhi yu Falu* (Politics and law) no. 6 (1991): 18-20; Chen Jian and Liu Min'an, "Jianlun cunweihui de falu diwei" (A brief analysis of the legal status of villagers' committees), *Zhengzhi yu Falu* (Politics and law) no. 6 (1992): 46-7. See also Liu, "Cunji zuzhi jianshe tantao," 39.
69   Some Chinese scholars have discussed the difference between "autonomy" *(zizhi)* and democracy. See, for example, Li Yuanshu, "Lun shehui zizhi" (On societal autonomy), *Xuexi yu Tansuo* (Study and exploration) no. 5 (1994): 92-3. Li is a researcher at the Institute of Politics, Heilongjiang Academy of Social Sciences.
70   See Gao, "Cunmin weiyuanhui zuzhi jianshe," 14.
71   See Tang and Dong, "Cunmin weiyuanhui zuzhifa," 11.
72   O'Brien, for example, suggested that village self-government meant democratic rights "packaged with increased state penetration." See O'Brien, "Implementing Political Reform," 59. See also Tang, "Jiaqiang nongcun jiceng minzhu," 23; and Ma, "Cunmin zizhi zuzhi," 19; "Wang Juntao on development of 'gray democracy,'" *Der Spiegel* (Hamburg), 3 July 1995, 118 (cited from *FBIS-CHI-95-128,* 5 July 1995, 35).
73   See (Civil Affairs Minister affirms village autonomy), *FBIS-CHI-95-223,* 20 November 1995, 29.
74   Vivien Pik-kwan Chan, "Town Poll Awaits Beijing Ruling," *South China Morning Post* (Internet edition), 27 January 1999; Vivien Pik-kwan Chan, "Beijing Indicates Recognition of Landmark Township Election," *South China Morning Post* (Internet edition), 1 March 1999.
75   Marc Blecher, "The Contradictions of Grass-roots Participation and Undemocratic Statism in Maoist China and their Fate," in *Contemporary Chinese Politics in Historical Perspective,* ed. Brantly Womack (New York: Cambridge University Press, 1991), 140. See also Zhou, "Guanyu cunmin weiyuanhui," 18.

Chapter 6: Cultural Distinction and Psychological Independence
1   Gabriel A. Almond and Sidney Verba, *The Civic Culture* (Princeton: Princeton University Press, 1963), 14-15, 32.
2   Gabriel A. Almond and G. Bingham Powell Jr., *Comparative Politics Today* (Boston: Little, Brown and Company, 1980), 4, 42-4.
3   Lucian W. Pye, *The Spirit of Chinese Politics* (Cambridge, MA: Harvard University Press, 1992), 236-7; Lucian W. Pye, "Tiananmen and Chinese Political Culture," *Asian Survey* 30, 4 (1990): 331-47; Lucian W. Pye, *The Mandarin and the Cadre: China's Political Cultures* (Ann Arbor: University of Michigan Press, 1988), 167.
4   Lowell Dittmer, *China under Reform* (Boulder, CO: Westview Press, 1994), 125-30.
5   Perry Link, "China's 'Core' Problem," in *China in Transformation,* ed. Tu Wei-ming (Cambridge, MA: Harvard University Press, 1994), 191-2.
6   Perry Link, Richard Madsen, and Paul G. Pickowicz, eds., *Unofficial China: Popular Culture and Thought in the People's Republic* (Boulder, CO: Westview Press, 1989).
7   See Andrew J. Nathan and Tianjian Shi, "Cultural Requisites for Democracy in China: Findings from a Survey," in *China in Transformation,* ed. Tu Wei-ming (Cambridge, MA: Harvard University Press, 1994), 97. See also Melanie Manion, "Survey Research in the Study of Contemporary China: Learning from Local Samples," *The China Quarterly* 139 (September 1994): 741-65.
8   Stanley Rosen, "Value Change among Post-Mao Youth: The Evidence from Survey Data," in *Unofficial China: Popular Culture and Thought in the People's Republic,* eds. Perry Link,

Richard Madsen, and Paul G. Pickowicz (Boulder, CO: Westview Press, 1989), 193-216; Stanley Rosen, "Students and the State in China: The Crisis in Ideology and Organization," in *State and Society in China: The Consequences of the Reform,* ed. Arthur L. Rosenbaum (Boulder, CO: Westview Press, 1992), 167-91.

9 Godwin C. Chu and Yanan Ju, *The Great Wall in Ruins: Communication and Cultural Change in China* (Albany, NY: State University of New York Press, 1993).

10 See Nathan and Shi, "Cultural Requisites," 95-123.

11 Peter R. Moody Jr., "Trends in the Study of Chinese Political Culture," *The China Quarterly* no. 139 (September 1994), 739.

12 See Tianjian Shi, *Political Participation in Beijing* (Cambridge, MA: Harvard University Press, 1997), 257-8.

13 Alfred L. Chan and Paul Nesbitt-Larking, "Critical Citizenship and Civil Society in Contemporary China," *Canadian Journal of Political Science* 28, 2 (1995): 293-309.

14 See Xue Liang Ding, *The Decline of Communism in China: Legitimacy Crisis, 1977-1989* (Cambridge: Cambridge University Press, 1994), 104-9, 141-65; Merle Goldman, Perry Link, and Su Wei, "China's Intellectuals in the Deng Era: Loss of Identity with the State," in *China's Quest for National Identity,* eds. Lowell Dittmer and Samuel Kim (Ithaca, NY: Cornell University Press, 1993), 125.

15 Bill Brugger, "From 'Revisionism' to 'Alienation,' from Great Leaps to 'Third Wave,'" *The China Quarterly* no. 108 (December 1986): 644-51; Bill Brugger and David Kelly, *Chinese Marxism in the Post-Mao Era* (Stanford, CA: Stanford University Press, 1990).

16 A discussion of this debate, including a translation of the main part of the Pan Xiao letter, can be found in Ding, *Decline of Communism,* 104-9.

17 Yang Kuisen, "Dangdai Zhongguo shehui sichao pinglun" (Comment on ideological trends in contemporary Chinese society), *Jilin Daxue Shehui Kexue Xuebao* (Jilin University social science journal) no. 5 (1990): 17-19; Liu Baiwen and Lü Fuxin, "Xiandai shehui: congxin renshi ziwo" (Modern society: Rethink the self), *Zhongguo Qingnian* (Chinese youth) no. 9 (1992): 12; Zheng Hangsheng, "Zhongguo shehui zhengzai da zhuanxing" (Chinese society is undergoing radical transformation), *Shanxi Fazhan Daobao* (Shanxi development herald), 8 April 1994, 4; Li Jingpeng, "Dangdai Zhongguo shehui liyi jiegou de bianhua yu zhengzhi fazhan" (Changes in the structure of social interests and political development in contemporary China), *Tianjin Shehui Kexue* (Tianjin social science) no. 3 (1994): 33-4; Dou Xiaomin, "Shichang jingji yu zhengzhi wending" (Market economy and political stability), *Zhengzhou Daxue Xuebao: Zhexue Shehui Kexue Ban* (Zhengzhou university journal: Philosophy and social science edition) no. 3 (1994): 9; Duan Yue, "Kunrao Zhongguo Qingnianren de shige lunli wenti" (Ten ethical questions that puzzle Chinese youth), *Zhongguo Qingnian* (Chinese youth) no. 5 (1995): 10-14; Liu Han, "Du Zouxiang quanli de shidai" (A review of *Toward the era of rights*), *Zhongguo Faxue* (Chinese legal science) no. 1 (1996): 110.

18 Shao Daosheng, "Shehui de fazhan yu daode de shuaitui" (Social development and moral decline), *Zhongguo Shehui Kexue* (Chinese social sciences) no. 3 (1994): 13; Shan Shaojie, "Dangdai Zhongguo: xinyang weiji yuanyu weishan zhi feng" (Contemporary China: Crisis of faith results from hypocrisy), *Zhongguo Shehui Kexue* (Chinese social sciences) no. 3 (1994): 16-17; Zhang Yu, "Shichang jingji yu jiazhi congjian" (Market economy and value reconstruction), *Zhongguo Shehui Kexue* (Chinese social sciences) no. 3 (1994): 19-20; Tang Can, "Xiangle zhuyi yousi" (Concerns over hedonism), *Zhongguo Qingnian* (Chinese youth) no. 12 (1992): 12-13; Shan Shaojie, "Guoren siliguan: leng de hanxin, re de zaodong" (The selfishness of Chinese: From freezing cold to boiling heat), *Zhongguo Qingnian* (Chinese youth) no. 10 (1993): 6-7.

19 Xing Fensi, "Xianjieduan Zhongguo shehui gaige de ruogan lilun wenti" (A few theoretical problems concerning China's social reform at the present stage), *Shehui Kexue Zhanxian* (Social science front) no. 1 (1988): 14; He Peiyu, "Lun minzhu zhengzhi de shehui jingji jichu" (On social, economic foundations for democracy), *Tansuo: Zhesheban* (Exploration: Philosophy and social science edition) no. 1 (1988): 24; Cai Tuo, "Shichang jingji yu zhengzhi fazhan" (Market economy and political development), *Tianjin ribao* (Tianjin

daily), 9 February 1993, 6; Jia Dongqiao, "Shichang jingji dui woguo zhengzhi de yingxiang qiantan" (A brief discussion of the impact of market economy on Chinese politics),
Shehui Kexue (Social sciences) no. 10 (1993): 27; Gu Benhua, "Shichang jingji tiaojianxia
quanli jiegou de zouxiang" (The way the structure of power changes under the condition
of market economy), *Hunan Shifan Daxue Shehui Kexue Xuebao* (Hunan Normal University
social science journal) no. 2 (1994): 18; Li Deshun, "'Huapo' yu 'papo'" ("Slipping down"
and "climbing up"), *Zhongguo Shehui Kexue* (Chinese social sciences) no. 3 (1994): 3.

20 Luo Jianhua and Gao Zhengang, "Lun minzhu jingshen" (On democratic spirit), *Guangming Ribao* (Guangming daily), 24 March 1989, 3; Huang Wansheng, "Xinquanweizhuyi
pipan wenda lu" (Criticism of neo-authoritarianism: Questions and answers), *Wen Hui
Bao*, 22 February 1989, 4; Qin Xiaoying, "Guilai ba, 'Wusi' shenhun – minzhu guannian
de gengxin yu minzhu guandian de xuanze" (Come back, the May 4 spirit: Renew
the concept of democracy and choose the ideas of democracy), *Huaren Shijie* (Chinese
world) no. 1 (1989): 21; Li Jiancheng, "Ziyou: shehuizhuyi minzhu de zuigao yuanze"
(Freedom: The supreme principle of socialist democracy), *Qiushi* (Seeking truth) no. 3
(1989): 40-1.

21 Liao Gailong, "Quanmian jianshe shehuizhuyi de daolu" (Road to all-round construction
of socialism), *Yunnan Shehui Kexue* (Social sciences in Yunnan) no. 2 (1982): 7; Wang
Ruoshui, (In defense of humanism), *Wen Hui Bao*, 17 January 1983, 3 (cited from *JPRS-
82880-16* no. 392, February 1983, 48); Li Lianke, (Do not negate Marxist humanism), *Shehui Kexue* (Social sciences) no. 7 (1983): 60-3 (cited from *JPRS-CPS-84-006*, 17 January
1984, 11-12); Yan Jiaqi, (The significance of differentiating between two implications of
humanism), *Guangming Ribao* (Guangming daily), 1 March 1984, 2 (cited from *JPRS-CPS-
84-024*, 28 March 1984, 58); Su Shaozhi, *Democratization and Reform* (Nottingham, England: Spokesman, 1988), 180; Tong Daling, "Renlei zai xin qimeng zhong" (Mankind in
new enlightenment), *Jingjixue Zhoubao* (Economics weekly), 23 April 1989, 1; Xie Weijian,
"Shehuizhuyi yu geren ziyou" (Socialism and individual freedom), *Shehui Kexue* (Social
sciences) no. 2 (1993): 29-30. See also the speech by Du Ruji in "Yongyu tansuo, tuijing
gaige – shoudu lilunjie zhaokai guanyu zhengzhi tizhi gaige zuotanhui de fayan" (Dare to
explore and promote reform: The speeches made at the symposium on political system
reform held by the capital's theoretical circle), *Makesizhuyi Yanjiu* (Marxist studies) no. 4
(1986): 6.

22 Weng Xianzhong, "Lun shehuizhuyi shichang jingji de wenhua jingshen" (On the cultural spirit of socialist market economy), *Zhongguo Shehui Kexue* (Chinese social sciences)
no. 6 (1994): 83-90; Yang Kuisen, "Shangpin yishi he renwen jingshen" (Commodity consciousness and humanist spirit), *Zhongguo Shehui Kexue* (Chinese social sciences) no. 6
(1994): 91-6; Han Qingxiang, "Shehuizhuyi shichang jingji yu ren de suzao" (Socialist
market economy and human development), *Zhongguo Shehui Kexue* (Chinese social sciences) no. 3 (1995): 123-30; Zhu Xinhua, "Xunzhao xin wenhua de lishi zuobiao"
(Searching for historical basis of a new culture), *Zhongguo Qingnian* (Chinese youth) no. 5
(1995): 15-17.

23 Min Qi, *Zhongguo Zhengzhi Wenhua* (Chinese political culture) (Kunming: Yunnan People's Press, 1989).

24 Zhang Mingdui, *Zhongguo "Zhengzhiren"* (China's "political person") (Beijing: Chinese
Academy of Social Science Press, 1994).

25 China Youth Research Centre Project Group, "1994-1995 Zhongguo Qingnian shehui
fazhan yanjiu baogao" (Research report on Chinese youth's social development: 1994-
1995), *Zhongguo Qingnian Yanjiu* (China youth research) no. 5 (1995): 4-12.

26 See Rosen, "Value Change"; Chu and Ju, *Great Wall in Ruins*; Shi, *Political Participation*;
Nathan and Shi, "Cultural Requisites."

27 Ronald Inglehart, *The Silent Revolution* (Princeton: Princeton University Press, 1977), 95-7.

28 See Chan and Nesbitt-Larking, "Critical Citizenship"; Inglehart, *Silent Revolution*, 302.

29 Pye, *Spirit of Chinese Politics*, 231.

30 See Rosen, "Students and the State," 169-70; Rosen, "Value Change," 201-2.

31 See Chan and Nesbitt-Larking, "Critical Citizenship," 294.

32 See Chu and Ju, *Great Wall in Ruins*, 224, 234.

33 See Shi, *Political Participation,* 250.
34 See Rosen, "Students and the State," 169-70; Rosen, "Value Change," 201-2.
35 Cao Yinghua and Li Huasong, "Dangdai qingnian xinyang de zhuangkuang yu qushi" (Contemporary youth's ideological condition and trends), *Zhongguo Qingnian Yanjiu* (China youth research) no. 5 (1995): 41-2. Cao Yinghua is a research member of the China Youth Research Centre. Li Huasong is an editor of *Zhongguo Qingnian Yanjiu.*
36 Wang Fuchun and Wu Xiaojian, "Guanyu Beijing daxue xuesheng minzhu yishi de diaocha baogao" (A survey report on the Beijing University students' democratic consciousness), *Zhengzhixue Yanjiu* (Political science research) no. 1 (1989): 27.
37 See Rosen, "Students and the State," 175-6.
38 See Ding, *Decline of Communism,* 141-65.
39 See Dittmer, *China under Reform,* 191-2.
40 See Ding, *Decline of Communism,* 126.
41 See Chu and Ju, *Great Wall in Ruins,* 157, 185-6, 280.
42 Cao and Li, "Dangdai qingnian xinyang," 42.
43 See Nathan and Shi, "Cultural Requisites," 112-15; Chu and Ju, *Great Wall in Ruins,* 55-6, 185-6.
44 Liu Haoxing and Xu Ke, "Shanghai shi wuzhong jiating jiajiao jiazhi quxiang de bijiao yanjiu" (A comparative study of the value orientations in family education of five types of families in Shanghai), *Shehui Kexue* (Social sciences) no. 1 (1995): 52. See also Stanley Rosen, "Students and the State," 177.
45 Xu Ming-Yang and Jia Daluo, "69 Percent of Couples Had Pre-marital Sex, Survey Says," *China News Digest,* 11 November 1996. Similar survey results were also reported in Rosen, "Value Change," 207-9.
46 Xiong Bo and Zheng Liedong, "Unmarried Couples Defending 'Living Together,'" *China News Digest,* 28 September 1996. Guo Dong, "Shihun yizhu yu qingren yizhu" (Those practising trial marriage and those having lovers), *Zhongguo Qingnian Yanjiu* (China youth research) no. 3, 1995, 36.
47 B. Michael Frolic, "State-Led Civil Society," in *Civil Society in China,* eds. Timothy Brook and B. Michael Frolic (Armonk, NY: M.E. Sharpe, 1997), 52.

Chapter 7: Conclusion

1 Andrew J. Nathan, *Chinese Democracy* (New York: Alfred A. Knopf, 1985), 64-5, 127, 130; Sun Yat-sen, *The Principle of Democracy (Minquan Zhuyi),* trans. Frank W. Price (Westport, CT: Greenwood Press, 1970), 35-8. (*Minquan zhuyi* literally means "the doctrine of the people's power.")
2 Nathan, *Chinese Democracy,* 228.
3 Willy Wo-Lap Lam, "Jiang's Theory 'Strains Ideology,'" *South China Morning Post,* 30 August 2000. For discussions of "three representatives" by regime theoreticians, see Chen Wei, "Shixian 'san ge daibiao' de lishi jingyan" (Historical experiences in realizing "three representatives"), *Xinhua News Agency,* 2 July 2000; Hu Zhenmin, "Yi 'san ge daibiao' de sixiang zhidao jingshen wenming jianshe" (Develop spiritual civilization under the guidance of the idea of "three representatives"), *Renmin Ribao* (People's daily), 11 July 2000, 9; Luo Shugang, "'San ge daibiao' yu dang de sixiang lilun jianshe" ("Three representatives" and the party's ideological and theoretical construction), *Renmin Ribao* (People's daily), 11 July 2000, 9.
4 See, for example, Liu Junning's distinction between "autocratic" and "democratic" politics in his "Shehui quanli, zhengzhi quanli, jingji quanli" (Social power, political power, economic power), *Gaige* (Reform) no. 4 (1988): 161. See also Chen Ziming, "Gaige zhongde zhengzhi yu jingji" (Politics and economy in the reform), *Zhengzhixue Yanjiu* (Political science research) no. 1 (1987): 7-9.
5 B. Michael Frolic, "State-Led Civil Society," in *Civil Society in China,* eds. Timothy Brook and B. Michael Frolic (Armonk, NY: M.E. Sharpe, 1997), 63.
6 Brantly Womack, "In Search of Democracy: Public Authority and Popular Power in China," in *Contemporary Chinese Politics in Historical Perspective,* ed. Brantly Womack (New York: Cambridge University Press, 1991), 61.

7   Barrington Moore Jr., *Social Origins of Dictatorship and Democracy* (Boston: Beacon Press, 1968).
8   Robert A. Scalapino, "Democratizing Dragons: South Korea and Taiwan," *Journal of Democracy* 4, 3 (1993): 70-83.
9   Vivienne Shue, "China: Transition Postponed?" *Problems of Communism* 41, 1-2 (1992): 158.
10 Robert A. Scalapino, "Modernization and Revolution in Asia," *Problems of Communism* 41, 1-2 (1992): 181.
11 Richard Baum, "China after Deng," *The China Quarterly* no. 145 (March 1996): 156, 161.
12 Frolic, "State-Led Civil Society," 52.

Glossary of Chinese Terms

Chinese	English
市場調劑	Adjustment by market
異化	Alienation
反左	Anti-left
社團；協會	Associations
資產階級自由化	Bourgeois liberalization
能人	Capable people
集中	Centralism, centralization
政府職能的轉換	Change the role of government
公民社會	Citizen society, society of citizens
市民社會	Civil society
宗族	Clan
階級敵人	Class enemies
階級鬥爭	Class struggle

人民內部矛盾	Contradictions among the people
信仰危機	Crisis of faith
一放就亂，一統就死	Decentralization leads to anarchy; recentralization leads to stagnation.
集中指導下的民主	Democracy guided by the centre
民主集中制	Democratic centralism
二元論；二元化	Dualism
二元分化	Dualist differentiation
政治經濟二元論	Dualism of politics and economy
國家與社會二元論	Dualism of state and society
少數人爭權奪利	A few people fighting for power and personal gains
四項基本原則	Four cardinal principles
人民的根本利益	Fundamental interests of the people
還權于社會	Giving power back to society
基層民主	Grassroots democracy
基層自治	Grassroots self-government
群體	Groups, social groups
利益分化	Interest differentiation
利益多元主義	Interest pluralism
解放思想	Liberation of the mind
管理公共事務	Management of public affairs

市場經濟	Market economy
群眾組織	Mass organization, mass association
群眾路線	Mass line
一元論；一元化	Monism
道德崩潰	Moral collapse
道德滑坡	Moral decline
新權威主義	Neo-authoritarianism
參與危機	Participation crisis
參與失敗	Participation failure
人民民主專政	People's democratic dictatorship
多元論；多元化	Pluralism
政治一元論；政治一元化	Political monism
政治多元論；政治多元化	Political pluralism
良性互動	Positive interaction
實踐是檢驗真理的唯一標準	Practice is the sole criterion of truth.
理性化的政治權威	Rationalized political authority
用法來治；法治；法制	Rule by law
法的統治；法治	Rule of law
求同存異	Seeking common ground while maintaining differences
小機關，大服務	Small bureaucracies providing big service

小政府，大社會	Small government and big society
社會協商對話	Social consultation and dialogue
社會管理	Social management, management of society
社會多元論；社會多元化	Social pluralism
社會主義市場經濟	Socialist market economy
社會自治	Societal autonomy
政府職能社會化	Societalization of government functions
身份社會	Society of ascribed status
社會的自我管理	Society's self-management
自發的社會權利	Spontaneous social rights
社會利益結構	Structure of social interests
主管部門 (掛靠單位)	Supervisory organization
國家興亡，匹夫有責	The fate of the country is everyone's responsibility.
物質不夠，精神來湊	The material is in short supply, so use the spiritual as a substitute.
一元化領導	The monist leadership, centralized leadership
一切向錢看	Think of money in doing everything.
權威轉型	Transformation of authority from one type to another
一致；統一	Unity
利益一致	Unity of interests
民間的	Unofficial, non-governmental

村自治	Village self-government
村民委員會	Villagers' committee
村民大會	Villagers' council
村民代表會	Villagers' representative assembly (VRA)
單位	Work unit

Bibliography of English-language Sources

Note: Author names and original-language titles of articles cited from online news agencies are not always available. A title in parentheses indicates a translation.

Almond, Gabriel A., and G. Bingham Powell Jr. *Comparative Politics Today.* Boston: Little, Brown and Company, 1980.

Almond, Gabriel A., and Sidney Verba. *The Civic Culture.* Princeton: Princeton University Press, 1963.

Baum, Richard. "China after Deng." *The China Quarterly* no. 145 (March 1996): 153-75.

Blecher, Marc. "The Contradictions of Grass-roots Participation and Undemocratic Statism in Maoist China and Their Fate." In *Contemporary Chinese Politics in Historical Perspective,* edited by Brantly Womack, 129-52. New York: Cambridge University Press, 1991.

Brugger, Bill. "From 'Revisionism' to 'Alienation,' from Great Leaps to 'Third Wave,'" *The China Quarterly* no. 108 (December 1986): 644-51.

Brugger, Bill, and David Kelly. *Chinese Marxism in the Post-Mao Era.* Stanford: Stanford University Press, 1990.

Chamberlain, Heath B. "On the Search for Civil Society in China." *Modern China* 19, 2 (1993): 199-215.

Chan, Alfred L., and Paul Nesbitt-Larking. "Critical Citizenship and Civil Society in Contemporary China." *Canadian Journal of Political Science* 28, 2 (1995): 293-309.

Chan, Anita. "Revolution or Corporatism? Workers and Trade Unions in Post-Mao China." *The Australian Journal of Chinese Affairs* no. 29 (January 1993): 31-61.

Chan, Vivien Pik-kwan. "Beijing Indicates Recognition of Landmark Township Election." *South China Morning Post* (Internet edition), 1 March 1999.

–. "Critical Chat Served with Tea in Beijing Bookstore." *South China Morning Post* (Internet edition), 5 February 1999.

–. "100 Zhong Gong Offices Shut Down." *South China Morning Post* (Internet edition), 1 February 2000.

–. "PRC: Book on Muslims' Sex Lives Sparks 'Outrage.'" *South China Morning Post,* 31 January 1996, 10.

–. "Town Poll Awaits Beijing Ruling." *South China Morning Post* (Internet edition), 27 January 1999.

Chu, Godwin C., and Yanan Ju. *The Great Wall in Ruins: Communication and Cultural Change in China.* Albany, NY: State University of New York Press, 1993.

"A CND Interview with Tong Yi." *China News Digest,* 9 August 1997.

"CPC Decision on Party Building." *Beijing Review* 37, 44 (1994): 10.

Di Palma, Giuseppe. *To Craft Democracies.* Berkeley, CA: University of California Press, 1990.

Ding, Xue Liang. *The Decline of Communism in China: Legitimacy Crisis 1977-1989.* Cambridge: Cambridge University Press, 1994.

Dittmer, Lowell. *China under Reform*. Boulder, CO: Westview Press, 1994.
—. "Ideology and Organization in Post-Mao China." In *Perspectives on Development in Mainland China*, edited by King-yuh Chang, 36-60. Boulder, CO: Westview Press, 1985.
Elklit, Jorgen. "The Chinese Village Committee Electoral System." *China Information* 11, 4 (1997): 1-13.
Falkenheim, Victor C. "Citizen and Group Politics in China." In *Citizens and Groups in Contemporary China*, edited by Victor C. Falkenheim. Ann Arbor: University of Michigan Center for Chinese Studies, 1987.
"Former Entrepreneur Sentenced to 20 Years." *Beijing Review* 36, 37 (1993): 7.
Frolic, B. Michael. "State-Led Civil Society." In *Civil Society in China*, edited by Timothy Brook and B. Michael Frolic, 46-67. Armonk, NY: M.E. Sharpe, 1997.
Goldman, Merle. "The Intellectuals in the Deng Xiaoping Era." In *State and Society in China: The Consequences of the Reform*, edited by Arthur L. Rosenbaum, 193-218. Boulder, CO: Westview Press, 1992.
—. "Politically-Engaged Intellectuals in the Deng-Jiang Era: A Changing Relationship with the Party-State." *The China Quarterly* no. 145 (March 1996): 35-52.
—. *Sowing the Seeds of Democracy in China*. Cambridge, MA: Harvard University Press, 1994.
Goldman, Merle, Perry Link, and Su Wei. "China's Intellectuals in the Deng Era: Loss of Identity with the State." In *China's Quest for National Identity*, edited by Lowell Dittmer and Samuel Kim, 125-53. Ithaca, NY: Cornell University Press, 1993.
Gu, Xin. "A Civil Society and Public Sphere in Post-Mao China? An Overview of Western Publications." *China Information* 8, 3 (1993-4): 38-52.
He, Baogang. "The Ideas of Civil Society in Mainland China and Taiwan." *Issues and Studies* 31, 6 (1995): 24-64.
"Hunan Incident Symptomatic of Social Upheaval." *China News Digest*, 20 January 1999.
Huntington, Samuel P. *The Third Wave*. Norman, OK: University of Oklahoma Press, 1991.
Inglehart, Ronald. *The Silent Revolution*. Princeton, NJ: Princeton University Press, 1977.
Jiang, Wandi. "Grassroots Democracy Taking Root." *Beijing Review* 39, 11 (1996): 11-14.
Keith, Ronald C. *China's Struggle for the Rule of Law*. New York: St. Martin's Press, 1994.
—. "Legislating Women's and Children's 'Rights and Interests' in the PRC." *The China Quarterly* no. 149 (March 1997): 29-55.
—. "The New Relevance of 'Rights and Interests': China's Changing Human Rights Theories." *China Information* 10, 2 (1995): 38-61.
Kelliher, Daniel. "The Chinese Debate over Village Self-government." *The China Journal* no. 37 (January 1997): 63-86.
Lam, Willy Wo-Lap. "Jiang's Theory 'Strains Ideology.'" *South China Morning Post*, 30 August 2000.
—. "PRC: Party Circular Warns of Spread of Illegal Trade Unions." *South China Morning Post*, 4 June 1996, 1. Cited from *FBIS-CHI-96-109*, 5 June 1996, 20.
—. "Scholars Vow to Promote Social Change." *South China Morning Post*, 7 June 1994, 11. Cited from *FBIS-CHI-94-109*, 7 June 1994, 32-3.
—. "Worker Unrest Said Threatening Social Stability." *South China Morning Post*, 6 December 1995, 19. Cited from *FBIS-CHI-95-234*, 6 December 1995, 22.
Lawrence, Susan V. "Democracy, Chinese Style." *The Australian Journal of Chinese Affairs* no. 32 (July 1994): 61-8.
Lieberthal, Kenneth. *Governing China: From Revolution through Reform*. New York: W.W. Norton and Company, 1995.
Lijphart, Arend. *Democracy in Plural Societies*. New Haven, CT: Yale University Press, 1977.
Link, Perry. "China's 'Core' Problem." In *China in Transformation*, edited by Tu Wei-ming, 191-2. Cambridge, MA: Harvard University Press, 1994.
Link, Perry, Richard Madsen, and Paul G. Pickowicz, eds. *Unofficial China: Popular Culture and Thought in the People's Republic*. Boulder, CO: Westview Press, 1989.
Lowe, Elizabeth. "China's House Churches." Paper presented at the conference on Modernization, the Church and the East Asian Experience held by the Boston Theological Institute in March 1996.

Ma, Shu-Yun. "The Chinese Discourse on Civil Society." *The China Quarterly* no. 137 (March 1994): 180-93.

McCormick, Barrett L. "China's Leninist Parliament and Public Sphere: A Comparative Analysis." In *China after Socialism*, edited by Barrett L. McCormick and Jonathan Unger, 29-53. Armonk, NY: M.E. Sharpe, 1996.

McCormick, Barrett L., Su Shaozhi, and Xiao Xiaoming. "The 1989 Democracy Movement: A Review of the Prospects for Civil Society in China." *Pacific Affairs* 65, 2 (1992): 182-202.

Manion, Melanie. "The Electoral Connection in the Chinese Countryside." *American Political Science Review* 90, 4 (1996): 736-48.

–. "Survey Research in the Study of Contemporary China: Learning from Local Samples." *The China Quarterly* no. 139 (September 1994): 741-65.

Mao Tse-tung. *On the Correct Handling of Contradictions among the People.* Beijing: Foreign Languages Press, 1957.

Meisner, Maurice. *Mao's China and After.* New York: Free Press, 1999.

Moody, Peter R., Jr. *Chinese Politics after Mao.* New York: Praeger, 1983.

–. "Trends in the Study of Chinese Political Culture." *The China Quarterly* no. 139 (September 1994): 731-40.

Moore, Barrington, Jr. *Social Origins of Dictatorship and Democracy.* Boston: Beacon Press, 1968.

Nathan, Andrew J. *China's Crisis: Dilemmas of Reform and Prospects for Democracy.* New York: Columbia University Press, 1990.

–. *Chinese Democracy.* New York: Alfred A. Knopf, 1985.

Nathan, Andrew J., and Tianjian Shi. "Cultural Requisites for Democracy in China: Findings from a Survey." In *China in Transformation*, edited by Tu Wei-ming, 95-123. Cambridge, MA: Harvard University Press, 1994.

Nevitt, Christopher E. "Private Business Associations in China: Evidence of Civil Society or Local State Power?" *The China Journal* no. 36 (July 1996): 25-43.

O'Brien, Kevin J. "China's National People's Congress Reform and Its Limits." *Legislative Studies Quarterly* 13, 3 (1988): 343-74.

–. "Implementing Political Reform in China's Villages." *The Australian Journal of Chinese Affairs* no. 32 (July 1994): 33-59.

–. *Reform without Liberalization.* New York: Cambridge University Press, 1991.

Oi, Jean C. "The Role of the Local State in China's Transitional Economy." *The China Quarterly* no. 144 (December 1995): 1132-49.

Panitch, Leo. "The Development of Corporatism in Liberal Democracies." *Comparative Political Studies* 10 (April 1977): 61-90.

Parris, Kristen. "Private Entrepreneurs as Citizens: From Leninism to Corporatism." *China Information* 10, 3/4 (1995-6): 1-28.

Pye, Lucian W. *The Mandarin and the Cadre: China's Political Cultures.* Ann Arbor: University of Michigan Press, 1988.

–. *The Spirit of Chinese Politics.* Cambridge, MA: Harvard University Press, 1992.

–. "Tiananmen and Chinese Political Culture." *Asian Survey* 30, 4 (1990): 331-47.

Rosen, Stanley. "Students and the State in China: The Crisis in Ideology and Organization." In *State and Society in China: The Consequences of the Reform*, edited by Arthur L. Rosenbaum, 167-91. Boulder, CO: Westview Press, 1992.

–. "Value Change among Post-Mao Youth: The Evidence from Survey Data." In *Unofficial China: Popular Culture and Thought in the People's Republic*, edited by Perry Link, Richard Madsen, and Paul G. Pickowicz, 193-216. Boulder, CO: Westview Press, 1989.

Rosenthal, Elisabeth. "While Defending Crackdown, China Admits Appeal of Sect." *New York Times* (Internet edition), 5 November 1999.

Saich, Tony. "The Search for Civil Society and Democracy in China." *Current History* 93, 584 (1994): 260-4.

Sautman, Barry. "Sirens of the Strongman: Neo-authoritarianism in Recent Chinese Political Theory." *The China Quarterly* no. 129 (March 1992): 72-102.

Saywell, Trish. "On the Edge." *Far Eastern Economic Review*, 25 February 1999.

Scalapino, Robert A. "Democratizing Dragons: South Korea and Taiwan." *Journal of Democracy* 4, 3 (1993): 70-83.

–. "Modernization and Revolution in Asia." *Problems of Communism* 41, 1-2 (1992): 180-1.

Schmitter, Philippe C. "Still the Century of Corporatism?" In *The New Corporatism*, edited by Fredrick B. Pike and Thomas Stritch, 85-131. London: University of Notre Dame Press, 1974.

Schram, Stuart R. "The Cultural Revolution in Historical Perspective." In *Authority, Participation and Cultural Change in China*, edited by Stuart R. Schram. Cambridge: Cambridge University Press, 1977.

–. "Decentralization in a Unitary State: Theory and Practice, 1940-1984." In *The Scope of State Power in China*, edited by Stuart R. Schram. Hong Kong: Chinese University Press, 1985.

–. *Mao Zedong: A Preliminary Reassessment*. Hong Kong: Chinese University Press, 1983.

–. "Party Leader or True Ruler? Foundations and Significance of Mao Zedong's Personal Power." In *Foundations and Limits of State Power in China*, edited by Stuart R. Schram. Hong Kong: Chinese University Press, 1987.

Schurmann, Franz. *Ideology and Organization in Communist China*. Berkeley: University of California Press, 1968.

Shi, Tianjian. *Political Participation in Beijing*. Cambridge, MA: Harvard University Press, 1997.

Shue, Vivienne. "China: Transition Postponed?" *Problems of Communism* 41, 1-2 (1992): 157-68.

Solinger, Dorothy J. "Urban Entrepreneurs and the State: The Merger of State and Society." In *State and Society in China: The Consequences of the Reform*, edited by Arthur L. Rosenbaum, 121-41. Boulder, CO: Westview Press, 1992.

Sorensen, Georg. *Democracy and Democratization*. Boulder, CO: Westview Press, 1993.

Stavis, Benedict. *China's Political Reforms: An Interim Report*. New York: Praeger, 1988.

Su, Shaozhi. *Democratization and Reform*. Nottingham, England: Spokesman, 1988.

Sun Yat-sen. *The Principle of Democracy (Minquan Zhuyi)*. Translated by Frank W. Price. Westport, CT: Greenwood Press, 1970.

Tatlow, Didi. "Mainland Academic Says Party 'Eliminated' at Grass Roots." *Hong Kong Standard*, 1 October 1994, 6. Cited from *FBIS-CHI-94-191*, 3 October 1994, 40.

Thurston, Anne F. *Muddling toward Democracy*. Washington, DC: United States Institute of Peace, 1998.

Unger, Jonathan. "'Bridges': Private Business, the Chinese Government and the Rise of New Associations." *The China Quarterly* no. 147 (September 1996): 795-819.

Unger, Jonathan, and Anita Chan. "Corporatism in China: A Developmental State in an East Asian Context." In *China after Socialism*, edited by Barrett L. McCormick and Jonathan Unger, 95-129. Armonk, NY: M.E. Sharpe, 1996.

"Village Officials Held in Tax Protest," *South China Morning Post* (Internet edition), 3 November 1999.

Wakeman, Frederic, Jr. "The Civil Society and Public Sphere Debate." *Modern China* 19, 2 (1993): 108-38.

"Wang Juntao on development of 'gray democracy.'" *Der Spiegel* (Hamburg), 3 July 1995, 118. Cited from *FBIS-CHI-95-128*, 5 July 1995, 35.

Ware, Robert. "What Good Is Democracy? The Alternatives in China and the West." In *Comparative Political Philosophy*, edited by Anthony J. Parel and Ronald C. Keith, 115-40. New Delhi: Sage Publications, 1992.

White, Gordon. "Prospects for Civil Society in China: A Case Study of Xiaoshan City." *The Australian Journal of Chinese Affairs* no. 29 (January 1993): 63-87.

–. *Riding the Tiger: The Politics of Economic Reform in Post-Mao China*. Stanford: Stanford University Press, 1993.

White, Tyrene. "Rural Politics in the 1990s: Rebuilding Grassroots Institutions." *Current History* 91, 566 (1992): 273-7.

Whyte, Martin K. "Urban China: A Civil Society in the Making?" In *State and Society in China: The Consequences of the Reform,* edited by Arthur L. Rosenbaum, 77-101. Boulder, CO: Westview Press, 1992.

Womack, Brantly. "In Search of Democracy: Public Authority and Popular Power in China." In *Contemporary Chinese Politics in Historical Perspective,* edited by Brantly Womack. New York: Cambridge University Press, 1991.

–. "Party-State Democracy: A Theoretical Exploration." *Issues and Studies* 25, 3 (1989): 37-57.

Wu, Fang. "A CND Interview with Tong Yi." *China News Digest,* 9 August 1997.

Xiong, Bo, and Liedong Zheng. "Unmarried Couples Defending 'Living Together.'" *China News Digest,* 28 September 1996.

Xu, Ming-Yang, and Daluo Jia. "69 Percent of Couples Had Pre-marital Sex, Survey Says." *China News Digest,* 11 November 1996.

Yan, Jiaqi. *Toward a Democratic China.* Honolulu: University of Hawaii Press, 1992.

Yang, C. Daniel. "China: Democracy at Grassroots." *China News Digest,* 14 January 1996.

Bibliography of Chinese Sources

Note: Author names and original-language titles of articles cited from online news agencies are not always available. A title in parentheses indicates a translation.

Bai Wei. "Luelun jingji gaige yu zhengzhi xiandaihua" (On economic reform and political modernization). *Rencai yu Xiandaihua* (Human resources and modernization) no. 1 (1986): 20-3.

Bao Xinjian. "Jiji tuijing shehuizhuyi zhengzhi xiandaihua" (Actively promote socialist political modernization). *Guangming Ribao* (Guangming daily), 14 December 1992, 3.

Bian Qingguo. (Declining role of village committees in population control work). *Renkou yu Jingji* (Population and economy) no. 92 (25 September 1995): 33-5. Cited from *FBIS-CHI-96-032*, 15 February 1996, 16.

Cai Tuo. "Shichang jingji yu zhengzhi fazhan" (Market economy and political development). *Tianjin Ribao* (Tianjin daily), 9 February 1993, 6.

–. "Zhengfu zhineng xintan" (A new exploration of government functions). *Tianjin Shehui Kexue* (Social sciences in Tianjin) no. 1 (1988): 23-7.

Cao Min. (Workers learn to protect their rights). *China Daily,* 24 January 1996, 1. Cited from *FBIS-CHI-96-017,* 25 January 1996, 10.

Cao Yinghua and Li Huasong. "Dangdai qingnian xinyang de zhuangkuang yu qushi" (Contemporary youth's ideological condition and trends). *Zhongguo Qingnian Yanjiu* (China youth research) no. 5 (1995): 41-3.

Chen Binhui. "Guojiade guanli zhineng xintan" (New exploration into the management function of the state). *Fujian Xuekan* (Fujian journal of learning) no. 3 (1991): 65, 69-71.

Chen Hefu. "Woguo minzhu zhengzhi jianshe de jianshi jichu" (Solid foundation for China's construction of democratic politics). *Zhengzhixue Yanjiu* (Political science research) no. 6 (1989): 47-52.

Chen Jian and Liu Min'an. "Jianlun cunweihui de falu diwei" (A brief analysis of the legal status of villagers' committees). *Zhengzhi yu Falu* (Politics and law) no. 6 (1992): 45-7.

Chen Shi. "Jingji gaige yu zhengzhi ziyou" (Economic reform and political freedom). *Gongren Ribao* (Worker's daily), 15 August 1986, 3.

–. "Zhengfu zhineng bixu zhuanbian" (The role of government must be changed). *Gongren Ribao* (Worker's daily), 15 May 1992, 3.

Chen Wei. "Shixian 'san ge daibiao' de lishi jingyan" (Historical experiences in realizing 'three representatives'). *Xinhua News Agency*, 2 July 2000.

Chen Xianglin and Liu Xijun. "Jingji tizhi gaige huhuanzhe zhengzhi tizhi gaige" (Economic system reform calls for political system reform). *Lilun Tantao* (Theoretical exploration) no. 1 (1987): 48-54.

Chen Zhen. "Minzhu shi renlei jingbu he wenming de jiejing" (Democracy is the crystallization of human progress and civilization). *Zhongguo Faxue* (Chinese legal science) no. 5 (1990): 10-13.

Chen Zhonghua and Ma Runqing. "Lun guojiade guanli zhineng" (On the management function of the state). *Guizhou Shehui Kexue* (Social sciences in Guizhou) no. 3 (1982): 1-7.

Chen Ziming. "Gaige zhongde zhengzhi yu jingji" (Politics and economy in the reform). *Zhengzhixue Yanjiu* (Political science research) no. 1 (1987): 7-11.

Chi Dao and Ji Ning. "Shehui xieshang duihua 'xin' zai nali?" (What is 'new' about social consultation and dialogue?). *Liaowang* (Outlook) no. 16 (1988): 18-19.

Chi Fulin. "Zhengzhi tizhi gaige dadao shenme mudi, baokuo naxie neirong?" (What are the objectives and substances of the political system reform?). *Liaowang* (Outlook) no. 8 (1987): 9-11.

China Youth Research Centre Project Group. "1994-1995 Zhongguo Qingnian shehui fazhan yanjiu baogao" (Research report on the Chinese youth's social development: 1994-1995). *Zhongguo Qingnian Yanjiu* (China youth research) no. 5 (1995): 4-12.

(Civil Affairs Minister affirms village autonomy). *Xinhua News Agency*, 20 November 1995. Cited from *FBIS-CHI-95-223*, 20 November 1995, 28-9.

(Clan influence on rural politics increases). *Zhenli de Zhuiqiu* (The pursuit of truth), 11 June 1995, 31-33. Cited from *FBIS-CHI-95-180*, 18 September 1995, 14-16.

(CPC to 'overhaul' grass-root party branches). *Xinhua News Agency*, 29 December 1994. Cited from *FBIS-CHI-94-250*, 29 December 1994, 33.

Cui Peiting. "Jianli shehuizhuyi shichang jingji tizhi yaoqiu shenhua zhengzhi tizhi gaige" (Building socialist market economy requires further political system reform). *Lilun Yanjiu* (Theoretical studies) no. 2 (1993): 1-7.

Cui Zhiyuan. "Yanjiu dangdai zhongguo zhengzhi de xindongxiang" (A new trend in the study of contemporary Chinese politics). *Jingji Shehui Tizhi Bijiao* (Comparison of economic and social systems) no. 5 (1995): 1-4.

Deng Xiaoping. "Shixian sige xiandaihua bixu jianchi sixiang jiben yuanze" (The four cardinal principles must be upheld in order to realize the four modernizations). *Zhongguo Zhengzhi* (Chinese politics) no. 5 (1987): 14-25.

Deng Zhenglai and Jing Yuejing. "Jiangou Zhongguo de shimin shehui" (Building civil society in China). *Zhongguo Shehui Kexue Jikan* (Chinese social science quarterly) no. 1 (November 1992): 58-68.

Dou Xiaomin. "Shichang jingji yu zhengzhi wending" (Market economy and political stability). *Zhengzhou Daxue Xuebao: Zhexue Shehui Kexue Ban* (Zhengzhou university journal: Philosophy and social science edition) no. 3 (1994): 8-11.

Duan Yue. "Kunrao Zhongguo qingnianren de shige lunli wenti" (Ten ethical questions that puzzle Chinese youth). *Zhongguo Qingnian* (Chinese youth) no. 5 (1995): 10-14.

"Faguo meiti zhi zhongguo dalu chuxian 'xin zuopai' fengchao" (French media reports the emergence of 'new left' in the Chinese mainland), *Zhongguo Shibao* (China times, Internet edition), 12 July 2000.

Fan Yongfu. "Xiang Gang de shehui zizhi he zixun xitong jiqi dui neidi jigou gaige de qishi" (Society's self-management and consultation system in Hong Kong and its implications for the institutional reform in the mainland). *Hainan Tequ Bao* (Hainan SEZ news), 26 October 1993, 3.

Gan Yang. "Ziyouzhuyi: guizu de haishi pingmin de?" (Liberalism: For upper class or common people?). *Huaxia Wenzhai* (CND Chinese magazine) Supplementary Issue no. 202 (10 January 2000). Reprinted from *Dushu* (Read books) no. 1 (1999).

Gao Changyun and Shi Yuan. "'Xiao zhengfu da shehui' de Hainan mushi – yizhong zhengzhixue de sikao" (The Hainan model of "small government and big society": A political science reflection). *Hainan Kaifa Bao* (Hainan development news), 23 September 1988, 3.

Gao Fang. "Zhengzhi tizhi gaige zhide sikao de jige wenti" (A few questions in political system reform that we should think about). *Jiaoxue yu Yanjiu* (Teaching and research) no. 6 (1987): 20-5.

Gao Jie. "Cunmin weiyuanhui zuzhi jianshe de beijing, xianzhuang he zhengce daoxiang" (The organizational development of villagers' committees: Its background, current situation and policy orientation). *Faxue Yanjiu* (Studies in law) no. 2 (1994): 11-15.

–. "Lun woguo cunmin daibiao huiyi zhidu" (On China's villagers' representative assembly system). *Faxue Yanjiu* (Studies in law) no. 2 (1995): 17-20.

Ge Xiangxian, Guo Yuanfa, and Song Jishui. "Gonghui yao zhenzheng daibiao zhigong liyi" (The labour union should truly represent workers' interests). *Liaowang* (Outlook) no. 17 (1988): 11-15.

Gong Zhihui. "Zhengzhi tizhi gaige zhongde zhengzhi wending" (Political stability in political system reform). *Shehuizhuyi Yanjiu* (Socialist studies) no. 5 (1993): 15-19.

Gu Benhua. "Shichang jingji tiaojianxia quanli jiegou de zouxiang" (The way the structure of power changes under the condition of market economy). *Hunan Shifan Daxue Shehui Kexue Xuebao* (Hunan Normal University social science journal) no. 2 (1994): 17-21.

Gu Jialing and Wu Zhilun. "Zhengzhi tizhi gaige de mubiao xuanze" (The choice of target for political system reform). *Zhengzhixue Yanjiu* (Political science research) no. 6 (1987): 1-10.

Gu Shicheng. "Zhubu jianshe gaodu minzhu de shehuizhuyi zhengzhi zhidu" (Gradually establish a highly democratic socialist political system). *Faxue Zazhi* (Journal of legal science) no. 1 (1982): 7-10.

Guo Daohui. "Fazhi guojia yu fazhi shehui" (Rule of law state and rule of law society). *Zhengzhi yu Falu* (Politics and law) no. 1 (1995): 17-20.

–. "Renquan, shehui quanli yu fading quanli" (Human rights, social rights, and legal rights). *Zhongguo Shehui Kexue Jikan* (Chinese social science quarterly) no. 3 (Spring 1993): 37-49.

–. "Shehuizhuyi ziyou – dangdai shehuizhuyi fade jingshen" (Socialist freedom: The spirit of law in contemporary socialism." *Faxue* (Legal science) no. 10 (1994): 2-6.

Guo Dingping. "Cong duoyuan shehui tanji zhengzhi gongshi" (Political common understanding in plural society). *Shehui Kexue* (Social sciences) no. 8 (1993): 28-31.

–. "Lun Zhongguo tese de tuanti zhengzhi" (On Chinese-style group politics), *Zhengzhi yu Falu* (Politics and law) no. 3 (1995): 23-8.

–. "Woguo shimin shehui de fazhan yu zhengzhi zhuanxing" (Development of civil society and political transformation in China). *Shehui Kexue* (Social sciences) no. 12 (1994): 52-5, 60.

Guo Dong. "Shihun yizhu yu qingren yizhu" (Those practising trial marriage and those having lovers). *Zhongguo Qingnian Yanjiu* (China youth research) no. 3 (1995): 35-7.

Han Qingxiang. "Shehuizhuyi shichang jingji yu ren de suzao" (Socialist market economy and human development). *Zhongguo Shehui Kexue* (Chinese social sciences) no. 3 (1995): 123-30.

Han Zhulin. "Xiao zhengfu, da shehui – guanyu zhengfu jigou gaige mubiao mushi de tantao" (Small government and big society: Explore the model for the reform of government institutions). *Shehui Kexue* (Social sciences) no. 3 (1989): 30-3.

He Peiyu. "Lun minzhu zhengzhi de shehui jingji jichu" (On social, economic foundations for democracy). *Tansuo: Zhesheban* (Exploration: Philosophy and social science edition) no. 1 (1988): 22-6.

He Zengke. "Guanyu shimin shehui gainian de jidian sikao" (Some reflections on the concept of civil society). *Xiandai yu Chuantong* (Modernity and tradition) no. 4 (1994): 41-8, 40.

–. "Shimin shehui gainian de lishi yanbian" (Historical evolution of the concept of civil society). *Zhongguo Shehui Kexue* (Chinese social sciences) no. 5 (1994): 67-81.

Hu Xiaoming. "Shehui tuanti wenti zhongzhong" (Various problems with associations). *Beijing Ribao* (Beijing daily), 20 November 1990, 3.

Hu Zhenmin. "Yi 'san ge daibiao' de sixiang zhidao jingshen wenming jianshe" (Develop spiritual civilization under the guidance of the idea of "three representatives"). *Renmin Ribao* (People's daily), 11 July 2000, 9.

Huang Hai. "Jinxing zhengzhi tizhi gaige de qiangda sixiang wuqi" (A powerful ideological weapon for the political system reform). *Renmin Ribao* (People's daily), 27 July 1987, 5.

Huang Shaohui. "Lun shehui xieshang duihua zhidu" (On the system of social consultation and dialogue). *Guangming Ribao* (Guangming daily), 7 December 1987, 3.

–. "Lun zhengzhi xietiao" (On political coordination). *Sichuan Shifan Daxue Xuebao: Sheke Ban* (Journal of Sichuan Normal University: Social science edition) no. 4 (1988): 1-5, 18.
Huang Wansheng. "Xinquanweizhuyi pipan wenda lu" (Criticism of neo-authoritarianism: questions and answers). *Wen Hui Bao*, 22 February 1989, 4.
Jia Dongqiao. "Shichang jingji dui woguo zhengzhi de yingxiang qiantan" (A brief discussion of the impact of market economy on Chinese politics). *Shehui Kexue* (Social sciences) no. 10 (1993): 12, 25-8.
(Jiang Chunyun on grass-roots political power). *Xinhua News Agency*, 21 November 1995. Cited from *FBIS-CHI-95-242*, 18 December 1995, 20-1.
Jiang Nanyang. "Shehuizhuyi gaige zhongde 'hunluan' zhuangtai jiqi duice" (The state of 'confusion' in socialist reform and the way to handle it). *Tansuo: Zhesheban* (Exploration: Philosophy and social science edition) no. 4 (1987): 29-32.
Jing Yuejing. "Shimin shehui yanjiu jiqi yiyi" (The study of civil society and its significance). *Xiandai yu Chuantong* (Modernity and tradition) no. 4 (1994): 28-33.
–. "'Shimin shehui yu Zhongguo xiandaihua' xueshu taolunhui shuyao" (A summary of the conference on civil society and China's modernization). *Zhongguo Shehui Kexue Jikan* (Chinese social science quarterly) no. 5 (Autumn 1993): 197-202.
Ju Xingjiu and Li Guangzhi. "Minzhu zhengzhi lilun shi zhengzhi tizhi gaige de lilun yiju" (The theory of democratic politics is the theoretical basis for political system reform). *Lilun Tantao* (Theoretical exploration) no. 4 (1988): 25-8.
Kung Shuang-yin. (China Confucius Foundation sues Ministry of Culture for illegal administrative interferences). *Ta Kung Pao*, 20 January 1996, A2. Cited from *FBIS-CHI-96-035*, 21 February 1996, 18.
Lang Yihuai. "Zhongguo shinian zhengzhi gaige de jiben zouxiang" (Basic directions in China's ten years of political reform). *Shehuizhuyi Yanjiu* (Socialist studies) no. 1 (1989): 11, 20-4.
Lei Dongsheng. "Shehui xieshang duihua zhidu zhi wojian" (My opinion on the system of social consultation and dialogue). *Hubei Shehui Kexue* (Social sciences in Hubei) no. 4 (1988): 51-2.
Lei Yun. "Lun tuidong woguo shehui fazhan de zhongyao maodun" (On important contradictions that promote China's social development). *Shehui Kexue* (Social sciences) no. 8 (1982): 41-2.
Li Chunling. "Hainan shehui zhongjie zuzhi de peiyu ji fazhan" (The nurturing and development of intermediate social organization in Hainan). In *"Xiao zhengfu da shehui" de lilun yu shijian* (Theory and practice of "small government and big society"), edited by Ru Xin et al., 274-313. Beijing: Social Science Literature Publishing House, 1998.
Li Deshun. "'Huapo' yu 'papo'" ("Slipping down" and "climbing up"). *Zhongguo Shehui Kexue* (Chinese social sciences) no. 3 (1994): 3-7.
Li Detian and Yuan Minwu. "Dui guojia zhineng de zairenshi" (Rethink the function of the state). *Lilun Yuekan* (Theory monthly) no. 4 (1986): 21-5.
Li Jiancheng. "Ziyou: shehuizhuyi minzhu de zuigao yuanze" (Freedom: The supreme principle of socialist democracy). *Qiushi* (Seeking truth) no. 3 (1989): 40-1.
Li Jing. "Minzhu wenhua yu Zhongguode minzhu jianshe" (Democratic culture and China's democratic construction). *Shehui Kexue* (Social sciences) no. 9 (1991): 15-18.
Li Jingde. "Zhengzhi tizhi gaige shi jingji tizhi gaige de baozheng" (Political system reform is the guarantee of economic system reform). *Guangming Ribao* (Guangming daily), 30 June 1986.
Li Jingpeng. "Dangdai Zhongguo shehui liyi jiegou de bianhua yu zhengzhi fazhan" (Changes in the structure of social interests and political development in contemporary China). *Tianjin Shehui Kexue* (Social sciences in Tianjin) no. 3 (1994): 31-7.
Li Kejing. "Woguode zhengzhi tizhi gaige yu zhengzhixuede fazhan – Zhongguo shehui kexue zazhishe zhaokai de 'zhengzhi tizhi gaige' xueshu zuotanhui zongshu" (China's political system reform and development of political science: A summary of the conference on political system reform organized by the Chinese Journal of Social Sciences). *Zhongguo Shehui Kexue* (Chinese social sciences) no. 4 (1986): 3-14.

Li Lianke. (Do not negate Marxist humanism). *Shehui Kexue* (Social sciences) no. 7 (1983): 60-3. Cited from *JPRS-CPS-84-006*, 16 January 1984, 11-12.

Li Mingyao. "'Liyi fenhua yu liyi xietiao,' 'zhengzhi minzhu yu zhengzhi wending' xueshu taolunhui zongshu" (A summary of the conference on "interests differentiation and interests coordination" and "political democracy and political stability"). *Zhengzhixue Yanjiu* (Political science research) no. 2 (1989): 33-6.

Li Peng. "Jiji tuijing xianji jigou gaige" (Actively promoting institutional reform at the county level). *Renmin Ribao* (People's daily), 7 July 1992, 1.

Li Ping, Shen Jian, and Ding Wang. "1987 nian gaige shehui xingli diaocha baogao" (Report on the 1987 survey on social psychology of reform). *Jingji Ribao* (Economic daily), 24 October 1987, 2; 27 October 1987, 2.

Li Wenshan. "Jiceng minzhu jianshe de xin xingshi" (A new form of grassroots democratic construction). *Xinhua Wenzhai* (New China digest) no. 4 (1989): 13-14.

Li Yuanshu. "Lun shehui zizhi" (On societal autonomy). *Xuexi yu Tansuo* (Study and exploration) no. 5 (1994): 89-95.

Liao Gailong. "Quanmian jianshe shehuizhuyi de daolu" (Road to all-round construction of socialism). *Yunnan Shehui Kexue* (Social sciences in Yunnan) no. 2 (1982): 1-8.

Liao Xun. "Lun 'da shehui, xiao zhengfu'" (On "big society, small government"). *Zhongguo Xingzheng Guanli* (Chinese administrative management) no. 8 (1988): 4-6.

Lin Yunong. "Lun shehuizhuyi minzhu fazhan yu jingji tizhi gaige de tongbu guanxi" (On the parallel development of socialist democracy and economic system reform). *Zhongguo Shehui Kexue* (Chinese social sciences) no. 5 (1986): 3-18.

Liu Baiwen and Lü Fuxin. "Xiandai shehui: congxin renshi ziwo" (Modern society: Rethink the self). *Zhongguo Qingnian* (Chinese youth) no. 9 (1992): 12-13.

Liu Han. "Du *Zouxiang quanli de shidai*" (A review of *Toward the Era of Rights*). *Zhongguo Faxue* (Chinese legal science) no. 1 (1996): 109-12.

Liu Haoxing and Xu Ke. "Shanghai shi wuzhong jiating jiajiao jiazhi quxiang de bijiao yanjiu" (A comparative study of the value orientations in family education of five types of families in Shanghai). *Shehui Kexue* (Social Sciences) no. 1 (1995): 50-4.

Liu Junning. "Shehui quanli, zhengzhi quanli, jingji quanli" (Social power, political power, economic power). *Gaige* (Reform) no. 4 (1988): 160-5.

Liu Wujun. "Shimin shehui yu xiandai fa de jingshen" (Civil society and the spirit of modern law). *Faxue* (Legal science) no. 8 (1995): 28-30.

Liu Xiaojun, Jiang Jinyong, Chen Jiaming, and Zheng Yu. "Zhengzhi tizhi gaige: lishi yu xianshi de sikao" (Political system reform: Reflections on the past and the present). *Tianfu Xinlun* (New ideas from Sichuan) no. 1 (1988): 1-8.

Liu Zhenwei. "Cunji zuzhi jianshe tantao" (Explore the construction of village-level organization). *Zhongguo Xingzheng Guanli* (Chinese administrative management) no. 1 (1988): 37-40.

Liu Zuoxiang. "Yanjiu quanli zhiyue wenti de lilun jiazhi he shijian yiyi" (The theoretical value and practical significance in studying the issue of restriction of power). *Zhengzhi yu Falu* (Politics and law) no. 1 (1992): 7-10.

Lu Pinyue. "Zhongguo lishi jingcheng yu shimin shehui zhi jiangou" (China's historical progress and the development of civil society). *Zhongguo Shehui Kexue Jikan* (Chinese social science quarterly) no. 8 (Summer 1994): 173-8.

Lu Xueyi. "Hainan sheng zhengzhi yu shehui tizhi gaige de shijian" (The reform of political and social systems in the Hainan Province). In *"Xiao zhengfu da shehui" de lilun yu shijian* (Theory and practice of "small government and big society"), edited by Ru Xin et al., 1-51. Beijing: Social Science Literature Publishing House, 1998.

Lu Zhen. "Shi nian fansi: gaige de si da wuqu" (Rethink the past ten years: Four big errors in the reform). *Shulin* (Books) no. 4 (1989): 2-9.

"Lun jiefang sixiang" (On the liberation of the mind). *Renmin Ribao* (People's daily), editorial, 4 July 1992, 1.

Luo Jianhua and Gao Zhengang. "Lun minzhu jingshen" (On democratic spirit). *Guangming Ribao* (Guangming daily), 24 March 1989, 3.

Luo Shugang. "'San ge daibiao' yu dang de sixiang lilun jianshe" ("Three representatives" and the party's ideological and theoretical construction). *Renmin Ribao* (People's daily), 11 July 2000, 9.

Ma Changshan. "Cong shimin shehui lilun chufa dui fa benzhi de zai renshi" (Rethink the essence of law according to the theory of civil society). *Faxue Yanjiu* (Studies in law) no. 1 (1995): 41-8.

–. "Cunmin zizhi zuzhi jianshe de shidai yiyi jiqi shijian fancha" (The organizational construction of village self-government: Its historical significance and its contrast with reality). *Zhengzhi yu Falu* (Politics and law) no. 2 (1994): 19-21.

–. "Luelun woguo shehui tuanti de falu diwei ji danhua qi xingzhenhua qingxiang" (On the legal status of China's associations and on reducing their tendency to become administrative entities). *Zhengzhi yu Falu* (Politics and law) no. 3 (1992): 35-7.

Min Qi. "Guanyu zhuanxingqi de Zhongguo zhengzhi" (Chinese politics in the transition period). *Xuexi yu Tansuo* (Study and exploration) no. 4 (1988): 77-9.

–. *Zhongguo Zhengzhi Wenhua* (Chinese political culture). Kunming: Yunnan People's Press, 1989.

Niu Fengrui. "Hainan de cunmin zizhi zhidu jianshe" (Building the system of villagers' self-government in Hainan). In *"Xiao zhengfu da shehui" de lilun yu shijian* (Theory and practice of "small government and big society"), edited by Ru Xin et al., 314-45. Beijing: Social Science Literature Publishing House, 1998.

Pan Debing. "Woguo xianxing tizhi jiegou yu shehui wenti" (China's present system structure and its social problems). *Zhengzhixue Yanjiu* (Political science research) no. 1 (1986): 22-5.

(PRC: Democratic Elections Come to Villages). *Xinhua News Agency,* 30 May 1996. Cited from *FBIS-CHI-96-109,* 5 June 1996, 35-6.

Qin Xiaoying. "Guilai ba, 'Wusi' shenhun – minzhu guannian de gengxin yu minzhu guandian de xuanze" (Come back, the May 4 spirit: Renew the concept of democracy and choose the ideas of democracy). *Huaren Shijie* (Chinese world) no. 1 (1989): 21-3.

–. "Shehuizhuyi minzhu yeying baokuo 'shaoshu yuanze'" (Socialist democracy should also include the "minority principle"), *Qiushi* (Seeking truth) no. 8 (1988): 20-3.

Qiu Zhen and Yu Chi. "Shilun woguode guoti he zhengti" (A tentative theorizing on China's form of state and form of government). *Xuexi yu Yanjiu* (Learn and study) no. 7 (1982): 14-19.

Research Office under the Central Organization Department. (Guard against "electoral bribery" in rural areas). *Renmin Ribao* (People's daily), 21 May 1996. Cited from *FBIS-CHI-96-116,* 14 June 1996, 18.

Rong Jian. "Cong zhengzhi he jingji de eryuanhua kan jingji gaige he zhengzhi gaige de guanxi" (The relationship between political reform and economic reform from the perspective of dualism of politics and economy). *Zhengzhixue Yanjiu* (Political science research) no. 6 (1987): 11-17, 27.

–. "Lun Makeside minzhu sixiang" (On Marx's democratic ideas). *Zhengzhixue Yanjiu* (Political science research) no. 3 (1987): 1-7.

–. "Makesizhuyi guojia xueshuo yu zhengzhi tizhi gaige" (Marxist theory of the state and political system reform). *Guangzhou Yanjiu* (Guangzhou research) no. 2 (1987): 24-30.

Rong Yiren. "Jianchi ba shijian zuowei jianyan zhenli de weiyi biaozhun" (Insist on taking practice as the sole criterion of truth). *Renmin Ribao* (People's daily), 15 June 1992, 5.

Ru Xin, He Bingmeng, Lu Xueyi, Liu Han, Jing Tiankui, eds., *"Xiao zhengfu da shehui" de lilun yu shijian* (Theory and practice of "small government and big society"). Beijing: Social Science Literature Publishing House, 1998.

Sha Chun. (Mainland center banned for violating taboo in investigating hot topics). *Ming Pao,* 12 September 1994, A2. Cited from *FBIS-CHI-1994-179,* 15 September 1994, 41-2.

Shan Shaojie. "Dangdai Zhongguo: xinyang weiji yuanyu weishan zhi feng" (Contemporary China: Crisis of faith results from hypocrisy). *Zhongguo Shehui Kexue* (Chinese social sciences) no. 3 (1994): 15-18.

–. "Guoren siliguan: leng de hanxin, re de zaodong" (The selfishness of Chinese: From freezing cold to boiling heat). *Zhongguo Qingnian* (Chinese youth) no. 10 (1993): 6-7.

Shao Daosheng. "Shehui de fazhan yu daode de shuaitui" (Social development and moral decline). *Zhongguo Shehui Kexue* (Chinese social sciences) no. 3 (1994): 11-15.

"Shaoshu yao fucong duoshu, duoshu yao baohu shaoshu – minzhu jianshe zhongde yige wenti" (The minority should be subordinate to the majority, and the majority should protect the minority: An issue in the development of democracy). *Guangming Ribao* (Guangming daily), 7 October 1986, 1.

She Dehu. "Youguan woguo shehui tuanti wenti de sikao" (Reflections on the problems concerning associations). *Qiushi* (Seeking truth) no. 17 (1991): 15-19.

Shen Rendao and Yang Ming. "Liyi jituan de gainian he fenlei" (The concept and typology of interest groups). *Zhengzhixue Yanjiu* (Political science research) no. 3 (1986): 19-22.

Shi Xianmin. "Zhongguo shehui zhuanxingqi de jiegou fenhua yu shuang eryuan shehui jiegou" (Structural differentiation in China's transitional stage and double dualist social structure). *Zhongguo Shehui Kexue Jikan* (Chinese social science quarterly) no. 5 (Autumn 1993): 55-65.

Shi Xuehua. "Lun shehui zhuanxing yu zhengfu zhineng zhuanbian" (On the social transition and changing the role of the government). *Tianjin Shehui Kexue* (Social sciences in Tianjin) no. 2 (1995): 19-26, 30.

"Shixing jiceng minzhu qunzhong shi zhubu you qunzhong ziji ban" (Implement grassroots democracy to gradually allow the masses to handle their own affairs). *Renmin Ribao* (People's daily), 5 December 1987, 3.

Shui Tian. "Daguancun li xuan cunzhang – Jilin nongmin 'haixuan' diaocha ji" (Electing the village chief in Daguan Village: An investigative report on the "sea elections" among peasants in Jilin Province). *Huaxia Wenzhai* (CND Chinese magazine) no. 389 (11 September 1998).

Situ Yan. "Zhongguo zhengzhi tizhi gaige de beijing yu qianjing" (Background and prospect of China's political system reform). *Zhengzhixue Yanjiu* (Political science research) no. 1 (1987): 1-6.

Su Shaozhi. "Zhengzhi tizhi gaige yu fandui fengjianzhuyi yingxiang" (Political system reform and the fight against the influence of feudalism). *Renmin Ribao* (People's daily), 15 August 1986, 8.

Sun Bingyao. "Xiangzhen shetuan yu Zhongguo jiceng shehui" (Township-level associations and Chinese society at the grassroots). *Zhongguo Shehui Kexue Jikan* (Chinese social science quarterly) no. 9 (Autumn 1994): 25-36.

–. "Zhongguo shehui tuanti guan-min erchongxing wenti" (The dual nature of China's associations). *Zhongguo Shehui Kexue Jikan* (Chinese social science quarterly) no. 6 (February 1994): 17-23.

Sun Guohua. "Minzhu jianshe bixu naru fazhi guidao" (The building of democracy must be in accordance with the rule of law). *Zhongguo Faxue* (Chinese legal science) no. 5 (1990): 6-9.

Sun Liping. "Guojia yu shehui de jiegou fenhua" (Structural differentiation of state and society). *Zhongguo Shehui Kexue Jikan* (Chinese social science quarterly) no. 1 (November 1992): 69-76.

Sun Xiaoxia. "Lun falu yu shehui liyi" (On law and social interests). *Zhongguo Faxue* (Chinese legal science) no. 4 (1995): 52-60.

(Take effective measures to strengthen building of villagers' committees). *Renmin Ribao* (People's daily) commentary, 21 November 1995, 4. Cited from *FBIS-CHI-95-250*, 29 December 1995, 18.

Tang Can. "Xiangle zhuyi yousi" (Concerns over hedonism). *Zhongguo Qingnian* (Chinese youth) no. 12 (1992): 12-13.

Tang Daiwang. "Shehuizhuyi chujijieduan de guojia zhineng" (The function of the state at the preliminary stage of socialism). *Zhengzhixue Yanjiu* (Political science research) no. 6 (1988): 16-18.

Tang Jinsu. "Cunmin huiyi yu cunmin daibiao huiyi" (Village assembly and village council). *Zhengzhi yu Falu* (Politics and law) no. 2 (1995): 10-13.

–. "Jiaqiang nongcun jiceng minzhu zhengzhi jianshe" (Strengthening construction of rural democratic politics). *Zhengzhi yu Falu* (Politics and law) no. 4 (1994): 21-4.

–. "Woguo cunmin weiyuanhui jianshe zhuangkuang yu zhanwang" (The current condition and the prospects of China's village committees). *Zhengzhi yu Falu* (Politics and law) no. 6 (1992): 42-4.

Tang Jinsu and Dong Chengmei. "Cunmin weiyuanhui zuzhifa (shixing) guanche shishi qingkuang diaocha baogao" (A findings report on the implementation of the Organic Law of Villagers' Committees [Trial Implementation]). *Zhongguo Faxue* (Chinese legal science) no. 2 (1992): 6-12.

Teng Pi-yun. (CPC's control over rural areas weakens, replaced by traditional forces or "capable people"). *Lien Ho Pao* (United Daily News) (Hong Kong), 18 July 1995, 8. Cited from *FBIS-CHI-95-163*, 23 August 1995, 163.

Tong Daling. "Renlei zai xin qimeng zhong" (Mankind in new enlightenment). *Jingjixue Zhoubao* (Economics weekly), 23 April 1989, 1.

(Trade unions urged to protect worker interests). *Xinhua News Agency*, 30 July 1995. Cited from *FBIS-CHI-95-146*, 31 July 1995, 32-3.

Wang Fuchun and Wu Xiaojian. "Guanyu Beijing daxue xuesheng minzhu yishi de diaocha baogao" (A survey report on the Beijing University students' democratic consciousness). *Zhengzhixue Yanjiu* (Political science research) no. 1 (1989): 24-34.

Wang Hongzhi. (Guarding against revival of clan culture.) *Renmin Ribao* (People's daily), 10 February 1996. Cited from *FBIS-CHI-96-035*, 21 February 1996, 20.

Wang Huning. "Jianli yizhong xinde zhengzhi fazhan guan" (Form a new concept of political development). *Zhongguo Qingnian Bao* (China youth news), 19 August 1988, 3.

–. *Minzhu Zhengzhi* (Democratic politics). Hong Kong: Joint Publishing [H.K.] Company, 1993.

–. "Zhongguo zhengzhi-xingzheng tizhi gaige de jingji fenxi" (An economic analysis of China's political-administrative system reform). *Shehui Kexue Zhanxian* (Social science front) no. 2 (1988): 107-15.

Wang Jiangang. "Duodang hezuo yu shehui zhengzhi wending" (Multiparty cooperation and social, political stability). *Zhongguo Qingnian Zhengzhi Xueyuan Xuebao* (The journal of the China Youth Political Institute) no. 6 (1993): 41-5, 49.

Wang Jianqin. "Dangqian woguo zhengfu jigou gaige weishenme nanyi tuijing?" (Why is it difficult to carry out government institutional reforms?). *Qiyejia Bao* (Entrepreneur's news), 6 January 1994, 3.

Wang Jue. "Minzhu zhengzhi de xinfeng" (New style of democratic politics). *Hongqi* (Red flag) no. 8 (1988): 28-9.

Wang Junchang. "Shehui gaige lilun chutan" (An initial exploration of the theory of social reform). *Zhejiang Xuekan* (Zhejiang journal of learning) no. 3 (1988): 9-13.

Wang Puli. "Lun minzhujizhongzhi de shizhi" (On the essence of democratic centralism). *Guangming Ribao* (Guangming daily), 7 October 1991, 3.

Wang Renbo. "Guanyu fenquan mushi de jiazhi sikao" (Evaluative reflections on the model of separation of powers). *Tansuo: Zhesheban* (Exploration: Philosophy and social science edition) no. 4 (1988): 33-6.

Wang Ruoshui. (In defense of humanism). *Wen Hui Bao*, 17 January 1983. Cited from *JPRS-82880-16* no. 392, February 1983, 48.

Wang Song. "Jingji liyi duoyuanhua yu dangdai Zhongguo zhengzhi fazhan" (Pluralism of economic interests and political development in contemporary China). *Tansuo yu Zhengming* (Exploration and debate) no. 10 (1994): 39-41.

Wang Song and Sun Li. "Lun jingji liyi duoyuanhua yu zhengzhi yitihua" (On pluralism of economic interests and political integration). *Zhongguo Xingzheng Guanli* (Chinese administrative management) no. 7 (1993): 24-7.

Wang Yaohua. "Tan zhengzhi tizhi gaige de changqi mubiao he jinqi mubiao" (On the long-term and short-term targets of the political system reform). *Lilunjie* (Theoretical circles) no. 5/6 (1988): 18-20.

Wang Ying. "Zhongguo de shehui zhongjianceng: Shetuan fazhan yu zuzhi tixi conggou" (The intermediary level of Chinese society: Development of associations and the rebuilding of the organizational system). *Zhongguo Shehui Kexue Jikan* (Chinese social science quarterly) no. 6 (February 1994): 24-36.

Wang Ying, Zhe Xiaoye, and Sun Bingyao. "Shetuan fazhan yu zuzhi tixi conggou" (Development of associations and the rebuilding of organizational systems). *Guanli Shijie* (Management world) no. 2 (1992): 186-96.

Wang Zhenhai. "Lun cun de shequ tezheng yu quanli jiegou" (On community characteristics and power structures of a village). *Zhengzhi yu Falu* (Politics and law) no. 6 (1991): 18-20.

Wang Zhenhai and Han Xijiang. "Dangqian cunmin weiyuanhui zuzhi jianshe chulun" (Our opinions on current organization building of villagers' committees). *Zhengzhi yu Falu* (Politics and law) no. 5 (1988): 7-10.

Weng Xianzhong. "Lun shehuizhuyi shichang jingji de wenhua jingshen" (On the cultural spirit of socialist market economy). *Zhongguo Shehui Kexue* (Chinese social sciences) no. 6 (1994): 83-90.

The Writing Group of the Scientific Socialism Teaching and Research Office of the CPC Central Committee Party School. "Lun shehuizhuyi shehui de maodun" (Contradictions of socialist society). *Guangming Ribao* (Guangming daily), 31 October 1983, 3.

Wu Cheng. "Tantan jiaqiang shehuizhuyi minzhu he fazhi" (On strengthening socialist democracy and the legal system). *Faxue Zazhi* (Journal of legal science) no. 1 (1982): 11-13.

Wu Jiaxiang. "Xinquanweizhuyi shuping" (Explaining neo-authoritarianism). *Shijie Jingji Daobao* (World economic herald), 16 January 1989, 12.

Wu Jiaxiang and Zhang Bingjiu. "Jijinde minzhu haishi wenjiande minzhu – Wu Jiaxiang and Zhang Bingjiu duihualu" (Radical democracy or stable democracy: A dialogue between Wu Jiaxiang and Zhang Bingjiu). *Guangming Ribao* (Guangming daily), 31 March 1989, 3.

Wu Yue. "Shehui guanli zhineng yu zhengfu jigou gaige" (Social management function and the reform of government institutions). *Qinghai Shehui Kexue* (Social sciences in Qinghai) no. 4 (1988): 4-7.

Wu Zhilun. "Bixu jianli zhengzhijia yu putong qunzhong de youji lianxi" (An organic relationship must be built up between politicians and ordinary people). *Zhengzhixue Yanjiu* (Political science research) no. 1 (1988): 24-9.

Xia Jun. (Guard against "rebound" of peasant burdens). *Renmin Ribao* (People's daily), 25 August 1994, 2. Cited from *FBIS-CHI-94-190*, 30 September 1994.

Xiao Rong. "Guanyu guojia minzhu zhidu de jianshe" (On the building of the state's democratic system). *Guangming Ribao* (Guangming daily), 26 January 1989, 3.

Xie Hui. "Quanli yu quanli de gongneng beifang" (The opposite functions of rights and power). *Ningbo Daxue Xuebao — Renwen Kexue Ban* (The journal of Ningbo University: Human sciences edition) no. 2 (1995): 96-104.

Xie Pengcheng. "Lun dangdai Zhongguo de falu quanwei" (On the authority of law in contemporary China). *Zhongguo Faxue* (Chinese legal science) no. 6 (1995): 3-13.

Xie Qingkui. "Zhengfu zhineng zhuanbian de hanyi" (The meaning of government role change). *Jingji Ribao* (Economic daily), 13 May 1993, 7.

Xie Weihe. "Shehui ziyuan liudong yu shehui fenhua: Zhongguo shimin shehui de keguan jichu" (The movement of social resources and social differentiation: Objective foundation for China's civil society). *Zhongguo Shehui Kexue Jikan* (Chinese social science quarterly) no. 4 (Summer 1993): 5-9.

Xie Weijian. "Shehuizhuyi yu geren ziyou" (Socialism and individual freedom). *Shehui Kexue* (Social sciences) no. 2 (1993): 29-32.

Xing Fensi. "Xianjieduan Zhongguo shehui gaige de ruogan lilun wenti" (A few theoretical problems concerning China's social reform at the present stage). *Shehui Kexue Zhanxian* (Social science front) no. 1 (1988): 8-14.

Xu Bin. "Zhengzhi tizhi gaige yu zhengti lilunde gengxin – guanyu guoti zhengti, minzhu jizhong guanxide zai renshi" (Political system reform and the renewal of the theory of political system: Rethink the form of state, the form of government, and the relationship between democracy and centralism) *Zhejiang Xuekan* (Zhejiang journal of learning) no. 5 (1987): 30-3.

Xu Guodong. "Shimin shehui yu shimin fa" (Civil society and civil law). *Faxue Yanjiu* (Studies in law) no. 4 (1994): 3-9.

Xu Hongwu and Li Jingde. "Zhengzhi tizhi gaige shi jingji tizhi gaige de baozheng" (Political system reform is the guarantee of economic system reform). *Guangming Ribao* (Guangming daily), 30 June 1986, 3.

Xu Yong. "Zhengzhi xiandaihua: shijie yu Zhongguo" (Political modernization: World and China). *Shehuizhuyi Yanjiu* (Socialist studies) no. 4 (1988): 8-13.

Xue Muqiao. "Jianli he fazhan zizhi hangye zuzhi" (Establish and develop autonomous industry organizations). *Renmin Ribao* (People's daily), 10 October 1988. Cited from *FBIS-CHI-88-201*, 18 October 1988, 34-5.

Yan Jiaqi. (The significance of differentiating between two implications of humanism). *Guangming Ribao* (Guangming daily), 1 March 1984, 2. Cited from *JPRS-CPS-84-024*, 28 March 1984, 58.

Yan Qin. "Guanyu zhengzhi tizhi gaige de ruogan sikao" (Reflections on political system reform). *Shehui-Shanghai* (Society-Shanghai) no. 9 (1992): 10-14.

Yang Haikun. "Shehuizhuyi chujijieduan liyiqunti lun" (Interest groups in the preliminary stage of socialism). *Zhengzhi yu Falu* (Politics and law) no. 2 (1989): 1-5.

Yang Kuisen. "Dangdai Zhongguo shehui sichao pinglun" (Comment on ideological trends in contemporary Chinese society). *Jilin Daxue Shehui Kexue Xuebao* (Jilin University social science journal) no. 5 (1990): 13-22.

–. "Shangpin yishi he renwen jingshen" (Commodity consciousness and humanist spirit). *Zhongguo Shehui Kexue* (Chinese social sciences) no. 6 (1994): 91-6.

Yang Zili. "Nongcun diaocha jishi" (Rural research notes). *Huaxia Wenzhai* (CND Chinese magazine) no. 413 (26 February 1999).

"Yao qieshi zhuanbian zhengfu zhineng" (The role of government should be truly changed). *Renmin Ribao* (People's daily), editorial, 5 August 1992, 1.

Yin Guanghua. "Zhengfu zhineng zhuanbian de san da nandian" (Three big difficulties in changing the role of government). *Jingji Ribao* (Economic daily), 15 April 1993, 7.

"Yongyu tansuo, tuijing gaige – shoudu lilunjie zhaokai guanyu zhengzhi tizhi gaige zuotanhui de fayan" (Dare to explore and promote reform: Speeches made at the symposium on political system reform held by the capital's theoretical circle). *Makesizhuyi Yanjiu* (Marxist studies) no. 4 (1986): 1-25.

Yu Haocheng. "Guanyu woguo zhengzhi tizhi gaige he fazhi jianshe de jige wenti" (A few questions on China's political system reform and legal system construction). *Wen Hui Bao*, 14 January 1989, 4.

Yu Keping. "Shehuizhuyi shimin shehui: yige xinde yanjiu keti" (Socialist civil society: A new subject of research). *Tianjin Shehui Kexue* (Social sciences in Tianjin) no. 4 (1993): 45-8.

Yu Qian. "Zhongguo jieshefa heri chutai lai?" (When will we have a Chinese law on associations?). *Shehui Baozhang Bao* (Social insurance news), 31 March 1989, 1.

Yuan Ming. (Democracy must be promoted in order to realize four modernizations). *Wen Hui Bao* (Wen Hui Daily), 10 January 1979, 1. Cited from *JPRS 73201* no. 507, 11 April 1979, 2.

Zhang Chengfu. "Xingzheng minzhu lun" (On administrative democracy). *Zhongguo Xingzheng Guanli* (Chinese administrative management) no. 6 (1993): 23-7.

Zhang Hailing. "Kua shiji de da lunzhan" (A great cross-century debate). *Huaxia Wenzhai* (CND Chinese magazine) Supplementary issue no. 202 (10 January 2000). Reprint from *Yazhou Zhoukan* (Asia weekly) no. 40 (10 October 1999).

Zhang Jingli. "Jiefang hongguan" (Macro-level liberation). *Renmin Ribao* (People's daily), 8 August 1992, 3.

Zhang Mingdui. *Zhongguo "Zhengzhiren"* (China's "political person"). Beijing: Chinese Academy of Social Science Press, 1994.

Zhang Qian. "Shehuizhuyi zhengzhi tizhi yu duoyuanhua" (Socialist political system and pluralization). *Lilun Xingxi Bao* (Theoretical information news), 26 September 1988, 4.

Zhang Weiqing. "Jiaqiang nongcun minzhu jianshe, miqie dangqun ganqun guanxi" (Strengthening rural democratic construction, establishing close ties between the party and the masses and between cadres and the masses). *Qiushi* (Seeking truth) no. 4 (1991): 36-40.

Zhang Yu. "Shichang jingji yu jiazhi congjian" (Market economy and value reconstruction). *Zhongguo Shehui Kexue* (Chinese social sciences) no. 3 (1994): 18-21.

Zhang Zhanbing. "Quanli guofen jizhong: zhengzhi tizhi gaige de jiaodian" (Overly centralized power: Focus of political system reform). *Tianjin Shehui Kexue* (Social sciences in Tianjin) no. 3 (1988): 27-9.

Zhao Chengxing. "Zhongguo minzhu zhengzhi lilun chutan – quanguo shouci minzhu zhengzhi jianshe yantaohui zongshu" (An initial theoretical exploration on the building of democratic politics in China: A summary of the first nationwide conference on the building of democratic politics). *Lilun Xingxi Bao* (Theoretical information news), 7 November 1988, 1.

Zhao Yongjin and Cao Zheng. "Zhigong quanyi de weishi" (Champion of workers' rights and interests). *Liaowang* (Outlook) no. 17 (1988): 16-17.

Zhao Zhongsan. "Jiceng minzhu zhengzhi jianshe de yizhong hao xingshi" (A good form of constructing grassroots democratic politics). *Qiushi* (Seeking truth) no. 2 (1988): 40-1.

Zheng Chengliang. "Shangpin jingji, minzhuzhengzhi de fazhan yu faxuede chonggou" (Development of a commodity economy and democratic politics, and the rebuilding of jurisprudence). *Zhengzhi yu Falu* (Politics and law) no. 1 (1989): 10-12.

Zheng Hangsheng. "Zhongguo shehui zhengzai da zhuanxing" (Chinese society is undergoing radical transformation). *Shanxi Fazhan Daobao* (Shanxi development herald), 8 April 1994, 4.

Zheng Shiping. "Lun Zhongguo zhengzhi tizhi jichu de gaige" (On reforming the foundation of China's political system). *Zhengzhixue Yanjiu* (Political science research) no. 1 (1986): 26-9.

Zheng Yongnian. "Jingji fazhan yu minzhu zhengzhi" (Economic development and democratic politics). *Guangming Ribao* (Guangming daily), 13 February 1989, 3.

Zhong Zhushan. "Nongcun jiceng dang zuzhi xianzhuang tanxi" (An analysis of the current condition of rural grassroots party organization). *Liaowang* (Outlook) no. 1 (1990): 12-14.

"Zhongguo nongcun paoli fankang yundong zaiqi" (The resurgence of violent resistance movement in China's rural areas). *Duowei Xinwenshe* (Duowei news agency), 12 September 2000.

Zhou Duo. "Yao jianjin minzhu, buyao jiduan zhuyi" (We need gradual democratization, not extremism). *Huaxia Wenzhai* (CND Chinese magazine) no. 482 (23 June 2000).

Zhou Jianming. "Cong shenfen guanxi dao qiyue guanxi zhuanbian zhi wojian" (My opinion on the transition from status relationship to contractual relationship). *Zhengzhi yu Falu* (Politics and law) no. 6 (1986): 9-11.

Zhou Yezhong. "Lun minzhu yu liyi, liyi jituan" (On democracy, interests and interest groups). *Xuexi yu Yanjiu* (Learn and study) no. 2 (1995): 70-6.

Zhou Yongchuang. "Guanyu bu shuyu jieji douzheng fanwei de shehui maodun" (On social contradictions that do not belong to the realm of class struggle). *Shehui Kexue* (Social sciences) no. 8 (1982): 28-9.

Zhou Zhongshu. "Zhengque renshi zhengzhi tizhi gaige de jinqi mubiao" (Correctly understand the short-term target of the political system reform). *Xuexi yu Jianshe* (Learning and construction) no. 5 (1988): 27.

Zhou Zuohan. "Guanyu cunmin weiyuanhui jianshe de jidian sikao" (A few reflections on the construction of villagers' committees). *Hunan Shifan Daxue Shehui Kexue Xuebao* (Hunan Normal University social science journal) no. 5 (1987): 18-21.

Zhu Changping. "Lun gongmin zhengzhi canyu de zhiduhua" (On institutionalization of citizens' political participation). *Ningxia Shehui Kexue* (Social sciences in Ningxia) no. 4 (1990): 15-19.

Zhu Qinjun. "Lun guojiade minzhu zhineng jiqi zai zhengzhi tizhi gaige zhongde xiaoying" (On democracy as a function of the state and its effect in political system reform). *Anhuisheng Dangxiao Xiaokan* (Journal of Anhui Provincial Party School) no. 1 (1987): 75-8, 84.

Zhu Xinhua. "Xunzhao xin wenhua de lishi zuobiao" (Searching for historical basis of a new culture). *Zhongguo Qingnian* (Chinese youth) no. 5 (1995): 15-17.

Zhu Xueqin. "1998: ziyouzhuyi de yanshuo" (1998: Liberal opinions). *Huaxia Wenzhai* (CND Chinese magazine) Supplementary Issue no. 202 (10 January 2000). Reprinted from from *Dushu* (Read books) no. 1 (1999).

Zu Xuguang. "Xietiao maodun shi minzhu dangpai canzheng de yige zhongyao fangmian" (Coordinating contradictions is an important aspect in the democratic parties' participation in politics). *Renmin Zhengxie Bao* (The people's political consultation news), 17 June 1988, 3.

Index

Alienation, 101-3. *See also* Ideological alienation; Political alienation
All-China Federation of Trade Unions (ACFTU), 57
Alliance for China's Development, 68
Almond, Gabriel, 97, 98
"Anti-left" theme, 33
Associations, 19, 22-3, 27, 48-9, 68-75; compared with villagers' committees, 92-3; control vs service functions, 56-61; corporatism, 52-62; in democratic villages, 84; emergence, 49-52; unofficial, 63-6
Attitudinal change, 85, 98-118
Authoritarianism, 12, 133; neo-authoritarianism, 21-2, 27, 125

Bai Hua, 101
Beijing, surveys, 108, 110
Beijing Institute for Research on Social and Scientific-Technological Development, 64
Berlin, Isaiah, 43
Birth control policies, 90
Brugger, Bill, 100

Cadres, 10; attitudes toward, 106-7; peasant-cadre relationships, 77-8, 85-6, 87-9
"Capable people," 89
CASS. *See* Chinese Academy of Social Sciences (CASS)
CDP. *See* China Democracy Party (CDP)
Centralism, 5-6, 9, 10, 16, 110-11, 120
Chamberlain, Heath, 69
Chan, Alfred L., 100
Chan, Anita, 70, 71
Change. *See* Attitudinal change; Cultural change; Democratization; Economic reform; Political modernization
Chen Shi, 34
China Democracy Party (CDP), 67
China Social and Economic Investigation Centre, 64
China Youth Research Centre survey, 104, 113-14
Chinese Academy of Social Sciences (CASS): conference on political reform (1986), 16, 25; political culture survey, 104, 106, 108, 109
Chinese social sciences. *See Zhongguo Shehui Kexue*
Chu, Godwin C., 99, 107, 114
Civil society, 3, 20, 35, 45, 119, 123; corporatism and, 68-73; debate on, 19-20, 24, 33, 36-9, 44; definition of, 69; emergence of, 62-8, 69, 122; positive interaction with state, 36-9
Clans, 88-9
Class struggle, 8, 9, 15, 120
Collective interests, 41
Collectivism, 5, 10-11, 17
Communist Party: attitudes toward, 106-7, 112; role in orthodox democracy, 6; village branches, 86-7, 90-1
Conferences, 46; on civil society (Shanghai, 1993), 37-8; on democratic politics (Changsha, 1988), 28-9; on the Party's Theoretical Work (1979), 123; on political reform (1986), 16, 25
"Contradictions among the people," 9, 15, 25, 120; views of Mao Zedong, 6-7
Corporatism, 138 n. 88; associational activities, 52-62; civil society and, 68-73; local, 59-61, 62, 71; pluralism and, 71; societal, 70-4
Criticism campaign, 32-3, 42

Printed and bound in Canada by Friesens

Set in Stone by Brenda and Neil West, BN Typographics West

Copy editor: Sarah Wight

Proofreader: Gail Copeland

Indexer: Christine Jacobs